Industry in Action

The Worker Directors

A Sociology of Participation

Peter Brannen
Eric Batstone
Derek Fatchett
Philip White

HUTCHINSON OF LONDON

Hutchinson & Co (Publishers) Ltd
3 Fitzroy Square, London W1

London Melbourne Sydney Auckland
Wellington Johannesburg and agencies
throughout the world

First published 1976
© P. Brannen, E. Batstone, D. Fatchett, P. White 1976

Set in Monotype Baskerville
Printed in Great Britain by The Anchor Press Ltd
and bound by Wm Brendon & Son Ltd
both of Tiptree, Essex

ISBN 0 09 124430 7

Contents

Editorial Foreword

A combination of factors makes it difficult for the practising manager or trade unionist to form a broad and forward view of modern industrial society and his or her role within it. Pressures of work and living, narrowing specializations, the increasing role of external influences particularly from government, and the pace and diversity of change all conspire against such understanding. The expanding demands of specialized functions have affected education and intellectual activity generally, compartmentalizing thought and knowledge and in particular tending to exclude social issues and values and to isolate industrial theory and practice from society in a dangerously unreal way.

Despite welcome developments in both the quantity and quality of education for industry, perspectives are still blocked by the preconceptions of yesterday and the pre-occupations of today. Even the younger manager attending a course has to make a considerable effort first to widen his view and then to integrate all that comes within it. The books in this series *Industry in Action* are designed to complement the individual efforts of those managers, trade unionists, students and others who wish to take this wider view. Within the framework set by the need to understand the complex forces which are re-shaping industry and society each book will impart the specialist knowledge and techniques relevant to its area of interest and seek to establish and explore the links between the specialism and technological, social, political and other influences which are relevant to them.

The related issues of industrial democracy, participation and 'workers on the board' are now commonplaces of discussion in British industry and trade unions as well as in the lecture and seminar rooms of our universities and polytechnics. References to the worker directors in British nationalized steel abound in these places and in management journals, but such references are usually superficial, and frequently misinformed. The reason for this has been that the only substantial study of the British Steel experiment has remained unpublished until the appearance of this book. It is now possible for those interested in the development of industrial democracy to study this comprehensive and authoritative work on one of the most important experiments in that field which has been made so far.

Against the background of a useful guide to change and adjustment in the steel industry and to the new organization under nationalization we are given the results of in-depth studies of the attitudes of and to worker directors and of their mode of operation in the new role accorded to them. It is especially interesting to have the issue of redundancy singled out and the scope for participation explored in that connection, with particular reference to the experience in British Steel. All this, it might be thought, is as much as can be expected from any one book. However, in addition, the authors have put their main subject matter both in its historical and sociological frames and also into a European setting, as well as attempting to connect the experience so far with probable developments in the future. The book is thus particular, both about worker directors in steel, and about participation in a broader more general sense. It is a most timely contribution to the ongoing debate on this topic.

K.J.W.A.

Preface

This book looks at some of the issues which are raised by having workers on the boards of industrial organizations and tries to put the current debate on this topic into a wider context. It is based on some of the material collected in the course of a research project on worker participation in the British Steel Corporation. This project was sponsored by both the British Steel Corporation and the Social Science Research Council and had the general support of the TUC. It was carried out by research staff representing a number of social science disciplines who were based at the universities of Bradford, Sheffield, Strathclyde and Wales (Cardiff); overall co-ordination of the research was undertaken from the first of these.

The process of collecting data and smoothing the path of the researchers was greatly facilitated by the existence of a steering committee composed of academics, representatives of the Steel Corporation, the TUC and the worker directors. It must be said that none of the interested parties on the steering committee attempted to impose their own conception of what the research should be about. In particular, the Steel Corporation, having agreed to support research in this area, were bold enough to leave the definition of research problems to the research workers and did not attempt to utilize the research to confirm their own prejudices; nor did they demand specific prescriptions as an end result. It might well be in the interests of both social science and industry if this open attitude to social science research was adopted more widely.

Many people associated with the Steel Corporation, management, trade unionists and ordinary employees, gave of their time and energy to provide us with information and help. We are grateful to them all. In particular, the late Lord Melchett and Mr Ron Smith deserve our thanks for giving us access to the corporation and opening many doors. We owe a special debt to the worker directors who for much of the time were the centre of our attentions. They allowed strangers to probe into their lives with a degree of openness and tolerance which we often found amazing. Whilst this book adopts in many places a critical stance towards the role of the worker directors, we infer no criticism of them as individuals. Needless to say, neither the Steel Corporation nor those associated with it are in any way responsible for the contents of this book.

Many people were of help to us in writing the book. In particular we would like to thank Ken Alexander, John Eldridge, and Ken Jones for their support and for their criticism. To the people who have typed successive drafts of this book and to Julia Brannen for help with editing the manuscript we also owe thanks.

P. BRANNEN

E. BATSTONE

D. FATCHETT

P. WHITE

Note: The manuscript for this book was substantially completed early in 1974. Whilst some minor modifications to the text have been undertaken since then, it has not been thought necessary or possible to update it more generally.

1 Introduction

'Participation' has become one of the vogue words of our time. Its widespread use in the media and in the rash of pamphlets and publications which have been produced since the 1960s has tended to mean that any precise, meaningful content has almost disappeared. Moreover, the area of social activity which is subsumed within the term 'participation' is also at least in part subsumed within other terms, such as 'industrial democracy' or 'workers' control'. Scott, for example, has argued that the term 'industrial democracy' ranges in meaning from outright workers' control of industry to the establishment of advisory and non-union committees. He adds that the term 'is in danger of becoming a shibboleth, so vague and ambiguous as to have little or no general meaning.'[1] This situation has led at least one author to conclude that any attempt at definition is doomed from the start.[2]

This terminological proliferation and confusion is, however, significant in that it draws attention to the multiplicity of objectives and meanings which are associated with 'participation'. One cannot assume that the idea of 'participation' has only one parentage. Discussions of 'participation' take place in the context of the analyses of a wide range of social problems which range from exploitation and alienation to productivity and inflation. It would be surprising if, given this multiplicity of aims and analyses, there were any consensus on the meaning of any one particular term, or even the suitability of any one term, to apply across the board.

Most authors use the term 'participation' to refer to an increase in the level of worker influence upon management.[t] Blumberg, for example, defines 'participation' as covering a wide spectrum of possible influence, which ranges from complete worker control to the dissemination of information on the part of management.[4] His definition (and similar definitions) is unsatisfactory, however, in that it maintains that the basic definitive characteristic is that of worker influence being greater than it would otherwise be. But some schemes of 'participation' have not been intended to increase workers' influence upon management; rather the reverse has been the case. Some schemes of joint consultation, for example, have been set up, less with the idea of permitting workers to express their views about the running of the plant, than to put across the company 'message'. Similarly, it is clear that other schemes set up to give increased influence have failed to do so to anything but the most marginal degree. The core of Blumberg's definition, however, that 'participation' is to do with a change in influence or control within the enterprise is important and serves to draw attention to another problem.

Most discussions of 'participation' are confined to institutions or processes which are termed participative and which have been set up with the manifest function of increasing worker influence or control in one or more areas. In this sense 'participation' is a relatively small part of the total system of worker influence over management. The institutions of collective bargaining (backed up by the strike weapon, the work to rule, etc.) are, in this country at least, a major source of worker control. More generally, however, control is exercised in the form of 'custom and practice' and the responsibilities which management themselves expect workers to exercise in the routine performance of their jobs. Less directly and less obviously it is exercised through occasional small-scale sabotage,[5] absenteeism and the act of voting with one's feet which we call labour turn-over. The influence and power exercised through these means is undoubtedly greater for the majority of workers than that derived from formal participatory schemes.

The central focus of this book, however, is on institutions which are seen as formal mechanisms of participation and in particular mechanisms which operate at high organizational levels. Most of the writings on this type of participation have been at the political and ideological level; there is little analysis of such schemes of participation in action. In this country, indeed, there has been little opportunity for such analysis. Research carried out in other European countries offers some insights, but even within this literature there are few detailed studies of the social relations of participation at board-room level. Moreover, variations in history, social structure and culture make comparisons from country to country difficult. (Some aspects of the European experience are, however, examined in Chapter 11.)

Whilst there have been few opportunities to examine in an empirical way what happens when workers are put on to company boards (or high-level management committees), in the last few years the questions of worker participation at board level has assumed a high degree of topicality. In a leading article in 1972 *The Times* argued for board-room participation as a palliative for shop-floor discontent.

It is a well-tried principle of British political life that to institutionalize protest is an effective way of channelling it into constructive ends. . . . There is some research data to suggest that commitment is likely to be increased when those affected participate directly in taking decisions. . . . Given an organization as complex as the modern corporation the presence of a workers' representative on the board is one route towards this goal.

That 'route' has become a matter of sharp public debate since that leader article was written. The draft fifth directive of the European Community and the proposed statute on the European company have forced management, trade unions and government to think out their positions. The TUC has now become a firm advocate of the supervisory board system and is pressing for half of these boards to be appointed by the work people through their trade union machinery.[6] These proposals go beyond the European system in advocating that the supervisory board should be the supreme body of the company and whilst taking into account views expressed at the AGM of shareholders it would not be bound by them. Individual unions are more ambivalent about board representation and some reject the idea. The CBI and the Engineering Employers' Federation are opposed to the supervisory board concept and feel that there should be no statutory obligation

3

on companies to have worker representatives on their boards. The 1970–4 Conservative government took a position probably nearer to the CBI than to the TUC. At the time of writing the current Labour government has still to pronounce. Whilst it is formally committed to legislate on industrial democracy and whilst in a major speech when in opposition Mr Wilson 'commended proposals formulated in Germany for two-tier boards', it seems to be having some difficulty in making up its mind. In a green paper on worker participation in Harland & Wolff, however, the government has stated that it 'would be prepared to consider proposals for board-level participation within the present legal framework which formed part of an overall programme of extension of industrial democracy in the yard'.[7] More recently a committee of inquiry has been announced.

It seems likely, however, that over the next few years there will be increasing worker representation on company boards whether this becomes statutory or not. The *Times* leader quoted above suggests at least some of the reasons for this. But will worker directors in fact 'institutionalize' protest and increase commitment? Is worker representation at board level industrial democracy achieved, or is it a recipe for imminent industrial chaos? Or will it be something else again? This book looks at one experience of board-room participation in British industry, the worker-director experiment in the British Steel Corporation. This experience was researched closely and has provided data which shed some light on the debate.

When the steel industry was re-nationalized in 1967 a very large organization with some quarter of a million employees was created. In the words of the then chairman of the Steel Corporation: 'It was essential to let people in this mammoth set-up feel they had some influence in the way its policies and future were shaped. We had little hope of carrying through nationalization unless we could get a spirit of genuine involvement.'[8] The corporation set out as a matter of policy to achieve this involvement through the introduction of comprehensive consultative machinery, the expansion of collective bargaining and the appointment of worker directors to group boards. It was the latter part of this tripartite strategy which received most

4

publicity, for it was the first time that workers had been given access as of right to high organizational levels within large-scale British manufacturing industry. The management journal *The Director* felt that 'it is not inconceivable that there will be some indigestion in the board rooms when the existing executive directors of the steel industry, men who have spent their whole lives at the job of being steel industry managers, are presented with their new worker-director colleagues on a plate.'[9]

The worker-director scheme was initially viewed by the Steel Corporation as a three-year experiment (which was subsequently extended to four years). Three part-time worker directors were appointed to each of four group boards. The appointments were made by the BSC Chairman, the late Lord Melchett, after consultations with the TUC and within the industry. They were to be paid £1000 per annum and to drop trade-union office. *The Times* characterized the schemes as 'faint-hearted'. Nevertheless it was unique and the Steel Corporation felt and the TUC agreed it should be evaluated.

The research project on which this present book is based was set up in the autumn of 1969 to study this experiment. Whilst the BSC scheme could not in any absolute sense be considered radical, nevertheless it provided an opportunity to study a participatory situation which was unique in this country. We saw this research as being primarily concerned with a description and analysis of the social relations of board-room participation as they were revealed through the worker-director experiment. We tried to create a research framework which allowed us to look at the forms of interaction entered into and played out, the norms and values which guided that interaction and the constraints and controls on interaction. Central to this were the sets of relationships in which the worker director was involved and the attitudes of all the actors in the set towards participation and towards the worker-director scheme. These attitudes would themselves be related to wider structural factors and more generalized sets of values. Central to this also was an examination of the relationships of power and influence, and the processes of decision-making in the BSC.

We created a research programme to try and meet these research aims. This programme involved interviewing a large sample of ordinary employees in the corporation, as well as a sample of shop stewards, management, and full-time trade-union officials. It also involved interviewing all members of the boards on which the worker directors sat, senior national executives of the corporation, the worker directors themselves and national trade-union officials. The formal interviewing programme was matched by a programme of observation at board meetings, meetings of working parties and other committees within the Steel Corporation structure and attendance at trade-union meetings and consultative meetings at which worker directors were present. Finally we examined documentary materials (minutes of meetings, internal memoranda, press cuttings, etc.) which were relevant to the development and operation of the worker-director experiment.[10]

A detailed and lengthy report which gave a preliminary overview of our findings was presented to the British Steel Corporation and the TUC in the autumn of 1971. The report was utilized in the evaluation of the worker-director experiment which both of these organizations then undertook. As a result of these evaluations changes were made in the worker-director scheme, the basic thrust of which was to allow the worker directors to be more involved with the trade-union structure. So, for example, worker directors were, subsequent to the evaluation, allowed to hold any lay trade-union office, and the appointment process for worker directors was organized so as to allow greater trade-union control over appointment and the possibility of greater grass-roots trade-union involvement in selection.[11]

This book examines the initial four-year period during which the worker-director scheme was evolved and operated. However, the problems which it highlights have a more general relevance. In the first part of the book we look at some aspects of the social context in which the scheme was introduced and in which it operated. Chapter 2 examines social and economic changes which have occurred in Britain (and in the western industrialized world more generally) since the second world war and their relationship to the revival of interest in participation. We also review briefly some of the more influential schools of thought on industrial participation in this period.

Chapter 3 looks at the varied meanings which people in the steel industry attach to the term 'participation', their attitudes towards participation and the way these are structured and patterned by their positions in the organization. Attitudes towards participation are also to some extent a function of the history of an industry; Chapter 4 outlines something of the economic and industrial relations history of steel, and the particular problems the industry faced on nationalization.

In the following chapter we describe the ways in which structural change, social and political pressures, and differing definitions of desirable levels of participation gave rise to the Steel Corporation's placing worker directors on its group boards. The group boards of the Steel Corporation were in formal organizational terms different from private enterprise boards; in terms of their actual operation, however, the difference may not have been great. In Chapter 6 we discuss this issue and how far the board room in any organization is the main forum for policy and decision-making. In the following chapters we look at the worker directors themselves and the role they played. The position of worker director was basically a new one in British industry. It was a part for which there was no script ready to hand. It was also a part which many did not understand and others thought irrelevant or non-legitimate. Chapter 7 looks at the characteristics of the men who took on the position of worker director and the ways in which they defined their role. Chapter 8 examines the way in which over time a particular definition of the role of worker director emerged, the activities of the worker directors, and some of the problems they faced. The board meeting constituted, by definition, the formal core of their activities and Chapter 9 examines the role they played on the board, and the evaluations which both they and others made of this role. The chapter also suggests that on the board, as in any other social situation, a continuous process of accommodation has to take place between the actors if stability is to be maintained. In that process of accommodation the rules will be, by and large, laid down by the most powerful, and accommodated to by the least powerful.

The worker directors often described themselves as 'neither

7

fish nor fowl', neither worker nor manager; this role, the role of the man in the middle, is never an easy one and in certain situations becomes very difficult to play, for example in the case of large-scale redundancy. In Chapter 10 we explore some issues raised by worker-director schemes in the context of this critical case. The penultimate chapter looks at some aspects of the European experience of high-level participation and attempts to see how far the themes which arose in the context of the BSC experiment find echoes in the experience of other countries. We suggest that despite particularistic aspects of the BSC scheme some general issues which are pertinent to the theme of high-level participation can be raised. The concluding chapter discusses these issues and the relevance of worker directors to our industrial culture. Finally we have added a postscript which attempts at a broad level of generality to suggest elements of a theoretical explanation for the current vogue for participation and similar vogues in the past.

Notes

1 SCOTT, W. H., *Industrial Democracy: A Revaluation*, Liverpool University Press, 1955, p. 7
2 LEVINSON, H., *International Trade Unionism*, Allen and Unwin, 1972, p. 205
3 See for example, *Industrial Democracy*, BIM Occasional Paper, OPNI, 1968
4 BLUMBERG, P., *Industrial Democracy, the Sociology of Participation*, Constable, 1968, pp. 70–1
5 WALTON, P., and TAYLOR, L., 'Industrial Sabotage, Motives and Meaning', in S. Cohen (ed.) *Images of Deviance*, Penguin, 1971
6 *Industrial Democracy*, Trade Union Congress, 1974
7 *Industrial Democracy*, Department of Manpower Services, HMSO, Belfast, 1975
8 Quoted in *Industrial Society*, January 1968
9 *The Director*, June 1968
10 Details are given in the Appendix
11 For details of these changes and for a view of the scheme from the perspective of a member of BSC management, see JONES, T. K., 'Employee Directors in the British Steel Corporation', in C. Balfour (ed.), *Participation in Industry*, Croom Helm, 1973

2 Participation in the sixties

There have been, during the course of this century, several periods during which there has been an upsurge of interest in, and indeed agitation for, institutional changes in industry which would allow employees to have a greater degree of control over the conditions of their working lives than was normal at the time.

The period from the mid-sixties onwards has seen the most recent of these upsurges of interest. Indeed a veritable participation explosion has taken place not only in the industrial sphere but in other spheres as well. The worker-director experiment in the British Steel Corporation was part of that explosion and must be understood within that context. This chapter examines some of the background to this revived interest and some of the ways in which it was articulated.

Britain along with other western capitalist countries entered after the second world war a period of growth, stability and high employment; this lasted long enough to appear as a new phase in industrial civilization and in the evolution of western capitalism. The major characteristics of this phase have been outlined by a number of commentators and can be briefly described.[1] Firstly, the application of an increasingly intricate and sophisticated technology to production. This technology has been developed at a rapid rate and on an organized basis. Large-scale industrial research has fused science, technology and industrial utilization into one system so that innovation becomes a function of planned development rather than sporadic invention. Sophisticated technology however requires a heavy investment of capital, the mobilization of large resources of technological skill, and the need for complex forms of planning. Thus the second characteristic has been the bureaucratization and concentration of production. Thirdly, the state has come to pay an increasingly important part in the economy; it accounts in its own right for a large part of economic activity and also plays a major role in economic planning.

Both technological and organizational change have led to profound changes within the occupational structure.[2] An increasingly large proportion of the work force is now employed in technical, professional and managerial jobs; there has been a great increase in the number of white collar jobs and a relative decline in the numbers employed in traditional manual jobs. Drucker has described these changes as a movement towards a 'knowledge society'.[3] The need of the economy for more specialists has meant that more and more people who have a close relation with production have had to acquire technical skills through the institutions of higher education and through technical colleges. These in turn have expanded in order to produce both the numbers and type of qualified manpower that the economy needs.

One further aspect of this new capitalism, clearly related to the others, needs to be noted; that is the increase in wealth and the standard of living of both middle and working classes which the new capitalism has brought and indeed needs to maintain given its dependence on large-scale consumption and mass production. The 1950s and 60s were periods of high productivity and high wages. 'The era of high mass consumption was generally achieved and the coming of the "affluent society" was at all events frequently proclaimed.'[4] At the same time, however, as total wealth increased the relative distribution of wealth changed little and the relative distribution of income only marginally.[5]

These developments have not proceeded without imposing considerable strain on the economic and social system; one effect of this strain has been an upsurge of interest in participative mechanisms. We now focus on just a few elements of the industrial economy of the 60s to illustrate the dynamics of this process. Firstly, a rapid rate of technological development has as its counterpart an accelerating rate of obsolescence and high capital costs. These factors led industry during the 60s to engage in more and increasingly sophisticated forms of planning in order to try and ensure the profitability of major projects. This planning involved the realistic prediction of costs and one central, though mercurial, element of this was labour costs. Secondly, the high cost of capital equipment (partly in the face of threatened international competition) spurred employers to attempt to maximize its use for in this way profitability was more likely to be assured. Increased capital utilization in its turn required fuller use and more flexible deployment of labour. For both planning and operational reasons, therefore, managers increasingly realized the need to try to re-assert their control over the work force[6] and to commit and involve workers in the goals of the enterprise.

Thirdly, the government was becoming more involved in the industrial sphere; this was partly a continuation of a trend which can be traced back to the nineteenth century, but it also reflected the increasing significance of the state as an employer and producer. It can be seen as associated with the importance of government contracts (particularly defence) to a wide range of companies, and with the developing role of the government in guaranteeing certain conditions of living to its citizens. Perhaps most importantly, it reflected the awareness that the government could and should manage the economy along Keynesian lines. The state itself had to be able to forecast and plan; it also therefore had an interest in controlling labour costs. The period of Labour government from 1964–70 illustrates these dynamics most fully. Serious balance of payments problems and an industrial infra-structure which was less advanced than that of many other industrial countries prompted the Wilson administration to actively sponsor techno-logical developments and industrial restructuring. Britain had to enter 'the white-hot heat of the technological revolution'.

However, many of the trends we have pointed to, whilst they involved the need to control labour as a factor of production, also strengthened the potential power of labour. Full employ-ment, high capital-labour ratios, integrated processes, the potential disruption to highly integrated plants, particularly in the face of strong competition, all meant that the costs which workers could impose upon employers were considerable. As industry developed and improved its performance, it became

II

ever more susceptible to the growing power of its work force. The legitimation for the further pursuit of industrial expansion rested – or such was the public myth – upon the prosperity it could bring to all. The 'welfare state' legislation after the second world war had created a web of social and welfare services which were thought to prevent anyone falling below a civilized standard of living. A set of minimal rights and expectations was established. Economic growth would lead to, and was essential for, the further extension of social reform. [7] In addition, for an increasing proportion of the working class, economic prosperity was creating a new affluence, and the promise of a constantly improving standard of living. They were told that they 'had never had it so good' but encouraged to the belief that it could be better. Expectations were further developed by the increasing flood of advertising and promotion essential to ensure the volume of sales which the growing production capacity of industry required. The development of industry, and the consumer society, was a promise of a growth in real standards of living; and workers pursued this promise, and to a degree were able to legitimate the use of their power in the pursuit of these goals, by reference to shared social beliefs in prosperity and consumption.

Inevitably this was an unstable situation in several respects. Rapid change meant the decline of some industries, particularly the heavy basic industries. The mines, railways and steel, for example, began to shed their work force dramatically. More generally, rationalization occurred, both in terms of new methods of working associated with particular new pieces of machinery, and also in the reorganization and relocation of major centres of production. Mergers and takeovers reached uprecedented levels. [8] Basic structural problems in the economy particularly the balance of payments and inflation became increasingly a matter of political concern. Whilst price inflation has been with us since the mid-thirties, the sixties and particularly the late sixties saw a more rapid rise in inflation than has been apparent outside of periods of war. Whilst there were a number of different diagnoses of the causes of inflation, wage control was seen as the primary element in the prescriptions for cure. So whilst on the one hand expectations of wage increases and a rising standard of living were not only held by the work force but constantly reinforced, on the other an incomes policy came to be seen as an essential economic tool. The Labour government of 1964–70 began to pursue such a policy which moved from the phase of generalized 'intent' through to restraint and wage freeze, and finally to compulsory powers which seriously threatened existing trade unions' rights and traditional workers' controls. In the opinion of one commentator 'All these developments stimulated not only opposition, but also counter-policies, at the centre of which explicit demands for extensions of workers' control were increasingly found'.[9]

At plant level, productivity bargaining became the vogue. Introduced primarily by American companies[10] it became a particularly British institution and received the sponsorship of the government. Essentially it was a new attempt to balance the conflict between reduction of costs and increases in wages, by buying out workers' job controls, or restrictive practices.[11] It therefore, at least theoretically, permitted greater utilization of labour and higher output, and at the same time satisfied the demands for significant wage increases without increasing costs. But productivity bargaining had several unintended consequences. It expanded the horizon of pay expectations and accelerated the wage spiral. Workers not involved in productivity bargains sought the maintenance of traditional differentials; while workers who were involved sought means of achieving equally large wage increases on negotiations subsequent to the original 'bargain': these tended to depend on traditional bargaining counters. The process of negotiation in productivity bargaining was itself significant. In large part, it was prompted by managements wishing to reassert what they saw as their proper authority and freedom of initiative against the intrusions of the work force. But this demanded both recognition of workers' traditional job controls and the attribution of a certain degree of legitimacy to such controls by management's very readiness to negotiate on the matter. Beyond that, however, the process of negotiating over the reduction of worker controls served to increase worker influence over managerial decision-making at other levels; to some degree, management had to 'open the books'.

Some managements also attempted to solve their problems by de-emphasizing the instrumental aspects of work. It became fashionable to assert that a worker does not live by bread alone.[12] The neo-human relations school[13] found fertile ground, particularly in the more technologically advanced industries, where it was not merely sufficient in many cases that the workers should avoid industrial action but where also lack of involvement, interest and responsibility could have calamitous and costly results.[14] In the age of affluence, man was not primarily economically motivated. The satisfaction of ego and self-actualizing needs became more important, and if industry would provide the required opportunities then the worker would respond. He would seek responsibility, employ his innate abilities and become committed to his task. Job enlargement and job enrichment were therefore seen by some as a solution to the problems of efficiency and productivity.[15] It was however industries which were most technically advanced which tended to take the lead in the redesigning of routine tasks. The best known and earliest exercises in job enrichment and job enlargement have taken place in chemicals, computers and electrical appliances. It is also in such industries that productivity bargaining was first introduced and staff status schemes for manual workers became most widespread. Managements in these industries have also been more prone than in other industries to question the effectiveness of traditional principles of hierarchical organization and attempts have been made to create more organic structures in which 'technicians' play a greater role in the decision-making processes.

By and large these participative experiments were introduced by managements sensitive to the imperatives of technology and the directions of change within the new capitalism. In other sectors, however, the pressure for increased participation tended to come from below. The thrust of technical change and of the concentration of productive resources has had the effect of decreasing the degree of workers' control; but as control has decreased at the point of production it has been asserted at other levels. The strategies most widely noted at the end of the sixties, which have increased in the seventies, have been those of the sit-in and the work-in. While such actions in the main were not primarily participative in terms of goals, there was a strong awareness of attempting to limit managerial prerogative. This was seen most clearly in the case of UCS where the work-in was not perceived primarily in terms of workers' control, but was rather couched in terms of protecting the right to work.[16] Similar strategies were apparent in the growth of industry or organization-wide shop-steward committees and the growing demand for further information about the operation of the enterprise.

The widespread structural changes we have noted and their consequences for decreased task satisfaction and control in some areas and increased control in others, the growing power of organized labour, and the need within the planning process to control labour as a factor of production, all led to a growing search for participative measures. In their attempts to improve company performance managers were increasingly constrained to recognize the power of their work force. At national level too, particularly when the Labour government was in power, the trade unions played an increasingly important role. Discussions between the TUC and the government were frequent, unions had representatives on development councils and a variety of bodies concerned with prices, incomes and industrial relations. The managed economy required that the managed be consulted and involved.

Moreover the broad changes within social and economic structures that we have described had implications for aspects of society other than the industrial and economic. From the sixties onwards participation became not only a modish catchword but also a programme of action in a number of spheres; in the churches and the schools, in the universities and colleges, in the institutions of central and local government, in the family as well as in industry. While to a degree each of these had its own specific explanations, they also reflected the more general developments in society and, more pertinently, probably served to reinforce each other. Within the industrial sphere at both the level of the firm and the level of the state, for managers, workers and government, participation became an important issue in the face of pressing economic problems.

At the beginning of the fifties, the trade unions were un-interested in participation. They stood firm by a view of collective bargaining and permanent opposition as being industrial democracy achieved. By the mid-sixties that position had changed. The TUC in its evidence to the Donovan Commission adopted a more flexible stance. It argued that the conflict of interest between employees and management did not present an overriding obstacle to worker representation at board level or indeed at other levels in the management hierarchy; a distinction needed to be made between the 'negotiating function of the employer and the overall task of management. Once this distinction is established, it can be seen that it does not detract from the independence of the trade unions for trade-union representatives to participate in the affairs of management concerned with production, until the step is reached when any of the subjects become negotiable questions as between trade unions and employers.'[17] The evidence went on to suggest changes in company law which would allow experiments in board-room participation. By the early 1970s, the TUC had developed and hardened its thinking on participation in management. In its green paper on industrial democracy it argued that

to be seen to be relevant, schemes of industrial democracy must be seen to be effective by workers at their own place of work. Yet some of the most basic aspects of the work situation and the security of that employment stem from decisions taken at extremely remote levels . . . It is for this reason that any policy for the extension of industrial democracy must operate at *all* levels, from shop floor to board room and indeed affect the process of national economic planning itself.[18]

It went on to argue that there should be an extension of the collective bargaining function and a statutory obligation on companies to disclose a wide range of information to employees and their representatives; it also advocated the creation of a two-tier board system on the German model, with a supervisory board with half of its members appointed by the work force and which had veto rights over both the management board and the annual shareholders' meeting.

This movement towards a more intense preoccupation with, and advocacy of, participation is also reflected in the thinking of political parties. In the sixties all three political parties began a debate over participation. The Liberals published their 'Plan for Partnership', a Labour working party produced a report on industrial democracy and the Conservative party discussed the need for consideration, consultation and co-operation in their 'Fair Deal at Work'.[19] Since that time the discussion of participation has assumed increasing importance in all parties. The introduction to a recent Bow Group pamphlet illustrates this dramatically:

The rebirth of the Conservatives as a governing party under Disraeli was made possible by the recognition that for democracy to function credibly, the franchise must be widened. The country is faced today with an issue of similar importance. The question now is not who has a right to elect the government, but who has a right to take part in those decisions in business and industry which immediately affect the lives of employees or have far reaching implications for society as a whole.[20]

Indeed, the matter has gone beyond the level of internal discussion. The Conservative government in 1973 announced that it would be producing a green paper on worker participation and it also announced that it was actively looking, along with both the CBI and the TUC, at ways of improving direct participation through schemes of job enrichment and enlargement. The 1974 Labour government has also announced that a bill to deal with industrial democracy will be one of its top legislative priorities. Since then it has set up a committee of inquiry to look at methods of implementing board-room participation.

Interest in participation has also increased amongst management. We have made reference to the increasing enthusiasm management has shown for particular forms of direct participation (for example, job enrichment and job enlargement). Apart from a torrent of articles in management journals and publications, several organizations have mounted experimental programmes, notably ICI.[21] There has also been increasing discussion of the role of the work force in relation to decision-making in the enterprise. The entry of Britain into the Common Market and the need to consider the EEC proposals on worker participation contained in the draft fifth directive of the

European commission and the draft statute for European company law have given increased emphasis to what was already a strong trend. As a recent commentary has pointed out, 'the press has been full of articles and comment on different aspects of worker participation in recent months. A year ago the possible development of a two-tier board system and employee directors would have been given only superficial study. Today it is the subject of widespread and serious consideration, along with other ways of achieving wider employee involvement.'[22] Recently the CBI has pronounced that they 'believe that what is now required is the development of methods allowing a wider degree of participation in the process of decision-making throughout British Industry'. This would involve the establishment of the practice of joint consultation at plant level, and the establishment of a company council at which 'members of the board, including the chairman and chief executive would make themselves available to discuss the annual figures, capital investment programmes, mergers or takeovers and other matters pertaining to the successful conduct of the company'.[23] Whilst these are hardly radical proposals, the significant point is that encouragement of worker participation is now formally part of CBI policy.

This renewed interest in participation by practical men whether they be workers, managers or politicians has been matched by an increasing output of analysis and prescription from academics and other commentators. We conclude this chapter by examining some of this writing as it not only reflects the aspects of social change with which we have been dealing but also provides the philosophies and vocabularies of this change.

PHILOSOPHIES OF PARTICIPATION

We will distinguish three types of participation philosophies which emerged during the period we have been discussing. The first of these is essentially a pluralist philosophy; Fox has summarized its main elements as follows:

the enterprise is not [seen as] a unitary structure but [as] a coalition of individuals, and groups with their own aspirations and their own perceptions of the structure. . . . It includes the notion that individuals and groups with widely varying priorities agree to collaborate in social structures which enable all participants to get something of what they want. The terms of collaboration are settled by bargaining. Management is seen as making its decisions within a complex set of constraints which include employees, consumers, suppliers, government, the law, the local community and sources of finance.[24]

This philosophy accepts the basic structure of authority and power in the enterprise but at the same time stresses the responsibilities of management in terms of maintaining and improving standards of living within the context of a rapidly changing economy.

Industry must rationalize and modernize at an increasing rate . . . The tempo of change seems to account in part for the unrest and the feeling of remoteness from decision making or influencing events which is arising in this as well as other countries . . . But the people want the material standard of life they are enjoying and the managers are in the main responsible for maintaining the economy so that they continue to get it.[25]

Intellectually this philosophy stems, ironically, from a rejection of formal participation; its emphasis and primary concern is on collective bargaining. Pluralism provides the industrial relations orthodoxy of our society; it stresses the normality of conflict and the existence of distinct workers' interests from a particular perspective but the aim is maintaining 'related but separate interests and objectives . . . in some kind of equilibrium'.[26]

At the end of the fifties the argument that industrial democracy was already with us was set out in ringing prose by Clegg.

The doctrines of collective bargaining which have been set out [here] constitute a practical and empirical creed, the creed of democracy achieved, of trade unionism which has arrived. They are fine doctrines to encourage men to protect what they have achieved from the corruption of Fascism or Communism. They may be useful guides to show how democratic society should be reconstructed . . . but they have little in common with the visionary doctrines of the early industrial democrats, for visions are not tough, nor practical, nor empirical.[27]

19

Blumberg has summarized Clegg's ideas as follows: 'The key elements in any system of industrial democracy are merely, 1 The existence of a trade union strong enough to oppose management and 2 A management which accepts trade unionism as a "loyal opposition" and is willing to compromise and come to terms with it in the interests of industrial harmony and unity.'[28]

The Cleggian view of industrial democracy was essentially embodied in the Donovan Report.[29] This again stressed the pluralistic framework of industrial relations but recommended the resolution of conflict primarily through adjustments in the institutional structure to place authority and initiative at plant level where balanced power and the possibility of broader agreements could be achieved. It also stressed managements' responsibilities for change. These views were significantly influenced by what Flanders called 'the challenge from below' that is, an awareness of the growing pressures upon management from 'an increasingly self-conscious and articulate labour force demanding its rightful share of power in industry.'[30] More recently this philosophy has been developed by McCarthy and Ellis and labelled 'management by agreement'.[31] Donovan, it is argued, failed to recognize the difficulties and implications of their recommendations. Donovan had been a great supporter of the idea of productivity bargaining but 'what Donovan failed to do was to discuss how certain other factors are making it progressively more difficult for even the most enlightened and well-meaning management to respond to union demands even where the Donovan conditions are met. These factors constitute the second challenge now facing British management.'[32] This 'challenge from without' is 'a complex of economic, technological and institutional pressures' of the kind we have already noted. These factors 'all tend to produce the need for a series of changes within the enterprise itself', which require changes within the work force. Productivity bargaining can be seen most clearly as an expression of the recommended reaction to these pressures. In Donovan terms, the 'trade off' in productivity bargaining was simple; 'the workers get higher earnings and management gets lower costs and higher productivity.' It is not, however, quite like that. 'Firstly, that simple idea requires new ways of thinking from management and makes massive new demands on managers and supervisors; secondly, it conceals a challenge to some long-established and cherished trade-union principles; and, thirdly, it represents a change in the socio-economic status of a group or groups of employees that sets up a chain reaction between rewards, roles and relationships throughout an organization.'[33] The spur to increasing the range of bargaining has impressed upon people the range of control which workers have, and the extent to which issues over which negotiation occurs have major reverberations upon the operation of the plant generally. Productivity bargaining then, by its very nature, stressed the centrality of workers in the managerial process.

The philosophy of management by agreement has derived largely from the working out of a framework and the realization of its full implications: 'authority must be shared with workers through an extension of the area of joint regulation.'[34] In operational terms 'this would entail a transformation of the normal processes of collective bargaining so that collective agreements are developed which cover subjects and areas of management decision-taking that extend well beyond those proposed by the Donovan Commission . . . there would no longer be any room for a doctrine of employer-reserved rights or "managerial prerogatives" '.[35] The distinctive element in this philosophy is, therefore, to lay stress upon an extension of collective bargaining as the means of promoting participation. It is still very much a collective bargaining *à la* Clegg approach – 'the customary rules of collective bargaining would still apply, each side would remain free to take what action it thought fit in the circumstances' (where there was disagreement).[36] McCarthy is at pains to stress that 'what has been proposed above is not a system of workers' control. It is a meaningful form of workers' participation in management . . . and could be said to represent a programme for promoting democracy. These proposals are not intended to challenge management's ultimate responsibility for manning the enterprise.'[37] The pluralist philosophy is basically conservative in that it in no way seeks to alter the basic authority structure within industry. Rather it seeks to make that authority structure more viable by promoting reforms which take into account the changing structure of advanced capitalist society and aim to contain conflict within the parameters of the planned economy.

The second philosophy we turn to is in direct contrast to this. It rejects the basic assumptions of pluralism, that society is segmented into groups who have equal access to power and resources, and whose interests can be mutually satisfied through constructive conflict. Fox describes the fundamental proposition of this philosophy as being

a belief that industrial society, while manifestly to some extent a congeries of small special interest groups vying for scarce goods, status or influence, is more convincingly characterised in terms of the over-arching exploitation of one class by another, of the property-less by the propertied, of the powerless by the more powerful. By this view, any talk of 'checks and balances' however apt for describing certain subsidiary phenomena, simply confines our understanding of the primary dynamics which shape and move society – a useful confusion indeed for the major power holders since it obscures the domination of society by its ruling strata through institutions and assumptions which operate to exclude anything approaching a genuine power balance.[38]

This philosophy then rests upon the view that industry is dominated by a conflict between the interests of capital and labour. It differs from the pluralistic management by agreement in that instead of trying to maintain 'equilibrium' it attempts to shift dramatically the balance of power, and ultimately to change the structure of industry and society more generally.

This goal is to be approached through the 'extension of industrial democracy' through a 'single channel of representation, based on trade-union organization and involving a further development of the scope of collective bargaining . . .' in order to challenge the prerogatives of management at all levels and 'on all the main facets of working life, including forward planning of manpower, rationalization and investment policies'.[39] The basic aim is to control management decisions and ensure that managements should not override workers' interests through the exercise of arbitrary power. Whilst at a tactical level many of the prescriptions which derive from this philosophy overlap with those derived from a pluralist perspective the basic assumptions and goals are clearly different. The aim is not joint regulation but workers' control:

> . . . all those demands which strengthen trade union powers and self-confidence have a control element within them. 'Control' is not at all identical with self-management: it implies a dual relationship in which one human party constrains [superintends, supervises] another. 'Workers control' is control over capitalists, limiting their powers to act as they will. It has to be developed to its farthest frontiers in order that with it can arise the understanding that capitalists are both unnecessary and inimical to the economic and moral well-being of the people.[40]

The pressing of participatory and control demands is a stage in the movement towards the creation of a system of workers' self-management. The basic question is 'whether the workers are to control their own destinies or to be subject to ever more intensive and minute control themselves as the power of the oligarchs becomes ever more arbitrary and ever more irresponsible'.[41]

Whilst the basic philosophy is shared by many social analysts, its working out as a participatory philosophy and practice in this country is most clearly identified with those associated with the Institute for Workers Control. In this form (unlike similar analyses further to the left) it is seen as a gradualist movement which works within current social structures and is committed to operating through the trade unions and the Labour party. Participatory forms which impose some real measure of worker control over management action, or at least the possibility of such action, are encouraged; other forms, such as some types of joint consultation are castigated as merely allowing workers 'to participate in the decisions of others'. A central demand is for the 'opening of the books'; that is for the maximum information to be made available to the work force. Worker representation on management committees and boards is seen as important within that context, as well as being a source of countervailing powers. Whilst the extension of the institutions of collective bargaining is encouraged, 'there is nothing impractical or unreal in the idea that workers should elect two sets of representatives to carry out two different functions – the traditional defensive role of the trade union bargaining

B

machine and the new offensive forms of worker control over management'.[42] Within these new offensive forms the sit-in and the work-in are seen as important tactics in promoting a more social definition of industry's goals.[43]

Both this two-power model of social relations and the pluralistic perspective discussed earlier, whilst their basic premises differ, start from a position which sees industry as consisting of groups with differential access to power and with interests that bring them into conflict. The final participatory philosophy we consider by contrast embodies an essentially unitary philosophy. Its frame of reference is not that of group conflict but rather a diagnosis of what leads individuals to behave the way they do.[44] Its ideas stem from 'behavioural science' and in particular psychology, and its emphasis is upon direct, rather than indirect, participation. Over the last thirty to forty years there have been three theories of human motivation which have been influential in the industrial area. The earliest, stemming from the work of Taylor, assumed the primacy of economic motives in man's orientation to work, and based its prescription for the control of work behaviour upon a simple set of financial rewards and punishments. The second followed as a critique of the behavioural assumptions of Taylorism. In the work that emerged as a result of the Hawthorne experiments, economic man was replaced by social man, and motivation was seen as a response to the social environment of the work place. This human relations school emphasized the necessity for non-authoritarian forms of supervision and the involvement of employees with the work group and the enterprise. It fostered various forms of what Child has called 'pseudo-participation' of which the joint consultative movement in this country might be considered one type.[45] However, the model of 'social man' proved unable to explain work behaviour with adequate consistency and led to the search for more complex formulations.

This search led to the third behavioural model of man, man as self-actualizing; this model and its applications have enjoyed considerable popularity in this country since the early sixties, particularly amongst management, and have led to a number of experiments to enhance job satisfaction.[46] The theoretical basis for much of the writing of the self-actualizing school has been Maslow's theory of a 'hierarchy of needs'. Briefly this states that human motivation is based upon the satisfaction of an ascending order of 'needs'; this moves from the satisfaction of basic biological requirements, through the needs for security and attention, to higher-order needs for esteem and self-actualization. Before self-actualizing needs become predominant, lower-order needs must have been largely gratified.[47] Maslow's work has acted as a catalyst for many applied behavioural scientists, the best known of whom is probably Herzberg.

Herzberg, in his work, stresses that the factors leading to job satisfaction are not simply the obverse of those leading to dissatisfaction. Dissatisfaction is different from non-satisfaction. Factors associated with job dissatisfaction derive from man's overriding need to avoid physical and social deprivation – and this is the 'Adam' conception of the nature of man. It is the 'Abraham' conception which is associated with job satisfaction – these factors concern man's need to realize his human potential for perfection. Man has a need to understand, to achieve, and through achievement to experience psychological growth, and these needs are great motivators. Within the work situation, management action in such spheres as pay, security and working conditions, merely serves to prevent dissatisfaction but fails to motivate the individual or give him real satisfaction. Only rewarding work, recognition, responsibility and opportunities for self-development can do this. Herzberg therefore recommends the design of jobs not with the Taylorist goal of exploiting the division of labour to increase efficiency, but with the aim of 'enriching' them in terms of motivating factors. This requires 'vertical job loading' – it does not mean adding another tedious, undemanding task to a worker, it is not merely an increase in variety which is required. The aim is to remove some of the constraints upon the worker role – to increase his area of discretion and responsibility and the challenge of work. In its pure form, this philosophy concentrates upon the individual rather than the work group.[48] Other approaches to job satisfaction, most notably in this country that of the Tavistock Institute, have stressed that individual needs at work must be seen within the context of the larger socio-technical

25

system. Emphasis is placed on matching the work group as a whole to the task as a whole and it is argued that in this way more scope is provided not only for the satisfaction of worker needs but also for enterprise efficiency.[49]

The work of Herzberg and others shares certain characteristics with the human relations school which it has virtually replaced. It views the enterprise in a unitary way and assumes that providing man's needs at work, of various orders, are satisfied, then his interests and those of management will coincide and he will be willing to accept and work at enterprise objectives. Whilst this philosophy presents a theory of the individual human being which leads to an attempt to humanize work, its basic aim is to reconcile individual motivation with organizational purposes. Indeed, Herzberg himself does not see the job enrichment techniques he advocates as being fully participative. 'Although there is no room for individual participation in the setting of goals, it is certainly possible that the ways in which these goals are to be reached can be left to the judgement of the individuals. . . . This is a reasonable solution to the problem of motivation, more reasonable than the usual formulation of participation. To expect individuals at lower levels in an organization to exercise control over the establishment of overall goals is unrealistic.'[50] Differential power and the possibility that different groups within the enterprise have different, and possibly conflicting, expectations of work are either not taken into account or discounted as pathological. It is for these reasons that several commentators have argued that this participatory philosophy is managerialist and essentially manipulative.

We have examined briefly three of the main philosophies of participation in the sixties. We have also tried in this chapter to suggest some of the reasons for the renewed interest in participation in this period, and offered a guide to some of the processes involved. For most of the rest of this book we look at participation and attitudes to participation in one particular organization, the British Steel Corporation. The nationalized industries are formally more committed to participation than most other industry in this country. Steel was nationalized in 1967, at a time when participation was very much in the air, and within this organization the principles of participation were taken further than they had ever been taken before in a nationalized industry. The BSC therefore provides us with an illustration of the way in which the general trends we have talked about were worked out within one organization, and with a case study of the social dynamics of one particular form of participation.

Notes

1   GALBRAITH, J. K., *The New Industrial State*, Penguin, 1969; DRUCKER, P., *The Age of Discontinuity*, Harper Row, 1969; KIDRON, M., *Western Capitalism since the War*, Weidenfeld and Nicolson, 1968
2   DRUCKER, P., op cit.; BRANNEN, P., 'Industrial and Economic Change and the entry into work', in *Entering the World of Work*, HMSO, 1975
3   DRUCKER, P., 'Knowledge Society', *New Society*, 24 April 1968; see also his book *The Age of Discontinuity*, Harper Row, 1969
4   GOLDTHORPE, J. H., et al., *The Affluent Worker in the Class Structure*, Cambridge University Press, 1969, pp. 5–6
5   For a recent discussion of this issue cf. ATKINSON, A. B., *Unequal Shares*, Allen Lane, 1972
6   FLANDERS, A., *Collective Bargaining: Prescription for Change*, Faber & Faber, 1967
7   CROSLAND, C. A. R., *The Future of Socialism*, Jonathan Cape, 1956
8   See for example GLYN, A., and SUTCLIFFE, B., *British Capitalism, Workers and the Profit Squeeze*, Penguin, 1972, pp. 143–7
9   COATES, K. and TOPHAM, A. J., *Industrial Democracy in Great Britain*, Spokesman Books, 1974, pp. 350–1
10 DANIEL, W. W., *Beyond the Wage–Work Bargain*, PEP, 1972
11 FLANDERS, A., *The Fawley Productivity Agreements*, Faber & Faber, 1964
12 DANIEL, W. W. and MCINTOSH, N., *The Right to Manage*, PEP, 1972
13 This is discussed more fully later in the chapter.
14 DANIEL and MCINTOSH, op. cit.; COTGROVE, S., et al., *The Nylon Spinners*, Allen and Unwin, 1971, especially Chapter 1
15 COTGROVE et al., op. cit., Chapter 2, for a useful summary of literature
16 MURRAY, R., *UCS: The Anatomy of Bankruptcy*, Spokesman Books, 1972
17 TUC, *Trade Unionism* (Evidence to the Donovan Commission), 1966
18 *Industrial Democracy*, Interim Report by the TUC General Council, 1973, p. 27
19 Liberal Party, *Opportunity Knocks*, New Directions No. 4, Plan for Partnership; Labour Party, *Industrial Democracy*, Working Party Report, 1967; Conservative Political Centre, *Fair Deal at Work*, 1968

27

20 *Employee Participation in British Companies*, Bow Group, June 1973, p. 1
21 PAUL, W. J., and ROBERTSON, K. B., *Job Enrichment and Employee Motivation*, Gower Press, 1971
22 *Employee Directors and Supervisory Boards*, Industrial Partnership Association, 1973, p. 8
23 *The Responsibilities of British Companies*, CBI, September 1973, p. 21
24 FOX, ALAN, 'A social critique of pluralist ideology', in J. Child (ed.), *Man and Organisation*, Allen and Unwin, 1973
25 *Industrial Democracy*, BIM Occasional Papers, 1968, p. 7
26 FOX, ALAN, 'Industrial Sociology and Industrial Relations', *Royal Commission Research Paper*, No. 5, HMSO
27 CLEGG, H. A., *A New Approach to Industrial Democracy*, Blackwell, 1960, p. 29
28 BLUMBERG, P., *Industrial Democracy, the Sociology of Participation*, Constable, 1968, p. 141
29 *Report of the Royal Commission on Trade Unions and Employers Associations, 1905–1968*, HMSO, London, Cmnd 3625
30 FLANDERS, A., *Industrial Relations: What is wrong with the system?*, IPM, 1965, ch. 5
31 MCCARTHY, W. E. J. and ELLIS, N. D., *Management by Agreement*, Hutchinson, 1973
32 Ibid., p. 91
33 COTGROVE, et al., op. cit., p. 41
34 MCCARTHY and ELLIS, op. cit., p. 96
35 Ibid.
36 Ibid., p. 105
37 Ibid., pp. 106–7
38 FOX, A., in Child, op. cit., p. 206
39 BARRATT-BROWN, M., *From Labourism to Socialism*, Spokesman Books, 1972, p. 185
40 COATES, K. and TOPHAM, A. J., 'Participation or Control', in K. Coates (ed.), *Can the Workers Run Industry?*, Sphere Books, 1968
41 Ibid., p. 240
42 Ibid., p. 238
43 BARRATT-BROWN, op. cit.
44 COTGROVE, et al., op. cit.
45 CHILD, J., *British Management Thought*, Allen and Unwin, 1969
46 See WILSON, N. A. B., *On the Quality of Working Life*, D.E. Manpower Paper No. 7, HMSO, 1973
47 MASLOW, A. H., *The Psychological Review*, 1945, SO, pp. 370–96
48 HERZBERG, F., *Work and the Nature of Man*, World Publishing Co., 1966
49 BROWN, R. K., 'Research and Consultancy in Industrial Enterprises: A Review of the contribution of the Tavistock Institute of Human Relations to the development of Industrial Sociology', *Sociology*, January 1967
50 HERZBERG, F., MAUSNER and SYNDERMAN, *The Motivation to Work*, Wiley, 1959, pp. 136–7

3 Vocabularies of participation

In the previous chapter we outlined some thoughts about the ways in which ideas about participation were related to social and economic changes in society in the sixties. We discussed at the end of the chapter participatory philosophies which have been put forward by academics and commentators who, in a sense, acted as the official proponents of particular viewpoints. In the main, their ideas are coherent and well developed. But how do they relate to the ideas of the ordinary person in industry whether he be shop steward or director, manager or worker? And how far do the ideas of shop stewards and directors differ and how far are they the same? We cannot offer any definite answers to these questions but in this chapter we attempt an examination of the ways in which a large number of people to whom we talked in the steel industry thought about participation.[1] Clearly there is likely to be some relationship between the formalized and documented arguments discussed earlier and the views of our respondents. The formalized arguments are part of the current repertoire of 'ideas in society'; they are related to, and emerge from, particular social and economic situations, they are a reflection of the problems which are facing management and workers in a multitude of production situations.

Unlike the views of the academics, however, the ideas of our respondents are not so clearly articulated and consistent. Ideas about participation and attitudes towards it will depend to varying degrees upon more general views about the nature of industry and society and the ordering of relationships within them. But more than that, when people talk about participation or take up particular attitudes towards participation, they are reflecting their own store of experiences within industry and their own hopes for the future. It is for this reason that we have used as a title for this chapter the phrase 'vocabularies of participation'. Participation, as we have pointed out earlier, is a word which means different things to different people. In talking about participation people are justifying the stance they take towards different forms of behaviour in industry. Our concern, however, is not with the view of individuals as such. In the words of C. Wright Mills, 'The differing reasons men give for their actions are not themselves without reasons.'[2] We are interested in the frameworks within which people think about participation and the ways in which particular orientations towards participation are located in particular social contexts. It is these two concerns which form the basis of this chapter.

In the first part of the chapter we want to examine the cognitive frameworks which people use in approaching participation. For heuristic purposes we distinguish four primary frames of reference: the nature of relationships in industry, efficiency and profit, hierarchy and expertise, and lastly satisfaction and involvement. Whilst analytically separate, in reality the frameworks overlap and any individual or group of individuals may be utilizing one or more of these frames of reference when he thinks about participation. Nor do they always hang together in neat paradigms. The imperatives of one framework may act as a constraint upon or even contradict the imperatives of another. Ambiguity, confusion, even contradiction, are perhaps more frequent than coherence. Differing frameworks may be drawn upon in different situations and over time the primacy of particular frameworks may be superseded by others. Nevertheless, particular sets of ideas fit most easily with specific structural positions and the interests associated with them. We show that these in turn are associated with varying definitions of participation, especially the level and areas where participation is felt to be most relevant. In the final section of the chapter we try to look in particular at the ways in which board-level participation is defined and relate this to the previous discussion. First, however, we examine each of the four primary frames of reference in turn.

RELATIONSHIPS IN INDUSTRY

The images which people have about industry and its essential relational structure are often central to the way in which they view participation. In this section we suggest that the general view of relationships within industry can be approximated to three models which we term dichotomous, pluralistic and unitary; these models also formed the basis of the philosophies of participation discussed in the last chapter. The dichotomous model of industry is based upon a notion that industry is divided into two opposing camps. The conflict between them is not capable of any basic solution within the current structure of society and is indeed the crucial characteristic of society. Amongst those who hold a dichotomous view of industry some have an alternative view of society in which radical changes in the balance of power will create a structure in which conflict will not be a basic element. Others are merely resigned to a power situation in which they are the permanent underdogs.

A dichotomous framework was more prevalent amongst the general sample of workers we interviewed than amongst other groups. 32% of these respondents saw management and workers as being essentially oppositional groups whilst 67% saw industry as basically a co-operative venture. (It is interesting that in this respect the general work force was more radical than its lay union representatives; amongst our general shop-steward sample only 16% held this view – so much for the public myths of shop stewards as the leaders of agitation.[3])

The sociological bases of dichotomous images amongst workers have been widely discussed.[4] The view has two implications in relation to participation: one is a revolutionary perspective that argues for structural change in society and the implementation of worker self-management; the other is a fatalistic perspective that accepts the divisions within society as permanent and adopts short-term hedonistic attitudes. This was the most common perspective amongst this particular category of workers. For both categories, however, management was seen as a threat and participation (other than full worker control) seen as an attempt to emasculate and incorporate the work force.

31

However, a dichotomous model of relations within industry was not only located within the general work force. It was to be found amongst those in more elevated positions in the organization, particularly amongst directors (the numbers holding such perspectives, however, were very small). For them conflict was an essential, permanent ingredient of industrial relations. Like the fatalistic workers, they saw the basic, divisive structure of society as given and immutable. They, through chance or ability, found themselves in particular structural positions which provided them with a certain set of interests and responsibilities solely concerned with profits and the welfare of the organization and its owners. These responsibilities could only be met by recognizing that in fundamental respects their interests conflicted with those of the work force. Like workers who held dichotomous views they rejected any degree of participation.

Amongst those who held dichotomous images, however, we can distinguish between what we might call 'hard' and 'soft' images. Up to this point we have emphasized hard images. The soft images were significantly more common. Whilst operating from a basis that there is a polarity of interests and whilst in certain cases holding a vision of an alternative society, those who held soft dichotomous images believed that open conflict must be avoided and institutions of compromise supported. Such a model was particularly common amongst full-time officials. Many, whilst expressing some form of belief in a 'socialist society', saw it as an impossible dream which had no bearing upon current strategies of action. In practice one tried to maintain and further one's own interests, to compromise, but never to join. Postures were basically oppositional, relative power was fairly clearly understood and bargains made which were restricted to certain areas. The fear of being 'tied in' is central to this perspective. Consultation and discussion, however, can be useful in so far as they delineate areas of real conflict and avoid conflict due to misunderstanding. Discussion served to clarify information and strategies relevant to negotiation. Schemes of participation were looked on with some unease. They merely blurred the lines. A few managers also held a similar perspective. They too had a fear of confusing roles and interests; the goals which they saw as paramount, those of efficiency and profit, could be compromised if workers or unions were to have too much influence upon managerial decisions. At the same time their goals could be achieved more easily if 'unnecessary' conflict was avoided.

The basic feature of the dichotomous model, whether it be of the hard or soft variety, is that whilst acknowledging duality it does not recognize the legitimacy of the position of the other side. In this respect it differs from our second model, the pluralist, the essential feature of which is that it recognizes several sets of legitimate interests. What contrasts the pluralist model with the soft dichotomous perspective is that the former holds that the balance of power between capital and labour is relatively equal and permits of meaningful contracts and compromises. The latter does not imply that there is equality of power; those holding it may not accept the practicability of working towards radical change, but they do not accept either that there is an equal balance of power or a set of interests that permit 'free' compromise.

The pluralist recognizes the legitimacy of these interests if only in a conditional manner and constrained by the 'rules of the game'. Pluralism was for many of our respondents pragmatic in the sense that it implied an unconscious and highly conditional acceptance of different interests largely based upon 'the way things work' and the perceived balance of power at any point in time. The pragmatists were not concerned with general ideas about relationship in industry; rather they saw themselves as 'having a job to do' and they attempted to balance interests in order to fulfil their primary goal. In this framework participation is one way amongst many of going about things; but it was seen as increasingly important because of the social changes which universal education, higher living standards, unionization and capital intensity had brought to industry.

This pragmatic pluralist framework finds its greatest expression amongst management. At one extreme and amongst a few managers concentrated in works which had a common company history, participation was clearly articulated as a form of manipulation. For others there was a realization that they 'could regain control by sharing it'.[5] Efficiency supersedes authority as a primary value – and participation is seen as a possible means to that end.

Some ordinary workers and a significant minority of union officials might also be labelled pragmatic pluralists. They also did not concern themselves with questions about the general nature of industrial relations. They were concerned with specific goals such as decreasing noise level in a mill, or increasing the bonus rate. The needs of management were given conditional legitimacy and in so far as participative procedures or institutions could be of some help, they were accepted and espoused.

The final model we turn to is the unitary model. Within this model, which was widely espoused by both management and workers, harmony and co-operation is seen as both normal, desirable and endemic, and accordingly the vocabulary of 'team spirit' and 'the family' is always apposite. Views as to the basis of this harmony varied somewhat amongst our respondents; some argued that since both sides derive their rewards from the successful operation of the company, similarly they have a common interest in capital investment. Others stressed that it was the product of teamwork itself – management and worker needed each other for the successful completion of their respective tasks. Good co-operation in itself would lead to rewards of both an economic and terminal nature on both sides.

Participation of a very limited kind is the very essence of a unitary managerial style; consultation at the face-to-face level is seen to be important. Consensus in itself legitimates the position of management, as long as the manager both maintains efficiency and ensures the involvement, commitment and happiness of the worker. One major means of doing this is consultation and 'keeping the worker in the picture'. Conflict is an aberration. Few of our management respondents explained conflict in terms of the existence of 'militants' or 'agitators'. More common systems of explanation related to poor communication or the view that those causing trouble were labouring under misconceptions which may be the product of past work experiences or poor training and teaching. These weaknesses required correction, and one instrument for this was participation.

Some workers and union officials also held similar explanations for lack of consensus. They, like management, attributed it to the failings of other workers; or, more importantly, failures were not infrequently laid at management's door – a particular manager's incompetence, ignorance or incivility. Managerial weaknesses may lead to greater demands for participation on the part of workers – to have a say in their job tasks, to be put in the picture and so on.

EFFICIENCY AND PROFIT

This second frame of reference is related to the overall goals of industry, and participation is judged as a means in relation to those goals. Efficiency is a major theme in arguments concerning participation and is often linked with the third frame of reference we shall be discussing, namely hierarchy and expertise. For management in particular their structural position in the organization demands that they should be primarily oriented towards profitable and efficient production. The great majority of our managerial respondents were concerned with the relationship between efficiency and participation, although there was a variety of perceived links. A few managers and directors felt that some minimal participation was necessary as a recognition of the demands of the work force and the changing culture of the enterprise. Not to concede something would be to go against the tide and ultimately be inefficient. At the same time, if participation were to reach any significant level, then the incompetence and ignorance of workers and their innate greed would breed inefficiency. Participation therefore must not be allowed to have any perceptible impact on managerial prerogatives or routine. 'Our job is not to hold workers' hands or have committees, it is to make steel.' Participation had to be limited to discussion and consultation in non-contentious areas, e.g. welfare or the details of the implementation of some capital investment schemes.

Another variant on this particular perspective argued that

35

if in our current society industry was to be efficient the work force had to be involved and carried along. Accordingly participation was put forward as a means of maintaining the involvement of the work force. Consultation procedures were seen as a means of forestalling trouble on the shop floor; of learning of problems early; of explaining matters to workers to ensure their commitment to management and managerial goals; of maintaining a harmonious relationship in the industry. The contribution which participation could make to efficiency was either seen, rather negatively, as the avoidance of disruption or, more positively, as the promotion of good teamwork. The latter not infrequently rested upon the view that if you treated people as human beings then they would be more co-operative.

The structural position of the worker in the enterprise does not lead him to place the same emphasis on efficiency *per se* as management. Indeed, his subordinate position in the organization, his limited share of rewards, together with the alienating tendencies of many jobs within industry, in many cases might lead in the opposite direction. However, in the steel industry commitment of the work force to efficiency appears to be high. This does not in the main have any connection with the fact that the industry is nationalized. The majority of the workers in our sample expressed a relatively high degree of job satisfaction and there was little variation between the various occupational groups, either shop floor or white collar. Moreover, other factors within the steel industry, such as traditional systems of seniority and payment, the interdependency between industry and community, the machismo and culture of the industry, all lead in the direction of a high degree of worker involvement in the success of the industry. For many workers and lay union representatives the extension of participation was seen as a means towards greater efficiency – not in the managerial sense of improving teamwork, but through permitting workers to exercise their skills and abilities. Management was often seen as being ignorant of how steel is really made – workers could tell them.

The efficiency and profit framework was particularly common amongst those who also held a pragmatic pluralist perception. This frame of reference when held by management in particular would appear to be potentially the most radical in the opportunities it created for participation. Management who held such a framework were willing to accept a high degree of participation if it would result in greater efficiency. These managers were primarily goal, rather than status conscious – efficiency was more important than authority. Respondents holding a hard dichotomous view amongst the work force showed little concern for efficiency within what they saw as the existing socially inefficient structure of industry; amongst management a dichotomous framework led to a stress on profits and a rejection of participation. Amongst workers holding a soft dichotomous perspective there was a rather uncertain concern with efficiency, which was seen in the existing system as crucial to their economic rewards, whilst for such managers participation was not seen as being related to efficiency. The unitary framework tended to be closely associated with efficiency amongst both management and workers. Participation, through promoting a common sense of enterprise, would play a major part in this.

It must be said, however, that the goal of efficiency was seen as a major limitation upon the extension of participation by many respondents from all groups. Many arguments here relate to ideas about authority and expertise. But other arguments related to the inefficiency of the democratic processes of decision-making: the difficulty of getting quick incisive decisions. This position was summed up in the often-used aphorism 'a camel is a horse designed by a committee'. Moreover, managers doubted the commitment of workers to the total enterprise which they felt to be essential; committees with workers on them were therefore suspect.

HIERARCHY AND EXPERTISE

Wherever there are industrial enterprises there are authority relations and a division of labour. It is to a frame of reference based upon these functional and scalar aspects of industry that we now turn. Such a perspective was most frequently articulated by management. Virtually all of our managerial respondents were sensitive to their authority status. The majority felt that their areas of discretion, both in terms of decision-making and the application of expertise, had been reduced because of nationalization.[6] Within this perspective participation was also seen as a threat. Arguments were put forward which stressed the legitimacy of management's position. Someone had to be in charge; participation raised the problem of 'too many chiefs, not enough Indians...'. Following from this was the argument of management's right to manage – some, particularly amongst the older directors, made reference to the rights of ownership. More generally, it was argued that, given it was management's job to manage, they must be given the rights and powers to do so; expressed at a more personal level, managers argued that since it was their heads which would roll if things went wrong, then they alone should make decisions.

These arguments rested essentially upon an assertion of the need to have a hierarchical authority structure. A second set of arguments related authority to achieved competence. In the main these arguments centred around some idea of professionalism; managers had the right to manage through the mere fact of having achieved managerial positions; this managerialist functional theory of stratification rested on the belief that those with ability achieved top positions; ergo those at the top had ability.[7] Younger, generally better-educated managers, stressed the fact of educational achievement in itself rather than acquired ability; education gave the manager a unique body of knowledge and skill necessary for the managerial role. The less formally qualified rested their claims to legitimacy upon the expertise acquired in the course of a managerial career, typically stressing their local knowledge of the perversities of their machinery and intimacy with their work force. Hence, participation must be limited in its impact upon managerial prerogatives and decisions, but it can nevertheless facilitate the exercise of managerial power. These arguments are essentially those discussed with reference to efficiency – participation as part of 'man management', as a source of information, a means of reducing conflict and strengthening managerial legitimacy.

The majority of workers at a general level also tended to accept the legitimacy of the management structure. Indeed, for the worker the contract of employment implies acceptance and taking orders from a 'boss'. Nevertheless, as we shall indicate later, there was a general desire for an increase of involvement over a wide range of areas of decision-making; that is, there was a significant demand for worker involvement in the management structure of the enterprise. At another level, however, challenges to management generally related to particular types of decisions and particular managers. The latter is often in effect a re-affirmation of the basic thesis of managerial expertise; it is minor rebellion, not revolution, in Gluckman's terms.[8] Particular managers were criticized for stupid decisions, being high-handed, working fiddles or lack of essential skills; the 'raw university bloke' who has 'learnt all his steel-making from books' was commonly criticized. Frequent changes of managers were similarly criticized, as was also the process of centralization. These arguments primarily concerned the failure of the Steel Corporation or of particular managers to employ workers' skills and experience. Because they have a detailed knowledge of the work, their views were seen as relevant to the exercise of managerial functions – hence participation was not merely a means of self-involvement, but a way of making some substantive contribution to the running of the works. Workers often accepted that their abilities did not stretch to matters of 'high finance' but it is noteworthy that when adverse rationalization plans were put forward workers were often ready and able to challenge management.

A significant number of workers argued also that their detailed knowledge from the point of production itself had a larger relevance. They saw the new professionals, the systems analyst, etc., dominating major decisions and argued that such people could not possibly develop relevant policies for they knew nothing about steel; the worker could counterbalance this by a sense of practical realism. This was seen as an important argument for worker directors. Some more junior managers also accepted this argument for worker participation at board level – their plans and ideas were also frustrated by ignorance at high levels. Indeed they saw members from their own ranks as potential worker directors for they themselves had this practical realism; but for this very reason worker participation was not required at their own level.

In so far as management more generally accepted these worker arguments they did so to a very limited degree – workers have limited ability, otherwise they would be managers. In addition workers are only interested in their own pockets and cannot be trusted to make managerial decisions.

Concern with the organizational and authority implications of participation also applied to the trade unions. Union officials, in particular, argued that the union and the system of collective bargaining were the best means of defending and promoting workers' interests and any system of participation must not endanger these. In addition schemes of participation, as we shall indicate later, pose threats to the organizational interests of the union. They could endanger the autonomy of the union, limit the exercise of officials' expertise and did not fit easily within the normal ways of doing things. Accordingly, participation was viewed with uncertainty.

SATISFACTION AND INVOLVEMENT

This final frame of reference has several elements, the central one of which relates to the dignity and fulfilment of the individual human being. The first of these elements refers to what we might term industrial suffrage. Whilst for the majority of workers material standards have risen since the second world world war, within the industrial system, in the words of one respondent, 'the worker is bound by chains – in these days of affluence they may be golden chains, but they are chains nevertheless'. The autonomy of the individual is more restricted in the industrial sphere than in other spheres of his life. Schemes of participation are one means through which the industrial system can begin to adjust to the sets of values which obtain in other spheres of society. This kind of perspective was particularly prevalent amongst lay and full-time union officials.

A second and closely related perspective was tied to the idea of frustration. The subordination of the worker within the industrial enterprise, his inability to be involved, creates frustrations. Such frustrations may take many forms, including managerial incompetence, waste and inefficiency, the lack of opportunity to employ one's knowledge, and inability to get simple matters rectified. Participation was seen as a means of changing this situation. For workers who adopted this perspective the crucial aspect was the removal of frustration itself, though it was also emphasized that more harmonious industrial relations and greater efficiency might result. In this sense it overlaps with the unitary perspectives mentioned earlier. Managers also emphasized participation as a way of obviating frustration. By and large, however, this was presented as a process of manipulative therapy. A similar view was that workers would feel happier if they thought their views were being considered; 'the beauty of participation is in the eye of the beholder'. Managers who held these perspectives tended to be in the category of pragmatic pluralists.

A third element in this framework is directly related to increased job satisfaction through positive ameliorative action in the job sphere itself. For many managers the demands of efficiency, allied with a general cultural evolution, called for a change in the system of control 'from the stick to the carrot'. Workers must be involved, they must be in the picture, they must be allowed to have more say. Management must wear a human face. At this point the framework is close to those ideas central to the human relations school. Personal fulfilment in the work situation will enhance efficiency; conversely efficiency can secure the happiness of the workers for an inefficient company can neither guarantee high wages nor security of employment. A number of workers also accepted this perspective for in steel there is a high awareness of communality of interests. But for other workers job satisfaction was an end in itself.

There were many people, however, in steel who rejected this view of man as needing total fulfilment within his industrial life. They argued that the individual worker is purely instrumental in his approach to work, and that therefore any participative schemes would be simply and solely exploited for financial ends. In fact it is worth remarking that very few of our worker respondents did orient themselves towards participation in terms of direct and immediate financial reward. A number of union officials did, however, stress the need for worker involvement as a direct result of threats to employment from closure decisions.

We have discussed at some length these four frames of reference in order to show something of the variety of factors which may inform people's approach to the idea of worker participation. The view of any individual may derive from one or more of these frames of reference; one perspective may limit or may support another. It will already be clear from our discussions so far that certain frames of reference are likely to find more support amongst management than amongst the work force; it should, however, also be clear that most perspectives are likely to spread through a number of groups in industry, though each perspective might be emphasized in a rather different way by each group. We now want to go on and look more closely at the distribution of particular orientations towards participation throughout various groups. Whilst this discussion is informed by what we have just written we have not attempted to organize the factors discussed in our analysis of frames of reference into neat paradigms which can then be discussed in particular groups. Reality is not neatly paradigmatic.

However, having said this, in ideal typical terms we can begin to argue that particular frames of reference tend to be most congruent with particular structural positions. The nature of industry is such that particular priorities have to be maintained by incumbents of various positions. So, for example, being a manager demands a concern with efficiency, which, as we have seen, is often buttressed by ideas of managerial prerogative; this is marginally modified by a perspective directed at job satisfaction and improved understanding through participation. Participation, however, if it is to be accepted to any significant degree, has to be seen as consistent with their primary goal of efficiency and profitability.

Similarly, workers in their work role may be expected to be

concerned with job satisfaction – it is this which facilitates the performance of their role. Their concerns with efficiency are in part a reflection of this. A significant minority of workers therefore have an interest in efficiency, in seeing a job well done, which implies a sympathy with what is primarily a managerial concern. Secondly, workers have their own interests which are typically expressed through trade unions. These interests may often be instrumental or economistic; they involve, in the present structure of society, two conflicting aspects – a conflict with management in terms of relative shares of rewards and at the same time an interest in efficiency, which ultimately is the condition for the continuation of a wage packet. But trade unions embody much more than this – while their economic emphasis may receive most public attention, this tends to hide a concern with the basic rights and dignity of the worker. These ideas, then, can be seen as uniquely congruent with trade-union activity.

We can, therefore, relate three of our four frames of reference to particular structural positions. But these differences in goals and priorities can, again, be linked to our first dimension relating to the nature of industrial relations. Hence, the expression of a unitary perspective fits most neatly with the economic interests of those in positions of authority and dominance in a society which rests primarily upon those goals which they espouse: as Fox states:

[This ideology] has its origins far back in the historical texture of class, status and power; in the constantly asserted and enforced 'right' of the master to demand unquestioning obedience from his servants. . . . Employers and managements may still succeed in inducing employees to share this frame of reference.[9]

Certainly the majority of workers are, generally, more anchored to such a unitary perspective rather than the opposite extreme of dichotomy. Hence, we find many workers concerned with efficiency; at the same time, the familistic rhetoric of unity permits concern, to a limited degree, with the idea of job satisfaction, and the optimum usage of workers' skills.

The dichotomous image is one which involves challenge to the existing structure – held by workers it rejects the priorities

43

of efficiency as defined by private profit, and accordingly the structure of managerial dominance and hierarchy is challenged. The dominant emphasis is upon the rights and dignity of workers.

Between these two extremes is the pluralistic frame of reference; it is, in essence, a compromise of either of these two perspectives to the apparent realities of the continued existence and strength of the other party – capital, or organized labour.[10] In the case of a few individuals from managerial groups, the existence of organized opposition to their efficiency interests has led not to an accommodative acceptance of that opposition but to a dichotomous definition which relates back to dreams of earlier, better, days. The compromise of pluralism, then can and does embrace all of the other frames of reference. The pluralist perspective is particularly concerned with the peaceable resolution of partially conflictual relations. Such concerns are found particularly strongly among those whose jobs involve them in dealing with these relationships – hence, over a half of management (and virtually the whole of our sample were either line or industrial relations managers) express such views, almost a third of full-time officials and a quarter of the stewards, but only 6% of the mass sample. But such relational concerns, important as they are, are not the primary consideration for these people, but are rather seen as means of facilitating, in practical terms, the achievement of more central goals. So, for example, two-thirds of those managers putting forward relational arguments for participation are in fact primarily concerned with its implications for efficiency.

In an attempt to clarify such arguments, we asked our respondents which reason was in their view the most important for participation – to increase efficiency, because it was a basic human right, or because it would increase job satisfaction. It is clear from Table 3–1 that the majority of managers and directors were concerned with efficiency; in the case of directors this was the overriding concern of the very great majority.[11]

Table 3–1

MOST IMPORTANT REASON FOR PARTICIPATION (%)

Single most important reason	Directors	Manage-ment	Full-time union officials	Stewards	Employees
To increase men's satisfaction with their work	24·0	13·5	21·0	32·0	38·1
Because it is basically a just and human right	—	14·5	37·0	23·0	11·1
To increase efficiency	52·0	39·0	26·0	36·0	36·0
Both to increase efficiency and men's satisfaction with their work	24·0	21·0	8·0	—	—
Other combinations	—	2·0	5·0	—	—
Other/don't know	—	10·0	3·0	1·0	3·9
There should be no participation	—	—	—	8·0	10·9
Total =	100·0%	100·0%	100·0%	100·0%	100·0%
N =	12	90	38	317	2379

Efficiency was less central to other categories, though it is interesting that there was a high emphasis on efficiency also amongst other groups, in particular shop stewards. Some explanation for this will be apparent from remarks earlier in this chapter. Those least concerned with efficiency were the full-time union officials whose stress upon the idea of industrial suffrage is once more clear. Finally, the arguments related to increased job satisfaction were primarily to be found amongst ordinary workers.

Emphasis placed by different groups, therefore, largely reflected the particular roles they played in relation to the production process. Management, as we pointed out earlier, conceived of participation primarily in relational terms, but

45

underlying this was a concern with efficiency; concern with this as we discuss below, and with their status within the authority structure, served to limit the degree of participation they favoured. Workers focussed more upon their own jobs and stressed the need to remove frustration and the opportunity to utilize most fully their own work-based knowledge and expertise. Full-time officials also reflected the nature of their role; their function is to further the interests of certain groups within the manufacturing organization. Hence they emphasized the rights of the individual over and against the organization. Shop stewards are both representatives and workers; as such their work involves an interest in the employing organization and in the union. The spread of answers amongst them reflected this diversity of interest and also the duality of their role as worker and trade unionist.

So far we have looked at the logic underlying participatory ideas and the implications of these, for the level at which participation is desired, have only been briefly touched upon. We now go on to consider this aspect in more detail, and in doing so indicate more fully differences in orientation towards participation amongst our respondents. We asked all respondents (other than the sample of ordinary employees) what level of involvement was implied by participation; Table 3–2 shows the responses.

It is interesting that the narrowest range of answers was found amongst directors and the broadest range amongst shop stewards. For directors participation was exclusively seen to be concerned with the exchange of information and ideas; for the majority it was workers making their views available to management and receiving information from management. The management sample responded in a similar way, though there was perhaps more apparent emphasis upon the reciprocity of the transaction. For full-time officials the exchange of information was the key meaning of participation – this relates back clearly to our earlier dicussion of dichotomous frameworks; however, almost a quarter of full-time officials saw participation in terms of joint decision-making or workers' control – that is they envisaged a structural change in managerial authority. A significant minority of stewards also

Table 3-2

THE MEANING OF PARTICIPATION (%)

	Directors	Management	Full-time union officials	Stewards
Workers merely being employed	—	—	—	8·5
Workers performing their normal tasks, job satisfaction	—	4·5	—	2·5
Workers being given information	19·0	5·5	7·0	9·5
Workers being involved; harmonius and co-operative relations between management and worker	13·0	19·0	4·0	23·5
Workers' opinions being considered; workers allowed to discuss the details of schemes	52·0	38·0	57·0	18·0
Workers and managers exchanging ideas	13·0	29·0		5·0
Workers and managers jointly making decisions, workers' control	—	1·0	25·0	19·0
Worker directors	3·0	2·0	2·0	5·0
Collective bargaining between workers and management	—	1·0	4·0	8·0
Other answers	—	—	1·0	1·0
Total =	100·0%	100·0%	100·0%	100·0%
N =	31	90	46	317

clearly articulated this view. However, the majority talked either in terms of exchange of information or discussion of their views with management, or in vague terms of being involved, which generally tended to mean a similar type of conception.

47

This point emerged a little more clearly in the replies to a forced choice question we put to both shop stewards and the general employee sample on the level of participation they desired.

Table 3–3

LEVEL OF PARTICIPATION DESIRED (%)

	Stewards	General employee sample
Management alone should make decisions	5·0	11·3
Management should make decisions but workers should be consulted	68·5	71·0
Workers and management should decide jointly	20·0	14·3
Workers alone should control the plants in which they work	4·5	2·2
Don't know or no answer	2·0	1·2

Total = 100·0 %   100·0 %
N = 317 and 2379

Here again it can be seen that while for a significant minority participation meant some radical change in the authority structure, for the majority of both samples participation was merely the opportunity to express one's views within the existing authority system.[12]

What is interesting at this general level is that directors and full-time officials constituted the polar groups in terms of spread of views on participation. However, when we begin to look at what respondents consider proper degree of worker involvement and influence within specific areas the pattern of responses changes. As can be seen from Table 3–4 the less important the area, the more willing were 'the professionals' to let workers be involved. More interestingly however, the position of directors vis-à-vis management and of full-time officials vis-à-vis shop stewards changed. Directors were willing to allow a greater degree of involvement of workers over all

areas than management and full-time officials were willing
to allow less involvement than either shop stewards or workers.

Directors have reached the top of their career structure.
They have high status, authority and power. They saw participation generally in terms only of discussion, discussion generally well removed from them within the organization, which
would not impinge on them directly, but which must have a
beneficial effect in terms of keeping management/worker
relations in the organization sweet. Management, on the
other hand, particularly more junior management, have less
influence and authority within the organization. Moreover,
they are in effect in the front line of the participative processes.
To allow participation, particularly in areas of major importance, would be a threat both to their authority and to
their sense of professionalism. Further, consultation and discussion take time and they saw it as inefficient particularly in
areas in which the only important dimensions of the decision
were technical; that is solely related to management and
production. In so far as workers' opinions needed to be taken
into account, they were nearer to the shop floor than directors
and therefore as good managers would 'pick up' or already
have the feel of workers' opinions.

Full-time officials are not so involved in the details of particular firms as the shop stewards and workers who are employed there. Most full-time officials feel that they have an
understanding of the way in which industry operates, particularly at its higher level, which is beyond that of their
members. Moreover, they tend to hold what we have termed
soft dichotomous views of industry; to see participation merely
as a means of collecting evidence for the defence and not to be
centrally concerned with the internal processes of the enterprise. They were therefore opposed to their members being
involved other than in peripheral areas. A high degree of
worker participation set problems for them in terms of their
self-conception, the role of the union and their status in relation
to their members. Whilst at a general level a large minority
argued for joint decision-making in industry, they were rather
in the position of St Augustine who cried, 'Lord make me
chaste, but not yet.'

49

Subject area	Level of participation desired	
Development plans	There should be no participation, manageme⬛ alone should decide	
	Workers should only be informed	Workers consulte⬛
	Discussions with workers but management decide	but management decide
	Workers and management should jointly deci⬛	
	Workers alone should decide	
Day-to-day organization of work	There should be no participation, manageme⬛ alone should decide	
	Workers should only be informed	Workers consulted
	Discussions with workers but management decide	but management decide
	Workers and management should jointly deci⬛	
	Workers alone should decide	
Welfare	There should be no participation, managemer⬛ alone should decide	
	Workers should only be informed	Workers consulte⬛
	Discussions with workers but management decide	but management decide
	Workers and management should jointly deci⬛	
	Workers alone should decide	

ARTICULAR AREAS (%)

	Directors	Management	Full-time union officials	Stewards	Employees
	5·0	22·0	9·0	14·0	25·3
	39·0	30·0	16·0 ⎫		
			⎬	39·0	29·0
	66·0	48·0	22·0 ⎭		
	—	—	14·0	45·0	42·9
	—	—	—	2·0	2·8
l =	100·0 %	100·0 %	100·0 %	100·0 %	100·0 %
=	18	87	44	317	2379

	Directors	Management	Full-time union officials	Stewards	Employees
	14·0	33·0	9·0	30·0	41·0
	7·0	12·0	3·0 ⎫		
			⎬	32·0	20·3
	79·0	55·0	65·0 ⎭		
	—	—	22·0	36·0	34·8
	—	—	—	2·0	3·9
l =	100·0 %	100·0 %	100·0 %	100·0 %	100·0 %
=	14	86	32	317	2379

	Directors	Management	Full-time union officials	Stewards	Employees
	12·0	1·0	—		
	—	2·0	5·0		
				Question not asked	
	88·0	97·0	62·0		
	—	—	33·0		
	—	—	—		
l =	100·0 %	100·0 %	100·0 %		
=	8	82	21	—	—

Further analysis reveals another set of interesting points. Only a fifth of managers and directors who favoured participation for human rights reasons were willing to accept discussions with workers rather than merely rights to information, compared to two out of five of management favouring such a level of participation who thought in terms of efficiency. There was a reverse pattern amongst shop stewards and full-time officials. Only one in five of these, who adopted an efficiency approach, favoured joint decision-making compared to a third of those who thought in terms of human rights. In other words, for these groups, those who favoured participation for reasons which were most congruent with their role tended to favour a greater degree of participation. That union representatives arguing in terms of rights should favour more participation is not surprising. It is, after all, a radical perspective. (It should be noted, however, that these tended to have dichotomous images; their responses often related to an ideal world; it does not follow from this that they favoured any increase in participation here and now – generally they were cautions if not opposed to systems of consultation because these involved some responsibility without leading to the more equal distribution of power.) But the reverse relationship existed with management – this apparently radical perspective reduced the level of participation acceptable to them. We would explain this in terms of the fact that this view is incongruent with their role. In other words, when managers express such views they are not denying that their primary role is efficiency, nor clearly are they denying the idea of managerial prerogative. Participation is seen less to promote than to limit their primary managerial goals. They therefore define the level of participation in minimal terms. Here then we see clearly the way in which the various frames of reference cross-cut each other.

In the sample of ordinary employees it was those who put forward idealistic views who demanded the greatest degree of participation, but second were those who felt that efficiency was the primary reason. Both of these views can be seen as congruent with the role of worker once we look at the ambivalent nature of that role. Ambivalence exists in two respects;

first, both 'rights' arguments as trade-union members and 'managerialist' arguments, as members of a production organization, are to some degree congruent with their roles; secondly, their commitment to management interests fosters what is effectively a challenge to the position of management because they feel their skills could be more fully employed.

An interesting variation between groups appears when we look at the level of participation desired by those thinking in terms of satisfaction. It was only among stewards that this view was associated with the demand for a relatively high level of participation (i.e. compared to others in their respective groups). The incongruency argument might be applicable to managers and possibly full-time officials, but it clearly cannot be applied to shop-floor workers themselves. What would appear more plausible is that satisfaction was essentially a task-related, task-confined, idea for the majority of respondents. However, the role of shop steward impresses upon its incumbent the larger structural implications of job satisfaction – for it is he alone whose primary task is negotiation over factors which lead to frustration on the shop floor. The worker merely experiences those frustrations, managers are merely aware of them, full-time officials are more concerned with larger issues. But for the stewards much time is spent tracing the causes of his members' dissatisfactions through the management hierarchy. They above all others have impressed upon them the idea that satisfaction can more easily be attained by major changes in the authority structure of the plant.

THE IDEA OF WORKER DIRECTORS

Respondents' attitudes towards the idea of worker directors influence their behaviour towards them; but, in addition, their attitudes serve to illuminate their more general idea of participation, particularly since worker directors are involved at what is taken to be the pinnacle of managerial power and decision-making. Views concerning worker directors essentially reflect the variations noted in attitudes towards workers having a say in 'macro' decisions.

53

In Favour of Worker Directors:
They could influence decisions, limit the power of other directors
They could represent, express shop floor viewpoints
They would improve understanding and communication
Workers would feel represented
They could pass information to workers
It is the right of workers to have a say, it is a move towards workers' control
They could improve wages and conditions
They could pass information to the directors
Other

Total in Favour
Uncertain about Worker Directors

Opposed to Worker Directors:
It is management's job to manage
Workers lack the skill, ability to be in the board room
They would have no influence on decisions
It is impossible to be on two sides, workers' and the board's at once
They would be under no union influence
Workers would not be interested in being represented on the board
They would have no meaningful function
They would take over the functions of the unions
Workers would have too much power
They would forget they were representing workers
They would be drawn in, incorporated by other directors
Other

Total Opposed

---

*Respondents often gave more than one answer so that figures do not total 100%.

WORKER DIRECTORS (%)

Directors	Managers	Full-time union officials	Stewards	Employees
—	4·0	7·0	10·5	1·3
31·0	26·0	29·0	52·5	40·2
31·0	13·0	7·0	18·5	14·3
4·0	2·0	7·0	—	—
4·0	3·0	17·0	19·0	11·8
4·0	—	7·0	4·0	3·5
—	—	—	1·0	1·5
—	—	—	12·5	11·4
10·0	10·0	13·0	6·0	10·5
56·0	42·0	65·0	88·5	74·6
10·0	8·0	11·0	—	7·3
8·0	4·0	4·0	1·0	2·2
17·0	31·0	7·0	2·5	9·6
—	10·0	9·0	5·0	2·2
10·0	11·0	7·0	3·0	0·9
—	9·0	4·0	—	—
—	1·0	—	—	0·5
10·0	8·0	2·0	—	—
—	—	2·0	—	—
—	—	—	—	0·5
—	—	—	—	—
—	—	—	1·5	—
4·0	9·0	7·0	1·5	4·7
34·0	50·0	24·0	11·5	18·1
= 48	90	46	317	2379

55

But concern with the need for influence in the corridors of power and in macro decisions on the part of workers we interviewed may well be exceptional, reflecting the particularly traumatic period which the steel industry was experiencing. Because of this, the support for the idea of worker directors which we find may be greater than would otherwise be the case. On the other hand, it would appear that for some stewards in particular experience of worker directors has reduced their enthusiasm.

For directors, the group who have had the most intimate experience of the worker directors, experience has had the reverse effect. In subsequent chapters we will see that initially many directors were shocked by the thought that workers would sit with them round the board-room table. But experience taught them that worker directors did not mean 'socialism coming at us'; while therefore, they might have been expected to be the most opposed to such ideas, they were not.

Those most opposed to the idea of worker directors were those whose position would be most challenged by them – that is, managers. For them it was a threat to suddenly find subordinates becoming superiors, putatively less capable people accelerating up *their* career structure; and there was also the danger of their activities being reported to their superiors. These were the group who felt 'cut out' by worker representation at board level. The ideology which they espouse is guarded by their directors, primarily because of ideas of managerial prerogative, ability and the nature of the management structure.

On the 'other side' of industry it was the full-time officials who were most hesitant about worker directors. Opposition to the idea derived from various sorts of arguments. First, the less radical amongst them tended to accept both the skills and the status of management. Their role brought them into contact with these skills and they respected them. For others their oppositional role required that they kept the two sides of industry clearly demarcated – only in this way was anything to be achieved. Again, they themselves are 'professionals' and are opposed to any system which challenges the function of their organization or their role, as the worker director might.

A few of the sample of ordinary employees also accepted the need for managerial skills, but they and their shop-floor representatives were the greatest supporters of the idea of worker directors.

Not only, then, was there a broad pattern of support reflecting structural position, but there was also a variation according to reasons put forward for participation. So, half the managers and directors whose reasons for supporting participation were most congruent with their structural position, were in favour of worker directors, compared with only a third of those putting forward idealistic arguments. A similar variation of congruency with structural position was found among the union groups, although it was relatively small – largely because the most radical respondents saw worker directors as a form of incorporation. Further, those who believed participation would promote efficiency through the use of shop-floor knowledge, were among those most strongly in favour of worker directors.

Not surprisingly, therefore, arguments in favour of worker directors largely reflected those for participation. Understanding was the strong theme among directors; contact with the shop floor would provide better information on which to base decisions – hence it was knowledge of the shop floor which was important. Worker directors would reflect the shop floor, not represent it.

The desire for the link between the top and bottom of the organization was the crucial argument; those who felt this most strongly were the stewards who suffer more than most from this distance. But for the union side, this element of merely helping directors to understand what really went on, to give them a breath of realism, was combined with the desire to represent their views and interests. They wished to influence decisions in a real sense. It is difficult to distinguish these two elements among the majority of workers and stewards, for they believed there was an essential consistency between their interests; if workers were to have more say, then not only would workers' interests be better served, but also those of management, at least in terms of efficiency. Some found it impossible to believe that if directors really knew what happened, and how things really operated, they would not make the decisions workers wanted them to. Others felt the need to know what was happening – few appeared to see this as a tool in negotiation. The views of some directors were similar – if workers knew their problems, they would co-operate; for many, it was all a question of knowledge. The possibility of knowledge increasing conflict was rarely considered.

In this chapter we have attempted to look at, in general terms, attitudes towards participation and worker directors in the steel industry. What we have tried to emphasize is that attitudes towards worker directors reflect more general views on the subject of participation. But such views do not exist in isolation; rather they themselves involve ideas about the nature of industry, the goals of actors themselves and their positions in the larger social structure. However, we have shown that frequently attitudes towards participation reflect a range of ideas which are often conflicting and confused. The importance of this is that it suggests the potentially dynamic nature of actors' views on the question of participation. The following two chapters look at the conditions which led to the expression of such change in the shape of the worker-director scheme in BSC.

Notes

1 The material in this chapter is taken from interviews with directors, managers, full-time trade-union officials, lay trade-union officials and ordinary employees; cf. Appendix A

2 MILLS, C. W., 'Situated Actions and Vocabularies of Motive', in I. L. Horowitz (ed.), *Power, Politics and People*, Oxford University Press, 1963, p. 440

3 See in this respect also COUSINS, J. M., 'The Non-Militant Shop Steward', *New Society*, No. 488, 1972

4 LOCKWOOD, D., 'Sources of Variation in Working Class Images of Society', *Sociological Review*, 14, 1966; BULMER, M., *The Occupational Community of the Traditional Worker*, Proceedings of a SSRC Conference, January 1973

5 FLANDERS, A., *Management and Unions: The Theory and Reform of Industrial Relations*, Faber & Faber, 1970, p. 197

6   We have described in a later chapter the centralizing tendencies of the Steel Corporation. The majority of management we talked to felt that in a number of fields their areas of discretion had been narrowed. Moreover, they also felt that they were further removed from the real centres of power and in that sense were less able to influence things. A number of them also noted what they felt to be an increase in trade-union influence since nationalization.

7   See BURNS, T. and STALKER, G. M., *The Management of Innovation*, Tavistock, 1966, especially Chapter 10, 'The Man at the Top'

8   GLUCKMAN, M., *Custom and Conflict in Africa*, Blackman, 1969, ch. 5

9   FOX, A., *Beyond Contract: Work, Power and Trust Relations*, Faber & Faber, 1974, p. 250

10   Ibid., ch. 6

11   It will be seen that, in this and subsequent tables in this chapter, the total number of directors, managers and full-time officials in each category varies. This is related to problems inherent in interviewing such people, utilizing a relatively unstructured schedule and having a variable amount of time with each individual. It was not possible to cover all of our question areas with every individual. Whilst we have no reason to believe that the pattern of responses of those who, for reasons of time, were unable to respond to particular questions would have been different from that of those who did respond, nevertheless the analysis here must be seen as exploratory rather than definitive.

12   This table is interesting in relation to the earlier figures which indicated that a dichotomous framework was more prevalent amongst our sample of ordinary workers than amongst shop stewards. It is likely that the fatalistic aspect of this framework is less widespread amongst shop stewards than amongst ordinary workers.

4 Change and adjustment in steel

From the last quarter of the eighteenth century the iron and later the steel industry have played a key role within the British economy. In a very real sense the history of the industry revolves around its attempts to deal with a number or problems with which it has been continuously faced. These relate to technological innovation and development, the need for high capital investment and increasingly large-scale plant, international competition, and crises and fluctuations in demand. Response to these problems has meant attempts to restrain and control prices, competition, and investment, which have not only involved inter-firm arrangements but also political pressure by the steel owners for government protection. Conversely government help and protection has also led to increased state intervention and control culminating in the acts of nationalization.

Economic historians have seen the inability of the steel owners to solve the basic problems of the industry in any satisfactory manner as being the root cause of its poor economic performance. Burn, for example, attributes the relative failure of the industry in the period up to the beginning of the second world war to seven factors: the relatively slower rate of growth without amalgamation of British companies; the construction of only relatively small new plants in Britain after 1885; the failure to construct new plants in areas where raw materials were cheapest; the limited integration of processes; the preference in Britain for vertical rather than horizontal amalgamations; the limited and 'immature' development of associations to control price and output in comparison to Germany; and finally the failure of British industry to employ collective action on matters other than price and output (e.g. standard sections).[1]

The plight of the steel industry in the face of strong international competition in the early twentieth century was overcome mainly by the demands of war and the reconstruction boom which followed the first world war for a few years. The war meant a respite from international competition; 'the search for markets was replaced by a search for raw materials. Instead of association to keep prices up there was state control to keep prices down. The state intervened too to secure an unheard-of pooling of knowledge and resources, and to promote an unparalleled expansion of productive capacity.'[2] Although the efficiency of the industry was improved during the war, 'partly on account of the patchwork character of much of the new building, and partly through the insufficient supply, or the neglect, of adequate technical advice, and the lack of experience, many of the faults which had for long characterized the industry remained'.[3] A report of a departmental committee during the war stressed the need for expansion of production and considerable reorganization to permit the concentration of production in large efficient plants and the buying of raw materials. Although some amalgamations did occur, notably the beginnings of the United Steel Company, the pattern of vertical rather than horizontal mergers was more typical. Similarly, collective action was somewhat limited. But the war did mean that 'the contacts between firms were far more intimate during the war than ever before, and though after its close individualism remained, so to speak, rampant, more of the possible services of joint action were commonly observed'.[4]

The slump following the reconstruction boom led the industry to seek protection as output fell and for much of the time plants were working at only half or one-third of capacity. But protection did not come until the thirties; in 1932 a $33\frac{1}{3}\%$ duty was imposed on imports, with the result that output rose and with the assurance of continued protection firms were encouraged to rebuild and add new plant, although 'the old habit of patching remained characteristic'. The imposition of the tariff, however, also involved greater political pressure for the reorganization of the industry; the newly established British Iron and Steel Federation, along with the Import Duties Advisory Committee 'in effect . . . became responsible for fixing prices, controlling competition, subsidizing high-cost producers and supervising the development plans of the industry'. However,

suppression of competition rather than technical reconstruction and rationalization of the industry appears to have been the primary object of the controlling authorities. The principles of plant specialization and integration of units were only tentatively applied [for example, in the building of a new integrated steel works at Corby], while only scant attention was paid to the question of extending best practice techniques.[5]

The failure to adopt large-scale production can be most clearly seen by the fact that in 1930 the twenty largest British firms had a combined output of steel which was less than one-third of the output of one American company (the United States Steel Company). Not only, however, did the protection afforded the industry mean a revival of output, but, more significantly, 'an industry that had once been a stronghold of individualism and unregulated competition was henceforward a highly organized and protected industry with regulated prices and centralized trading, an industry that had "come into politics" to stay'.[6]

The second world war again saw an expansion of the industry, with the building of new plant; but this reconstruction within the industry was of the kind to maximize short-run output rather than to increase long-term efficiency. Of equal significance, the war effort saw the expansion 'in breadth and in depth' of the central control of the industry. Such close control, along with an attempt to plan the future of the industry more carefully, continued after the war; not only were there close controls, but in addition co-operation continued on a wider range of activities, including a joint research establishment. The peak of such control was reached with the Labour government's somewhat hesitant attempt to nationalize the steel industry in 1949.

While the Conservative government quickly de-nationalized

the industry in 1951 control remained in the form of the Iron and Steel Board. The board's role was, however, permissive in that it could not coerce individual companies into investment and other strategies with which they disagreed. As a partial consequence firms had an autonomy which, according to critics, led to unnecessary and wasteful duplication of steel-making facilities. Essentially the industry did not change its ways; concern with the maintenance of the autonomy of individual companies, and of private profit tempered only by considerations of the potential of public opinion, meant limited reorganization and the policy of patching; essentially the continuation of a decades old habit which served merely to make any real reorganization more difficult.

By the 1960s the position of the steel industry still reflected many of the problems which had plagued it throughout its history. Its competitive position was weak in the face of a world-wide surplus capacity which arose partly because of the increased scale of modern steel plant and partly because of the emergence of former net importers as net exporters of steel.[7] Japan was a prime example of expansion. Its industry had a 25% share of world exports in 1966 as compared to 7% some eight years previously. The combination of surplus capacity and the exigencies of large-scale production forced steel-makers throughout the world to dispose of their surpluses, often through exports, at barely profitable prices. Again reminiscent of the thirties British steel-makers attempted to soften the impact of surplus capacity and competition by common pricing policies, but in 1964 the Restrictive Practices Court found these policies to be 'not advantageous' arguing that any individual producer should be at liberty to depart from a common price, if he so wished.[8]

The impact of surplus capacity and of the costly scale of steel investment underlay the industry's performance in the 1960s. These are reflected both in the declining British share of world trade (from 8% to 6% between 1958 and 1967) and in the progressively worsening profit performance of steel which are indicated in Table 4–1.

Table 4–1

RATIO OF PROFITS:
CAPITAL EMPLOYED IN STEEL COMPANIES, 1958–67

1958	*1959*	*1960*	*1961*	*1962*	*1963*	*1964*	*1965*	*1966*	*1967*
17·3	15·7	18·8	12·4	8·2	7·1	10·7	9·7	5·7	3·5
				(6·6)	(4·8)	(7·3)	(6·7)	(3·8)	(1·9)

(The figures exclude four new steel works which had not yet reached full potential by 1967. Inclusion of these effectively reduces the ratios from 1962 onwards: see figures in brackets.)

Source: BSC, *Finance for Steel*, May 1969

The allegations that the British steel industry was not reaping the full economies of scale, induced some commentators to draw a connection with the apparently low productivity levels in Britain. Although such measures are fraught with difficulties, international comparisons of productivity performance between 1955 and 1967 showed the British figures to reflect an upward trend, but less favourably so than any other major steel producer save the USA (Table 4–2).

Table 4–2

STEEL OUTPUT/MAN HOUR IN FIVE COUNTRIES, 1955–67
(1957 = 100)

	1955	*1960*	*1965*	*1966*	*1967*
USA	104·1	97·5	120·0	122·4	118·6
France	102·5	127·8	144·7	151·5	159·1
Japan	81·3	131·5	209·1	245·3	304·7
UK	95·6	106·7	120·5	125·5	125·6
W. Germany	92·4	116·1	130·3	133·7	147·2

Source: P. C. Jackman, in *Monthly Labor Review*, August 1969

During the 1960s the major form of steel-making in Britain was by the 'open-hearth' process, which has a production-cycle time of approximately eight hours. However, internationally the oxygen steel-making process had been gradually supplanting the earlier technique because of the high, fast and economical tonnages obtainable (cycle times can be reduced to forty minutes). Despite the existence of new techniques, the relatively more costly open-hearth processes accounted for two-thirds of all British production in 1967.

In the mid-sixties the British Iron and Steel Federation set up a committee to investigate the future needs of the industry. In its report (the Benson Report) the committee underlined the superiority of oxygen steel-making and recommended it for the new high-capacity melting shops which would be the basis of the industry in the seventies.[9] This committee envisaged that the 'main works comprising the industry in the mid-seventies will normally have to be appreciably larger than is the average works at present.'[10] In specific terms, therefore, a strip works would have an annual capacity of 5 million tons while a multi-product works (also based on the oxygen process) would have a minimum capacity of $3\frac{1}{2}$ million tons. The developments required to achieve these figures can be gauged from Benson's own figures, for in 1966 the industry had no steel works over 4 million tons capacity, and out of the thirty-four major plants one had a 3–4 million ton capacity and two fell within the 2–3 million ton range. Benson's analysis entailed an increased concentration upon coastal-based steel complexes, and the corollary of redundancy and works closure was clearly envisaged. Indeed, the report estimated that the work force would decline by 100 000 between 1965–75, a very high rate of job loss even for the steel industry. The report argued that the future development of the industry should take the form of integration into a few companies and a handful of technologically advanced steel works. Benson, therefore, preached the doctrine of economies of scale, especially because the success of many foreign steel industries was said to have been based upon the extensive exploitation of massive steel complexes, well placed to obtain large supplies of raw materials.

THE NATIONALIZATION OF STEEL

Benson's plans for the reorganization of steel under private enterprise were, however, forestalled by the renationalization of the industry in 1967. The policy of the Labour administration, which had come into power in 1964, towards steel nationalization needs to be looked at within the context of its overall economic strategy. Shanks has maintained that the world-wide phenomenon of growing economic expectations 'has meant that Governments everywhere . . . have to accept a commitment to (economic) growth'.[11] Yet such a commitment has in turn forced governments to play an active role in ensuring the industrial success upon which growth is based. In attempting to play a more active role than its predecessors, the 1964 Labour administration identified technological change and industrial revitalization as major potential growth inducers. Perceiving the role of expectations as an important determinant of business investment, the government endeavoured to break out of the 'stop-go' policy, which, it argued, had periodically unsettled business confidence prior to 1964. It aimed, instead, to sustain high and steady levels of demand and investment in new plant and equipment. The National Plan[12] can be seen as a global attempt to 'reduce the area of the unpredictable to a manageable series of clear alternatives'.[13] The plan was also designed to identify 'the areas where there are weaknesses and where we should concentrate our resources'.[14]

The process of technological change may, however, be frustrated by the increasing complexity and cost of modern technology and frictions which may prevent a smooth introduction of new techniques. The Labour government defined its role here as that of catalytic agent and provider and underwriter of capital. In addition to the newly created Ministry of Technology's active intervention in the British computer industry, other aspects of policy concentrated on industrial modernization and rationalization. The UCS merger was promoted by the government, and although the combine obtained financial subvention from a variety of sources the government played the predominant role. At the same time, the conditions sought by Labour before it agreed to continued assistance for this 'new form of capitalism'[15] included 'changes in UCS management and tighter financial control [and] the agreement by the workers to co-operate fully in reorganization and measures for higher productivity – including substantial redundancy'.[16]

The UCS merger was but one indication of the government's active interest in industrial regrouping. Other examples included the Industrial Reorganization Corporation through which Labour wished 'to promote rationalization schemes to yield substantial benefits to the company in terms of increased exports and more rapid technological change'.[17] The British business community was ambivalent towards the government's initiative. There were inevitably those who refused to co-operate with the policy and to recognize the legitimacy of the government's role as a quasi merchant bank. However, other industrialists were actively co-operative.[18] The rationale underlying the IRC was that mergers would provide economies of scale, protection for groups of firms engaged in costly investment projects, capital to finance (at least in part) these projects and a base the better to combat international competition. The last point explains the government's welcome of the GEC/AEI/EE merger of 1968 from which a company emerged 'capable of fighting the European giants on equal terms'.[19]

Shanks has suggested that governments can take two paths in their dealings with industry. There can either be the 'high road of partnership', which would seem to be typified by Labour's national plan, or government can take the 'low road of intervention'.[20] As far as steel was concerned, Labour favoured a policy of intervention rather than a partnership of equals. Direct government involvement in steel dates, as we have seen, effectively from the inter-war period. At that time the industry's management and major unions successfully sought a protective tariff on steel imports, but the industry had to agree to a government request that steel be reorganized. In fulfilment of its undertaking, the industry set up the British Iron and Steel Federation (BISF) which initiated a system of uniform pricing and cross-subsidization throughout the industry. It was during this period, too, that the major steel union made its first demands for nationalization, although different interpretations have been put on this initiative. Burn, for instance, has argued that the union's case 'came singularly close' to a plea for cartelization.[21] Hughes interpreted the case not as a matter of 'socialist conviction' but as a means of salvaging the industry. It was, he maintained, an inevitable product of 'very conservative' steel institutions.[22] Banks, by contrast, has defined the union's case as a recognition that the major steel union no longer had confidence in management's technical ability, and that the demand for nationalization constituted a frontal questioning of the capability of steel management.[23]

The industry was, as we have noted, briefly nationalized in the late 1940s, but it was subsequently de-nationalized in 1951. Nevertheless, the industry continued to accept (partly willingly and partly under pressure) a measure of public influence. For instance, the Conservative government during the fifties 'went to great lengths to demonstrate that a fully adequate means could be found to assert the public interest in steel while it remained in private ownership'.[24] This assertion was exemplified by the ISB's collaboration with the steel companies in the preparation of their investment plans as well as by its overseeing of the determination of maximum steel prices. A further example was the decision to locate a strip mill at Llanwern (Wales) and another at Ravenscraig (Scotland), rather than one larger mill at either of these places. The first was publicly owned, the second privately, although Ravenscraig was also built with help from public funds.

The industry was therefore increasingly facing a major dilemma; although all connected with steel recognized the necessity for modernization and technological change, the increasing cost of steel plant in association with unfavourable return on capital rendered it increasingly difficult for the industry to provide the required capital from its own resources. The prospect of government assistance was therefore a tempting one, although the attractiveness was tempered by the potential control which government might seek as a *quid pro quo*. Further, the industry was impelled to extend the policies of standardization initiated during the inter-war period; but a policy of restrictive pricing policies, while insulating the industry from internecine (or healthy) competition (depending upon one's standpoint), also invited charges that steel was taking advantage of its 'monopoly position' and thereby infringing the 'national interest'.

These factors have to be borne in mind when considering the Labour government's arguments for nationalization between 1964 and 1967. The white paper on 'Steel Nationalization' emphasized the significance of the industry as a capital goods and export-based industry. Labour argued that steel's poor performance could not be 'reconciled' with the national interest and with 'the proper functioning of private enterprise itself'.[25] During the debates on the white paper and the subsequent bill, the case for nationalization was amplified with stress throughout being placed upon the 'economic facts' underlying the reasons adduced.[26]

There was little doubt that nationalization was the only solution as the government saw it. Thus, Fred Lee (the first Minister of Power) rejected the so-called 'BP solution' for steel which would have given the government 51 % share ownership in the industry. 'State Capitalism', he said, 'is the only way, a position in which the government is by far the senior partner with the industry itself accepting the instructions of the government.'[27] Lee articulated the most important argument for nationalization as being that the 'steel companies were far too small to take advantage of the latest techniques of production and direction. . . . Common ownership will make it possible to work out the best pattern of organization.'[28] To the argument that the companies should be encouraged independently to regroup and amalgamate into larger units, the reply was that, 'one cannot produce a board which can go to the private steel owners and persuade them to amalgamate when it means some of them losing their jobs, many losing their power and old dynasties being broken up'.[29] More importantly, a process of independent mergers was in principle unsatisfactory for industrial size confirmed economic power and once private mergers started to occur the industry 'would be getting to be a state within a state'.[30]

Nationalization was also held to be an integral part of national planning. The National Plan, for instance, had referred to the need for 'fundamental changes in the industry', in order to make possible positive control and planning of investment, production and marketing.[31] It was also argued that the planning and handling of redundancies, a concomitant to the rationalization of the industry, was more effectively done under public ownership. In the debates on nationalization a Treasury minister reminded the House how efficient nationalized industries can be in the management of redundancy. Referring specifically to coal and the railways, he argued that 'large-scale redundancies were achieved without major difficulty of any kind as a result of improved labour relations which are possible only with a nationalized industry'.[32]

This then was Labour's case for nationalization. In common with the Benson Report, prime attention was placed upon the need for the industry to modernize and re-group. To be sure, the government differed from Benson in prescribing 'state capitalism', but both shared the view than an unprecedented crisis might overtake the industry unless quick and decisive reorganization took place.

STRAIN AND ADJUSTMENT

We have been emphasizing up to this point the centrality of technological, organizational and market factors to change in the steel industry. It is clear, however, that these changes could not take place without inducing strain in the social relationships of production, particularly management–worker relationships. From the perspective of workers in the industry there may be a number of reasons for resisting change. Alterations may be perceived as redundancy-inducing and of critical significance to workers whose skills are specific to one industry, and whose communities are steel-dependent; they may also have an unfavourable impact on the level of earnings or on earnings growth. Finally, technological change may destroy those workplace relationships and tasks on which workers put high value.

From a management perspective workers may vitiate the return on capital investment embodied in new equipment, especially where production is concentrated in a few integrated steel plants. Strikes may be one source of reduced return on capital, but informal work-group relationships and practices may also contribute towards a sub-optimal utilization of plant. Sub-optimalization might, for example, arise from 'over-manning', excessive overtime and demarcation. Management therefore must attempt to convince workers of the need to accept technological change and its subsequent implementation. Within the steel industry the management of change has been remarkably smooth. Both unions and managements have stressed the legitimacy of, and need for, change, and have co-operated in institutional devices to exploit new technology. Until recently the incidence of strikes in steel has been relatively low compared to other traditional heavy industries. More specifically, however, many of the disputes that have occurred have derived from the differing bases of organization of the various unions in the industry and competition for 'new' or 'revised' jobs which have occurred as a result of technological change.

As will be seen from Table 4–3 there were seventeen unions involved in the steel industry immediately after nationalization. BISAKTA (or ISTC) is the principal union and was estimated in 1968 to contain almost 50% of the industry's employees; traditionally it has been this union which has set the pattern for management–worker relations in the industry. The union was formed in 1917 as a result of the merger of seven unions. Similar developments were also occurring in the industry among steel employers.[33] At shop-floor level BISAKTA members are organized into a series of branches, each branch generally co-terminous with the appropriate steel works' function. BISAKTA then is an industrial union with an organization at work level which mirrors the production process. Each branch has traditionally operated as a discrete unit and high value is placed on branch autonomy; branches are, however, subject to the external constraint of strong union discipline and tight centralized union control. BISAKTA has assigned to itself (and in fact has been assigned by the

Table 4–3

BRITISH STEEL CORPORATION:
TRADE UNIONS AND MEMBERSHIP, SPRING 1968

Union	Total membership in steel[1]
Iron and Steel Trades Confederation (BISAKTA/ISTC)	105400[2]
National Union of Blastfurnacemen	19600[2]
Transport and General Workers Union/National Association of Clerical and Supervisory Staffs	17500[2]
National Union of General and Municipal Workers	12800[2]
National Craftsmen's Co-ordinating Committee[4]	22300[2]
Amalgamated Union of Building Trade Workers	3000[2]
Clerical and Administrative Workers Union	3500[3]
Association of Scientific, Technical and Managerial Staffs	4100[3]
Grand total	188200

[1] These totals include employees in the iron and steel sectors who, although employed by the BSC, were party to other agreements such as those of the Engineering Employers Federation. CAWU – subsequently renamed APEX – and ASTMS were recognized by the BSC in locations where the EEF agreements apply for approximately 1000 CAWU and ASTMS members.
[2] Includes small percentage in private sector of steel industry.
[3] Excludes private sector membership.
[4] The Committee consisted of ten unions.

Source: Report of a Court of Inquiry under Lord Pearson into the dispute between the BSC and certain of their employees, Cmnd 3754, August 1968

employers) a role which is consistent with its perception of the industry and the place of trade unionism within it. Thus, steel has been defined by BISAKTA's leaders not as 'a forum for permanent hostility' where the protagonists are 'engaged in a ceaseless class struggle', but as 'a joint enterprise where divergent interests could be reconciled by discussion and negotiation against a background of common interest in an efficient, thriving and prosperous industry'.[34]

Indeed, BISAKTA has played an active role as representatives' disciplinarian and active promoter of technological change, as exemplified in the shift towards continuous working in 1947. In that year, the union concluded an agreement with the employers which entailed weekend working in order to bring British practice in line with foreign experience, but over 1000 steel workers refused to accept the new arrangements. The unions' response was to issue an ultimatum to the recalcitrants that if the agreement was not adhered to, the men would be expelled from the union; expulsion would be tantamount to the sack in a steel works' closed shop situation. A steel union official whom we interviewed outlined the union's case to us: 'If we allow people to get away with this we shall no longer retain our self-respect, and can we expect employers to sit at the negotiating table with us if we are not able to say we are prepared to, and capable of, honouring agreements to which we are joint signatories?' The official then went on to say, 'I know of no other union who would have dealt with it in that way.'

Whilst there has been some resistance to change on the part of the work force, as illustrated by the above example, in the main the co-operative ethos of union leaders has been a reflection of the general attitudes of steel workers, amongst whom, as we have noted in earlier chapters, there has been found a general commitment to the industry. There would seem to be several sources from which this commitment springs. Firstly, acquired skills are specific to steel on the production side and, whilst on the one hand there has been a high degree of job control, it tends to create also a 'locked-in' effect on the place of employment of the steel worker. These effects are enhanced at the works level by a system of seniority which is union controlled and permits approved progression in the steel plant, but which inhibits transferability from one steel works to another. Secondly, the tonnage bonus payment system in steel has contributed towards a level of earnings which has industrially been one of the highest in Britain. Furthermore, in so far as technological change enhances productivity and the unions benefit from such change through bonus negotiation, and to the extent that the effort of the group

73

can have a material impact upon earnings, then steel workers might have been expected to have a positive financial attachment towards technical change. The commitment to steel which is generated by the socio-technical system in the plant is re-inforced in many cases by the dependency of the surrounding community on steel as a sole or major source of employment.

This sense of co-operative commitment seems also to have both informed, and been derived from, much of the formal industrial relations machinery in the industry. Solutions to the problems created by the technological development of steel were often found in mechanisms which acknowledged the work force as something more than a mere factor of production. Conciliation boards which were widespread in the industry at the turn of the century are a good example of this. They were started at the joint initiation of management and unions in order to forestall costly strikes. Costs to employers would include the potential loss of trade which strikes might cause. Costs to workers would include the replacement of striking workers by an unemployed but willing pool of labour. Furthermore, conciliation buttressed the role of the unions, for management asserted that a strong union, prepared to enforce adherence by steel workers to procedure, was essential to the functioning of any board. This assertion was attractive to the unions at a time when trade union mortality was high.

The payment system in operation in the industry up to the second world war also provides an illustration of the co-operative commitment of the work force. Until 1940, and the onset of a controlled iron economy, a selling price sliding wage scale operated in steel, which took the form of a relationship between supplements to the basic rate and changes in the price of steel products.[35] Mutual advantages were apparent in the sliding-scale arrangements, for they 'avoided constant bickering over wage changes with each alteration in the prosperity of the industry'.[36] The employers were attracted to a system which guaranteed flexibility in wage costs, and given the cyclical fortunes of steel, this was an important guarantee. As for the workers, although steel productivity may often have been low in international terms, it nevertheless did increase as a result of technical innovation. In so far as productivity had a favourable impact on earnings (notably through tonnage bonus payments), then this would partly compensate for a sliding scale which led to flexibility in wages both upwards and downwards.

There were, nevertheless, some critics of the sliding scale. The Webbs, for example, pointed scornfully at 'sturdy trade-union leaders' who meekly accepted 'the capitalists' axiom that wages must necessarily fluctuate according to the capitalists' profits . . . '.[37] Yet, we have seen that both employers and unions espoused conciliation and sliding scales because of mutual advantages; not simply in terms of industrial relations stability but because the arrangements (and their effects) encouraged commitment by workers to the industry and its fortunes. Furthermore, as the Webbs made clear, sliding scales reflected the force of tradition and they could only continue to operate as long as managers and workers shared common economic assumptions about how wages should be fixed and regulated.[38] Significantly, the sliding scale was abolished in 1940 and not during the previous decade when wages were relatively more depressed and when 'assumptions' might not have been expected to have been shared.[39]

Payment systems more generally in steel have been based on a system of de-centralized plant and departmental bargaining. Plant-level bargaining in steel has been associated with complex payment systems with differing bases of payment for production, craft and ancillary workers. Piece-work featured widely in the industry and variations in pay-packet structure were also introduced through tonnage bonus schemes, shift allowances, cost of living allowances, and abnormal conditions premiums. This type of system is prone to 'wage drift' and despite the absence of data on 'drift' in steel it is plausible to assume that it did occur. From one perspective wage drift can be seen as a form of shop-floor control over earnings. From another perspective, however, it indicates a lack of managerial control over the utilization and payment of labour, and it may be part of the sub-optimal utilization of capital equipment. It indicates a need to alter the relationships between men and management as defined in the payment system in order to promote the more efficient operation of the technology.

75

Productivity bargaining is a recent example of this. It was not unique to steel, but that it was promoted in steel and elsewhere during the 1960s confirms the view that steel's problems were a reflection of a wider economic malaise. Productivity bargaining attempted to fund wage increases through improvements in efficiency, as we have already pointed out, and it was enthusiastically promoted by steel management, who paid special attention to various inefficient labour practices especially among craftsmen. At the Port Talbot works of the Steel Company of Wales (SCOW), for example, there had been a problem of increasing labour costs, which management aimed to reduce by improved work-place organization and manning reductions.[40] At a more general level, there were at least four interrelated advantages to steel management. First, it was widely held 'within the industry as well as outside it' that manpower utilization could be appreciably improved in steel.[41] Second, productivity bargaining was seen as a means of enhancing profitability and managerial control of steel works operations. Third, if efficiency was to improve, then the industry would be in a better position to meet international competition, for the British steel industry's labour productivity performance was relatively low. However (and fourth), although sub-utilization of capital arose in part from inefficient labour practices, the nature of these practices forced management to negotiate generally with work groups and to seek from them a change in attitude. In other words, because the behaviour of work groups had given rise to a variety of practices which simultaneously protected their interests yet inhibited capital utilization, management could only achieve greater efficiency through recognition of inter-dependency rather than through managerial fiat.

This brief illustration of some of the ways by which adjustments in the relations of production took place in the steel industry would not be complete without some reference to joint consultation. Joint consultative schemes in the industry appear to have had their origins mainly in the 1920s and were associated in some cases with the ideas and recommendations of Whitley. Others appear to have been associated rather more with the atmosphere of the later 1920s and the fear of workers following the example of the Russians. Such fears on the part of management were fostered by the General Strike and best indicated by the Mond–Turner talks. In addition, this period once again saw the steel industry in a particularly difficult position internationally. We find, it would seem, a convergence of new schemes to promote discussion between unions and management – or at least workers and management – and the demands for protection for the industry against international competition.

The most complete system of joint consultation within the steel industry was developed by the United Steel Company. This particular company established works councils in the majority of their works in 1929 with the following stated aims:

(1) enabling the company to take work people into their confidence in outlining plans for development and explaining the state of trade;
(2) enabling work people to have the ear of management in ventilating grievances;
(3) fostering the growth of welfare activities, accident prevention and social services;
(4) promoting efficient working.

The councils were composed of work people directly elected from departments rather than through the unions, along with management. In addition, as time passed, a variety of sub-committees dealing with such matters as production, safety and welfare developed; and consultative committees were established at a departmental level. It was only in 1963 that some of these consultative committees became trade-union based, though it was not until the early seventies that all became trade-union based.

Whilst joint consultation became relatively widespread throughout the steel industry, both its usefulness to management and its importance as a vehicle for stabilizing relationships between management and the work force varied over time. As with joint consultation in other industries, it fell into disfavour with the trade unions in the 1950s, and came to be seen as a purely managerial instrument. The system within

77

United Steel, for example, was described by one of our informants as being merely a means 'for the vicious manipulation of the work force'. Nevertheless, the concept of consultation seems to be acceptable to the majority of steel workers and the Steel Corporation has, though with some difficulty, been able to revive the system in co-operation with the trade unions.

CONCLUSION

We have tried in this chapter to examine something of the process of change and development in steel and to suggest that whilst the industry has been faced with recurrent problems, relationships between men and management have remained relatively smooth, partly because of the general orientations of workers and unions towards the industry and partly through the introduction of various mechanisms which have helped to adjust strain in the relations of production.

We have also shown that by the mid-sixties it was clearly recognized that the industry was on the verge of major changes. The Benson report had pointed to the necessary future structure of the industry, but, whilst it had outlined the ends, it did not touch upon the means by which to achieve them. The Labour government took the argument further and advocated nationalization as the only means to achieve the major changes which were felt necessary.

It was anticipated that nationalization would be accompanied by the 'necessary and desirable centralization of the main policy decisions'.[42] As this process got under way after 1967 several important implications became apparent, of which two will be mentioned here. As the sole employer the new corporation would inevitably have to standardize labour-relations practices throughout the industry. Thus productivity bargaining, job evaluation and the wholesale reform of payment systems were encouraged by the corporation, although many of the changes would take years to accomplish. The corporation also attempted to standardize the principles of union membership by encouraging white-collar unionization. This policy was in sharp contrast to that of the private steel companies who had vigorously opposed their white-collar staff joining unions. Three unions, BISAKTA, CAWU and ASTMS, began to recruit actively for membership and a number of inter-union disputes broke out. The Pearson court of inquiry was set up to investigate the problem. In evidence to the court BISAKTA made clear its abhorrence of such disputes, but it also revealed its concern lest its inevitable loss of membership in the contracting production area of steel might not be offset by recruitment in the white-collar area.

This recruitment dispute was certainly one factor which encouraged the formation of the Steel Industry Trade Union Consultative Committee on which all the major unions in the steel industry were represented. The hope was that this committee would not only minimize the chances of future interunion disputes but would also create a body which could directly liaise with the Steel Corporation on points of common industry-wide interests.

Another implication of nationalization sprang from the merger of fourteen formerly independent companies. In this respect it might be argued that the corporation could only achieve stable management-worker relationships were it to succeed in gaining the loyalty of its newly acquired work force. Even if this fund of goodwill towards the corporation existed, it was likely to be heavily tested by the corporation's labour-relations policies. The reform of payment systems, for example, could have unfavourable implications for the work force. At the individual level, earnings opportunities and job control might be circumscribed, while at the institutional level branch and shop-floor union autonomy might be curtailed.

Loyalty, however, would be more heavily strained by the anticipated programme of rationalization and redundancy which was envisaged. One aspect of the rationalization programme was that steel workers would be required to acquire new technical skills and jettison old ones. It also meant that the industry's employment composition would alter as a consequence of technological change, notably in the proportionate reduction in the number of production workers. When considered in the context of BISAKTA's traditional commitment to steel, the industry's managers could not automatically expect an equivalent commitment from a proportionally growing group of non-production manual workers. Given these prospects, it is not coincidental that attention was again focussed upon ways of accommodating labour–management relations to these strains. According to Richard Marsh, in many ways the most important question for nationalized steel was to devise ways of securing 'the full involvement of the workers in the efficiency of the nationalized steel industry'.[43] In essence, therefore, major changes could only be achieved smoothly through policies which actively promoted commitment and a readiness to change amongst the work force. The process of adjustment would require to be planned, for it was unlikely to be achieved by some industrial equivalent of osmosis.

Notes

1 BURN, D., *Economic History of Steelmaking 1867–1939*, Oxford University Press, 1940, pp. 220 et seq.
2 Ibid.
3 Ibid.
4 Ibid.
5 ALDCROFT, D. H., *The Inter War Economy 1919–1939*, Batsford, 1970, p. 173
6 SAYERS, R. S., *History of Economic Change in England, 1880–1939*, Oxford University Press, 1967
7 AMPHLETT, J., 'Where has all the Surplus Capacity Gone?' *British Steel*, No. 8, February 1970
8 *Restrictive Practices Agreements, Report of the Registrar 1.7.64–30.6.66*
9 *The Steel Industry: The Stage 1 Report of the Development Co-ordinating Committee of the British Iron and Steel Federation*, 1966 (known as the Benson Report)
10 Ibid., para. 68
11 SHANKS, M., 'The Irregular in Whitehall', in P. Streeter (ed.), *Unfashionable Economics: Essays in Honour of Lord Balogh*, Weidenfeld and Nicolson, 1970
12 *The National Plan*, Cmnd 2764, 1965
13 SHONFIELD, A., *Modern Capitalism*, Oxford University Press, 1965, p. 67
14 BROWN, LORD GEORGE, *In my Way: The Political Memoirs of Lord George Brown*, Gollancz, 1971, p. 119
15 Ibid., p. 123

16 WILSON, H., *The Labour Government 1964–70: A personal record*, Michael Joseph, 1971
17 *The Industrial Reorganisation Corporation*, Cmnd 2889, 1966, p. 676
18 BROWN, LORD GEORGE, op. cit., p. 102
19 WILSON, op. cit., p. 561
20 SHANKS, op. cit.
21 BURN, op. cit.
22 HUGHES, J., 'Steel Nationalization and Political Power', *New Reasoner*, August 1957
23 BANKS, J., *Marxist Sociology in Action*, Faber & Faber, 1970, pp. 104–5
24 SHONFIELD, op. cit., p. 96
25 *Steel Nationalization*, Cmnd 2651, 1965
26 *Hansard*, vol. 711, col. 1572, May 1965
27 Ibid., col. 1578
28 Ibid., col. 1581
29 *Hansard*, vol. 732, col. 1345, July 1966
30 Ibid., col. 1241
31 *The National Plan*, op. cit.
32 *Hansard*, vol. 732, cols 1352/3, July 1966
33 Although several unions may have decided to merge as a counterweight to amalgamations on the employers' side, two additional contributory factors can also be cited. First, there had been a protracted inter-union dispute in 1909 which led thereafter to discussion and correspondence over spheres of influence between the Steel Smelters and Iron Workers Unions. Second, the TU (Amalgamation) Act was passed in 1917 in order to facilitate amalgamations.
34 Anon., *Man of Steel*, 1951
35 SHARP, I. G., *Industrial Conciliation and Arbitration in Great Britain*, Allen and Unwin, 1950, pp. 59–61
36 Ibid., p. 59
37 WEBB, S. and B., *The History of Trade Unionism*, Longmans, 1902, p. 324
38 WEBB, S. and B., *Industrial Democracy*, Laymans, 1897 (quoted in J. E. T. Eldridge, *Industrial Disputes: Essays in the Sociology of Industrial Relations*, Routledge & Kegan Paul, 1968, p. 156)
39 It may be, of course, that assumptions may not have been shared, but that steel workers had no alternative but to accept the principle of wage reductions at a time of heavy unemployment. The existence of the sliding scale, incidentally, may be one reason why BISAKTA was virtually alone, in the trade-union movement of the 1930s, in pressing for tariff reform.
40 Royal Commission on Employers Associations and Trade Unions, *Productivity Bargaining and Restrictive Labour Practices*, Research Paper No. 4, 1967
41 Benson Report, op. cit., p. 177
42 *Steel Nationalization*, op. cit., para. 25
43 *Hansard*, vol. 737, col. 1798, January 1967

5 Genesis of the worker-director scheme

We have seen in the previous chapter that in 1967 the newly nationalized steel industry was on the threshold of major changes. The Steel Corporation was required to transform the industry into a viable and competitive unit; central to this strategy was a process of rationalization which involved policies of works closure, as well as the building of new high technology plant. The new corporation needed to seek the co-operation of its work force to carry through these changes for without that co-operation economic success would have been at worst unobtainable, at best evanescent. But the change process itself meant that such co-operation would need to be worked for very hard.

In this chapter we want to examine some of the factors that led to the organizing committee for the Steel Corporation becoming involved with worker participation at board level.[1] These factors included the corporation's organizational and operational problems, the corporation *qua* nationalized industry, the role of key personalities in the corporation, the representations made to the committee by spokesmen for the trade-union movement and the ongoing debate, both within the industry and beyond it, on the issue and meaning of 'worker participation'.

WHY WORKER DIRECTORS?

After the election of a Labour government in 1964 and the policy commitment to renationalize the steel industry, provisions were made to involve the steel unions in the running of the industry; these provisions went beyond those offered to the unions in the nationalization measures of the 1940s. One such provision was that the corporation be statutorily required to consult with the unions before finishing its report on organization. Another was contained in the white paper on steel nationalization[2] where the proposal was made to set up an Iron and Steel Advisory Committee, along the lines of a 'Little Neddy'. The ISAC would comprise government, management and union representatives who could discuss development in the industry in the context of rational economic planning. Given these provisions, and given also that the new corporation was statutorily required to enter into collective bargaining and joint consultation arrangements with the appropriate unions, why was it thought necessary to provide yet another forum for involvement in policy-making in the worker-director scheme?

One suggested reason concerns the traditionally posited inter-connection between the principles of worker participation and nationalization. Participation in this context has been viewed from a variety of standpoints, notably as a right to which workers in a publicly owned industry should be entitled, as a means of allowing workers a voice in the determination of 'their' industries' policies and as a means of facilitating the speedy introduction of those organizational, manning and technological changes which may stem from nationalization itself. However, from the 1950s onwards there had been increasing disillusionment within certain sections of the labour movement because of the lack of impact that the 1940s nationalization measures had had upon management–worker relationships in the industries concerned. While some regarded the experience as a vindication of the belief that no change could have been expected to occur, others tempered their disappointment with pleas for new thinking. Hughes, for example, referred to the lack of 'bold experiments characterized by the nationalized industries' preoccupation with sterile forms of joint consultation and collective bargaining'.[3]

Seizing on these issues of 'sterility' certain groups put forward demands in the 1960s for experimentation in the sphere of participation. The National Craftsmen's Co-ordinating Committee (NCCC) of the steel industry, for instance, called in early 1967 for major advances in worker participation after the nationalization of steel. Their proposals, amongst other things, urged the selection of the vice-chairman and four members of the main board from a panel of names submitted by the trade unions, the ratification by a group workers' council of the appointment of the group managing director, the right of the group workers' council to receive reports on all policies and to ask for detailed costings for all departments, and the ratification of the appointment of a board chairman at plant level by the plant workers' council who were also empowered to elect half of the plant board.

Calls for advancement in board-room participation within the public sector as a whole were also made by the TUC and the Labour party at about that time; it is important to observe that these calls represented a change in attitude in relation to previous policy discussions. In 1944, for example, the TUC had doubted whether 'it would be in the interests of the work people of a nationalized industry to have, as directly representative of them, members of a controlling board who would be committed to joint decisions . . . it was essential . . . that the unions should maintain complete independence'.[4] The TUC did not however exclude the possibility that some board members be drawn from 'appropriate' workers' organizations as long as those appointed surrendered their union offices. Similarly the Labour party's manifesto of the same year saw advantages in the appointment to nationalized boards of 'representatives of labour', provided that the appointees possessed 'managerial ability'.[5] The stress on ability was reminiscent of the 1932 debate in the Labour party on the London Passenger Transport Bill, during which Herbert Morrison emphasized that only through ability could efficiency in public corporations be assured. Moreover, 'efficiency' would be compromised if the boards were comprised of sectional interests.

Subsequent practice in the nationalized industries from the 1940s was partly influenced by the stances then adopted by the TUC and the Labour party. The practice, for instance, perpetuated the conventional wisdom that full-time trade-union officials were those most 'able' to sit on boards. In cases where they were given full-time (functional) posts they were asked to resign from their unions, and in other instances, part-time board members were drawn from the range of full-time officials of unions unconnected with the industry concerned. The issue of 'sectional interests' was resolved in that they were appointed to the boards by the appropriate minister or corporation chairmen; as board members, therefore, they were neither appointed by, nor accountable to, a shop-floor electorate.

Yet, by the mid-1960s both the TUC and the Labour party had adopted revised positions on the issue of board-room participation. The TUC, referring to its 1944 proposals, admitted that it had then made the problems of the trade unions' function 'unduly sharp'.[6] This recantation, coupled with an acquired experience of running nationalized industries, induced the TUC to recommend a 'new approach' in those industries. To this end, it therefore suggested that 'union representatives of work people employed in those industries [should] participate in the formulation of policy and in the day-to-day operation of those industries. These appointments should be made "at each level in the management structure".' In its proposals, the Labour party sought experiments in placing 'representatives of workers directly concerned on the boards of publicly owned firms and industries. . . . This representation should not be confined to full time officers of the union.'[7]

There are several points to note in the recommendations of the NCCC, the TUC and the Labour party. Firstly the call was for experimentation and departure from traditional practice. Secondly, attention was focussed on management boards at all levels in the organization. Thirdly, the call was being made for board membership to be drawn from within the industries themselves. Fourthly, these members would be preferably lay, rather than full-time, union officials. This last suggestion was partly a recognition of the increased role and importance of shop stewards in British industry since 1945, but it was not unrelated to doubts as to the unique and useful role that full-time officials could play on nationalized boards. One full-time union official we interviewed summarized these doubts in this way.[8] He spoke of retired or almost retired officials on public boards who 'played no role at all because they are then divorced from their unions; they're on a pension;

they need or they welcome the extra £500 to £1000 a year and the main aim is not to run across any of the powerful decision-makers in case their contracts are not renewed'.

The organizing committee for the steel industry, therefore, was deliberating on the future corporation at a time when calls for participative experiments in nationalized industries were being widely articulated in the Labour party and trade-union movement.

Moreover, as we have pointed out in an earlier chapter, the 1960s had seen a more general growth in interest in, and demand for, participation in a number of social institutions, particularly in educational, religious and industrial institutions. The theme was very voguish in management circles and the mood and reasons for interest from this particular perspective are perhaps well summed up in an extract from a British Institute of Management publication in 1968:

The Royal Commission on trade unions has just reported. The Select Committee on nationalized industries has been looking at the problem. A Labour party working party has reported on the future development of industrial democracy and other political parties and pressure groups have published their views. In a highly industrialized society forced to undergo great technological change and to find new ways of holding if not raising the standard of living people feel that democratic processes work badly. This creates unrest and tension; radical relief will be required to avoid an explosion. We need not look far abroad to see the dangers. Soon we must take new measures to realize the main ideals of industrial democracy whilst safeguarding the wealth producing industrial framework.[9]

The organizing committee were certainly sensitive to the need for new measures and experimentation. Moreover, the act of nationalization and the debates surrounding it had set the scene for increasing worker participation in the industry. We have noted that the corporation was statutorily required to develop joint consultative committees in steel, but the form of consultation differed from that embodied in the legislation of the late 1940s, again a reflection of dissatisfaction with existing standards. The major departure can be seen in S.31, sub-section 2(a) of the Act, where the corporation was required to 'make available to those persons [i.e. consultative committee members] at a reasonable time before the discussion is to take place, such information in their possession relating to the subject, as after consultation with those persons, appear to the corporation . . . to be necessary to enable those persons to participate effectively in discussions'.[10] The minister's agreement to this amendment was warmly applauded by certain MPs. Ian Mikardo, for instance, thanked Marsh, the minister, 'in the warmest terms', while Stanley Orme saw the amendment as a 'long overdue frontal attack on managerial functions in this country'.[11] The amendment was also a partial reflection of the more general demands for industry to 'open its books' to the workers.[12] The mood at the time in the steel industry was described by one national union official we talked to in this way:

'. . . now the industry was going to be held by the nation and the role of the worker would have a far more important part. I think there was that feeling there and I think it was consciousness on the part of the corporation of that really . . . there was constant pressure [by the unions] that they wanted the requirements of the Act to be met and that consultation in the industry would be meaningful and effective.'

For some people, and given the 'consultative' amendment, the participation question could have ended there. But the organizing committee deliberately and specifically set out to go beyond the legislative requirements. The question they posed themselves, as one committee member put it, was 'How in fact can you go further than the state required you to go. . . ?' An advance on the statute would be an attestation of the corporation's willingness to innovate, not from any statutory requirement, but of its own volition. The committee was also seeking to make an impact in an industry where inter-union friction had been a frequent occurrence. 'In that atmosphere [a committee member told us] if you were going to make an impact you were probably going to think a bit less convention-ally than you might otherwise have done.'[13]

The proposals from the NCCC were, in a sense, on the table before the organizing committee. How far did these influence the desire to innovate and the direction of innovation? In evaluating the impact of the NCCC proposals upon the thinking of the committee (together with proposals prepared at about the same time by the Institute for Workers' Control[14]) it may be important to distinguish between the impact in principle, and the impact in regard to detail, for committee members and corporation personnel seemed to make such a distinction. A committee member assessed the IWC's impact as nil, but the NCCC's proposals were 'extremely helpful'. He went on to say, nevertheless, that one could not say that 'this' (i.e. the worker-director scheme) came out of 'that' (i.e. the NCCC document). 'The ideas I think came about almost concurrently. . . .' Another corporation official was even more sceptical: 'I honestly do not believe that [the NCCC document] had any influence at all.' However, the role of the proposals (and calls for experimentation) *were* important as a catalyst; this is clear both from the organizing committee's papers and our interviews. In February 1967 (prior to the committee's first meeting with the NCCC) the papers show that the committee was taking into account 'the need for the corporation to grasp and keep the initiative in the face of pressures from various interests for workers' participation in extreme form'. The NCCC proposals were instanced as an example of this.

By the end of March the committee was clear that it needed 'to keep the initiative – not as a political gimmick – but to forestall those who might seek alternatively to impose such upon the committee'. It is not clear here as to the likely source of this 'imposition' but it must be remembered that the bill had yet to receive the Royal Assent and a 'motivated' group of MPs and ministers may have been expected by the committee to attempt to seek impositions. (That this was highly unlikely in *fact* will be shown later.) The TUC, too, might have been inclined to bring pressure to bear, and the committee accordingly decided (at the beginning of April) to bring the TUC into discussions 'in view of the importance of maintaining the initiative'.

The need for initiative was also reflected in our interviews. A senior corporation executive spoke to us about the expectations amongst the unions after nationalization that they would have a greater say in, and control over, management in the industry. Indeed, 'at one end of the spectrum . . . the craftsmen's groups were seeking [a] . . . veto over management. . . .' The decision was therefore taken that, 'rather than get into a long drawn out struggle with different groups of people, it was better to take the initiative.'

The role of the NCCC, then at a formative stage, was important, but what impact did parliamentary pressure seem to have? We have seen that manoeuvring in the Commons had contributed towards the 'consultative' amendment, but it seems unlikely that the same group of MPs were instrumental in the initiation of the worker-director scheme. The NCCC had ruled out the enlistment of help from MPs on the grounds that 'all sorts of decisions of expediency can be taken in the Commons' and that they wished to make a 'straightforward demand' for an experiment. What then of Ministerial influence? It seems that Richard Marsh's role was fairly significant, for, as one committee member surmised to us, the Minister 'welcomed the fact that we were thinking in our own right about things and willing to experiment'.

Another committee member remarked to us that Lord Melchett and Marsh were 'very close together in those days [and that] if Marsh had held a contrary view I am sure that Melchett would not have gone ahead with it'. We are referring, nevertheless, to 'negative' influence, that is, to the possibility that Marsh might have vetoed something to which he objected.

Turning now to the 'positive' influence of significant individuals, major importance can be attached to the interaction between Lord Melchett and Ron Smith (respectively chairman and board member in charge of personnel and industrial relations), especially during the early days of the committee. Historical influence had impinged upon each, for Smith was the former General Secretary of the UPW which was the only union to have passed consistently for fifty years at their annual conferences motions demanding an extension of industrial democracy. He had also in his early years had some contact with guild socialism. Lord Melchett, by comparison, was the grandson of Alfred Mond, an initiator of the Mond–Turner conferences of the late 1920s, who had actively supported both industrial rationalization and schemes of employee participation during the inter-war period.

It is important for our purpose to note that these two men were the first to be given permanent appointments to the committee, and as a consequence Smith had a unique opportunity to suggest to Melchett the need for experimentation and new thinking. And, just as Smith seemed to be intent on formulating new ideas, so the chairman designate seemed receptive to them. As the organizing committee grew in numbers, however, its composition came to reflect opinions less favourably disposed towards the idea of workers on boards. In the words of one committee member, 'the committee as a whole was not overrunning with enthusiasm for the idea, but it wasn't practically opposed to it . . . but the important thing was that the chairman was interested'. Because of the possibility that scepticism would be shared by many associated with steel, stress was accordingly placed upon the organizational advantages likely to accrue from the scheme and from the participative processes which it typified. The committee itself, for instance, accepted that 'the success of the corporation cannot be determined by management above . . . it must have the involvement of employees at all levels.'

The minister, we were told, initially reacted very strongly to the more radical NCCC's proposals and had 'no sympathy at all for the idea'. He was alleged to have said, 'Why the hell are you not going to the Gas Industry, the Electricity Industry or the National Health Service – all these industries can jog along and not worry whether they make money or not. Why come to this industry? It's got to be revolutionized, it's got to be streamlined, it's got to be competitive.' Yet, although the minister did not legislate for the appointment of worker directors, he did refer elsewhere to the importance of participation: 'I do not believe that major reforms in the industry can be carried through unless we carry the men with us.'[15]

For its part, the NCCC informed the organizing committee in February 1967 that 'major changes . . . could only be made smoothly if the unions had a say in the decision-making process'. Michael Foot said that major changes in steel were more likely to be accomplished 'if management will explain and discuss with working people what are the profound changes which will have to take place'.[16] Many people, therefore, stressed the 'instrumental' value of participation. Other considerations in the same vein pointed to the size of the new corporation and the remoteness of the boards from the people working in the industry. The creation of worker directors would, albeit imperfectly, bridge the gap. The need for the workers to comprehend and to accept the goals of the organization, and for them to be committed to these goals, was also thought by some to be an important consideration. One committee member to whom we spoke admitted that he was less than fully committed towards the idea: the scheme was 'a step in the non-wrong direction'. In so far as the scheme did have merits, he perceived these in 'educative' terms. His argument pointed to the capital intensity of steel and to the damage which strikes could accordingly inflict. He hoped that worker directors who became aware of the damage which strikes cause 'would modify their attitudes and they in turn would educate their colleagues'.

The trade-union reaction to the idea of a worker-director scheme was mixed. We have noted the role played by the NCCC proposals. Not all of the craft unions were, however, in favour of such a scheme; the electricians' union in particular opposed the scheme, taking the line that management should manage, whilst the unions should form a permanent opposition. The draughtsmen's union was also strongly opposed, but rather from the perspective that until there was a radical change in the structure of industry and society, any form of participation was not only playing management's game, but would be detrimental to worker interests. The main union in the industry, BISAKTA, took the position that looking after worker interests was its affair, and whilst some marginal advantages to steel might accrue from worker directors, they were basically 'surplus to requirements', and a 'well-intentioned gimmick'. The blastfurnacemen's union took a similar line, and saw in the creation of such schemes an implicit criticism of its own officials. Of the two general unions, the T. & G.M.W. seems to have felt that this was a tentative step towards much greater worker control; the G & MW had no really firm views at all. Pressure from the unions, then, was very much centred within the NCCC and came, in particular, from its convener John Boyd, who was the main and most enthusiastic and consistent union supporter of a worker-director scheme.

Thus far, we have attempted to show that the new thinking in the early days of the corporation was a response both to generalized and specific demands for experiments. The development of the ideas was stimulated by a few key actors who sought to mould the thinking into forms which would advance the policies of the new organization. It remains now to deal with the details of the emerging scheme.

THE BARE BONES OF THE SCHEME

The initiative which was seized by the organizing committee was, however, subject to constraints of both a constitutional and an organizational kind. The constitutional constraints concerned the system of appointment in a nationalized corporation, for the minister alone is empowered to make appointments to the main board of a public corporation. As one organizing committee member put it to us, the committee could only contemplate experimental action in those areas which were under the control of the corporation itself. The committee had therefore to concentrate on levels below that of the main board. At the same time, the committee purposely de-limited the involvement of worker directors to the group board level, and rejected the idea that worker directors be involved in management committees at works level. This decision (contrary, it may be remembered, to the suggestions of the NCCC and the TUC) was justified in order to avoid 'interference [by worker directors] in day-to-day management functions which normally are exercised at company or works level'. In more general terms, the delimitations confirmed that the worker directors would be 'involved in the making of policy', but not in policy implementation.

The committee seemed briefly to flirt with the idea of

appointing 'full-time worker directors, with the responsibility for some functional duties'. These appointees, it was suggested, should preferably be close to retirement age so as to avoid the difficulties which might attend the ex-worker director on his return to the shop floor. We were informed that this suggestion was a product of the committee's secretariat, but it was rejected on a variety of counts, including considerations of equity and 'management efficiency'. According to the committee's papers, 'if the worker is the best man for the [functional director] post he should be appointed to it by virtue of his merits and an open promotion policy; and if he is not the best choice management efficiency will suffer in consequence'. The committee's views were also modified on the issue of the source of recruitment of worker directors. At its first meeting it spoke in terms of candidacy 'below management' level but by April it had become aware (indeed, it had been *made* to become aware) 'that limitations to shop-floor participation would lead to intense dissatisfaction in the staff grades, including middle management and supervisors'. By April, therefore, the potential catchment area was re-drawn to embrace any level 'from middle management down'.

Another suggestion which was explored was that the worker directors be appointed to those boards unconnected with their places of employment. According to the committee, a problematic relationship between supervisory staff and supervised board members would hopefully be avoided. Other arguments mentioned to us by a committee member included the possibility that 'cross membership' would enable 'cross fertilization' of problems and solutions, and 'it would also remove this great difficulty that the division couldn't get at him because he was in a different division . . . '. In the event this position was modified after discussions with the trade unions.

The committee also discussed the relationship of worker directors to their unions. They felt that it should be a condition of appointment that trade-union positions should be surrendered. The committee's case on this issue was that it would be untenable for a negotiator (perhaps on his union executive) to be simultaneously a member of a board which decided the parameters of (management) negotiating policy. One committee member pointed out that the 'exclusion' decision was taken when the role of the boards had still to be clarified, and although it subsequently transpired that parameters were not generally determined by a divisional board, 'in the preliminary stages who was to know what the boards would be doing . . . ?'[17] In the early days, too, the committee also deliberated whether to create a corporation plus divisions or groups, or whether to form a holding company with four major groups. Were the latter to have been decided upon, then the principle of corporate responsibility would have extended to each board member. As a safeguard, therefore, the committee stressed as 'fundamental' the principle of corporate responsibility in its discussions with the unions.

Yet quite apart from the possible structure of the emerging corporation, it was decided by the committee at an early stage that worker directors would be expected to show paramount loyalty to the boards on which they were to serve. While the principle of corporate responsibility, *per se*, eventually became redundant, the worker directors were expected, by continuing to work at their own shop-floor jobs, to ascertain and express the views of the mass of people working in the industry rather than to protect and represent the views of workers in steel. In short, the principle of loyalty, according to the committee, was incompatible with the role of active union representative. These considerations also prompted the committee to suggest a system of appointment based finally on management discretion, for (consistent with Morrisonian principles) a worker director who was elected by, and accountable to, a shop-floor group, would be anathema to the principle of management responsibility.

The committee had also to show that the system of management appointment was 'not unfair' and partly for that reason the unions were asked to provide nominations, from which the final choice would be made by the corporation chairman. There were additional factors which influenced the committee's thinking on this matter. According to one committee member, for example, the decision to seek nominations was a tactical one, for the exclusion of the unions may have convinced them that the scheme 'was creating a new channel of communication and undermining their authority . . . it was really essential that we got them to work with us . . . '. Moreover, a role was devised for the TUC. It was decided to ask it to 'sift' the nominations from the constituent unions and to send the resulting short list to the corporation. In this way, the committee hoped 'to avoid the domination of the system by any particular or extreme group of workers'.

As we have pointed out earlier, whilst generally the trade unions were not enthusiastic about the idea of worker directors in steel, only two unions were totally opposed to the principle. Both the steel unions and the TUC discussed the worker-director scheme with the organizing committee during the period when proposals were being framed. Two of the proposals in particular proved to be contentious. The unions questioned the proposal that the worker directors should serve on the boards of groups other than those in which they worked. It was argued that if the advice of employees was important to the process of policy-making that advice would be more relevant if the worker director could draw on his own immediate experience. A situation was envisaged, for example, where a tin-plate worker would be serving on a board whose main concern was heavy steel where his experience and knowledge would be of limited value. This point was conceded by the organizing committee and it was agreed that appointments would be made to 'own' group boards.

The proposal that worker directors should not be trade-union representatives was also opposed by some unions. They argued that the effectiveness of the scheme would be reduced if the worker directors were not representatives; moreover, the dropping of trade-union offices might lead to the worker directors becoming distanced from trade-union attitudes and thinking. The organizing committee was not, however, prepared to compromise on this issue and the unions reluctantly withdrew their opposition. As one union official involved in the discussions put it: 'I had to agree with it; when you're fighting a battle you have to compromise or you get nowhere.'

CONCLUSIONS

By April 1967 the main outlines of the scheme had been formulated. There would be three part-time worker directors on each of the four group boards; they would work at their normal jobs when not undertaking board duties; they would be drawn from the group in which they worked; they would be appointed by the chairman of the corporation, preferably from trade-union nominees, and on appointment would have to relinquish any union posts they might hold. Whilst the corporation's aims for the scheme, once it had emerged, were not very clear, nor was the role which the worker should play very well articulated, it appears that there were three main strands in the corporation's hopes for the scheme.[18] Firstly it would act as a symbol of a new departure in industrial relations in the newly nationalized industry. Secondly, worker directors would provide the board with a new dimension in its discussions; they would bring to the board 'an experience which nobody else can bring'.[19] Finally, the scheme 'should be seen as a part of a serious effort on the part of the corporation to involve its very numerous employees in working out the future policies of the industry'.[20]

The scheme as it emerged was largely the creation of the Steel Corporation. The organizing committee had succeeded in grasping and maintaining the initiative. At the same time the scheme can also be seen as a compromise between the radical demands of the craft unions, the considerable hesitancy of the production unions about worker-director schemes, the doubts of many members of the organizing committee about allowing worker involvement at the highest organizational level, and the advantages other members of the committee saw in the scheme. The result of the compromise was an experiment whose structure and objectives were unclear even at a formal level. It might be argued that this was scarcely surprising in view of the nature of the enterprise and the numerous other major matters which top management and unions had to deal with at the time of nationalization. However, one can equally argue that any more specifically de-lineated scheme would not have got off the ground because agreement would not have been reached; the mere existence of the scheme satisfied the concerns of certain senior management people in cutting off demands for participation; the production unions who were generally uncertain about the whole idea could hardly object to such a bland scheme; and in the face of political problems it satisfied the NCCC, for they at least had achieved a marginal success which might be developed at a later date.

Notes

1 The general thinking of the organizing committee about the structure for the industry after nationalization can be found in the First Report on Organization which was published in August 1967 (Cmnd 3362)
2 *Steel Nationalization*, Cmnd 2651, April 1965
3 HUGHES, JOHN, *Nationalised Industries in a Mixed Economy*, Fabian Pamphlet 328, 1960, p. 30
4 TUC, *Interim Report on Post-War Reconstruction, Appendix D. 1944*
5 Labour Party, *Your Future*, 1944
6 TUC, *Trade Unionism*, Evidence to the Royal Commissions on Employers Associations and Trade Unions, 1966 (paras 259–62)
7 Labour Party, *Report of the Working Party on Industrial Democracy, 1967* (Recommendation XVIII)
8 This individual was not, nor had he ever been, a board member
9 BIM Occasional Paper OPN 1, *Industrial Democracy*, 1968, p. 8
10 *Iron and Steel Act 1967*, Part VI, S. 31, sub-section 2(a)
11 *Hansard*, vol. 739, col. 1203, January 1967
12 BARRATT-BROWN, M., *Opening the Books*, IWC Pamphlet No. 4
13 It became clear during our research that many people were under the mistaken impression that the corporation was statutorily required both to consult, and to appoint, workers to its boards. This impression may have arisen because the Act had not been closely read. Another factor may have been a less than rigorous definition and usage of terms. For example, a senior corporation executive justified the creation of the scheme (in part at least) as a means of avoiding 'suspicions that we are doing things behind the scenes and *not consulting fully*'. (Italics added)
14 Schemes for the democratization of the steel industry after nationalization were also put forward by various workers' control groups in the industry; cf. MEARLE, WILLIAM, 'Nationalized Steel', in Ken Coates (ed.), *Can the Workers run Industry?*, Sphere Books, 1968, p. 147
15 *Hansard*, vol. 739, col. 1200, January 1967
16 *Hansard*, vol. 739, col. 1824, January 1967

17 The corporation has subsequently modified the exclusion principle, allowing worker directors to continue as lay representatives.

18 It is interesting to note that, whilst references to all of these functions can be found scattered in various speeches and reports of meetings, they were nowhere expressed together, and in this way, until we wrote our initial confidential report to the BSC and the TUC on the scheme. They have, however, subsequent to that, been referred to in precisely that way. cf. TUC, *Industrial Democracy*, Interim Report, 1973, p. 23

19 MELCHETT, LORD, *Spectator*, 26.4.68

20 SMITH, RON, radio interview, 1.5.67

6 The organization

In an earlier chapter we indicated how views about worker directors were in part related to the way in which the board was seen as the effective locus of power in a company. Both inside and outside industry general folklore assumes that because the board is at the apex of the organizational structure then it is necessarily the centre of policy and decision-making. It is for this reason that many adherents to the idea of worker directors are attracted by the concept. In this chapter we examine the organization of the British Steel Corporation at that time, the role of both main, and divisional boards, and their relationship to policy-making. We also try to examine, in the light of available evidence, how far conclusions drawn from a nationalized industry can be related to private companies.

The Iron and Steel Act of 1967 took into public ownership the assets and activities of fourteen companies.[1] Unlike other nationalization legislation the Iron and Steel Act 1967 did not lay down any particular organization structure for the new entity. It was felt, given the problems which confronted the new organization, that the maximum flexibility should be left to those actually running it. To achieve this end an organizing committee was appointed by the government in September 1966 'to prepare for the nationalization of the industry and to start work on the future organization of the public sector'.[2]

The new corporation would employ over a quarter of a million people with plants located in all parts of the United Kingdom. An immediate organizational problem was therefore to devise a management structure which would allow this vast industrial empire to work with some degree of unity and co-ordination. In addition the new organization would have to establish for itself some form of identity which would supersede

99

that of the old companies and replace it with a loyalty to a group of executives dedicated to the success of the new entity. A further, and in the long term more important, objective of any new managerial structure would be to deal with the economic and technological problems facing the industry. The need to close old inefficient plants and to phase in new technologies, coupled with the prospect of abolishing, according to some estimates, 110000 jobs within the first ten years of existence, would confront any organization with a major challenge. As with the first need, that of creating a unified management structure, the economic decisions facing the industry also demanded a degree of centralization. A coherent plan, taking into account the various locations of existing capacity, was called for. It was almost inevitable that such a plan would have to be determined centrally so as to avoid bias either towards the former companies or particular regions.

Mainly for these reasons it was felt that a head office with central policy determining functions would be needed. One of the alternatives suggested in the early planning stages was the establishment of BSC as a holding company, with policy being decided upon by the particular trading companies, but this would not satisfy requirements for central planning and control. Having decided upon a head office with significant control over policy, another, almost contradictory, difficulty remained. A highly centralized system might have drawbacks in dealing with the wide variety of problems which could be met at the point of production in an industry as diverse as steel. Some degree of local autonomy had to remain with management, and it would probably prove preferable and more efficient to control and filter that automony through a level of management which filled the vacuum between head office and the production units. Initially, this gap was filled by the creation of regional groups, which were based largely upon the old companies and which were given their own directors and boards. Apart from the possible organizational necessity which has been referred to, one of the less obvious attractions of having directors and boards at regional level related to the status and legitimacy it conferred upon these directors in dealing with both outside organizations, and their subordinates in the works. In the case of the group directors, the majority of whom were on the boards of the old private enterprise companies, this also ensured, to some extent, a continuity of status and softened the blow of nationalization.

This initial structure of head office and regional groups can be seen as emerging as a compromise between the conflicting needs of centralization and local autonomy. Furthermore, the new structure reflected to some extent the pace of implementation of nationalization, and the limited time available for the organizing committee to develop what its members might have considered a more ideal management structure. Most of the directors whom we interviewed, who were also involved in determining the original shape of the corporation, conveyed the impression that they had always considered the regional groups as a temporary expedient only. This proved to be the case, and in April 1970 the corporation changed over to a system of product and functional divisions. The main objection to the group system was that 'by its nature it impedes rationalization and the optimum utilization of the corporation's assets'.[3] This reorganization also had the additional consequence of largely destroying old company identities and boundaries and replacing the old steel barons with men who were committed to BSC.

Table 6–1

PRINCIPAL PRODUCT DIVISION STATISTICS, 1971–2

	General steels	Special steels	Strip	Tubes	Construc- tional	Chemical
Crude steel production (million ingot tons)	8·63	3·38	7·40	1·12	N/A	N/A
Gross turnover (£ million)	454·00	231·00	507·00	177·00	55·00	22·00
Number of employees	77100	36900	64700	37700	9600	1600

Source: *BSC Annual Report and Accounts, 1971–2*

The new divisions grouped similar products and technologies under common control, thereby removing potential competition across regional groupings. The six new product divisions covered all areas of iron and steel manufacture along with subsidiary chemical and construction activities, and each division in itself constituted a large organization. This is apparent from the data set out in Table 6–1 dealing with the six product divisions.

In addition to the six product divisions, six functional divisions were established, dealing, in line with traditional management practice, with such areas as finance, personnel and commerce. Each of the twelve divisions had its own managing director, although in the case of the product divisions, additional directors were appointed from the works groups and specialist functions. None of the product division directors was a member of the corporation's main board.

THE CORPORATION BOARD

The key body in the organization of the corporation, and the only one with formal decision-making power, was the corporation board. Unlike other formal committees in the organization, members of the corporation board were ministerial appointments and they had corporate responsibility for all the activities of the corporation. During the course of the research the board usually consisted of about twelve members, of which half were normally part-time directors. There was no worker director as such on the board, although a former worker director was appointed as part-time member. In that he replaced another ex trade unionist it can be assumed that he was seen as representing a shop-floor/trade-union viewpoint. (As employees are not one of the categories of individuals whom statute allows on to the main board he ceased to be an ordinary employee.)

Those members of the main board whom we interviewed suggested that main board meetings were highly formal and voting was not a normal activity. One board member summed it up this way: 'we've never voted on any policy, not since

I've been in the corporation. Like the leader of the Conservative party, policy emerges from discussions.' In fact it appears that the board in the normal course of events merely sanctioned policy options already decided upon.[4] In some respects it would appear that the majority of characteristics of the corporation board are common to all boards. We will note later that divisional boards were equally formal and ritualistic. Pahl and Winkler[5] have also observed similar characteristics for a small number of private enterprise boards they have studied.

Given the relative unimportance of the main board in policy formulation, the question remains as to how policy emerges, and the manner in which various alternatives are filtered, to provide an acceptable strategy. A senior executive of the Steel Corporation described its policy-making process in the following way: 'we have twelve divisions, six of them resident at head office, six of them product divisions. Now the six at head office are divided functionally and they are formally charged with the responsibility for generating policy programmes and procedures.' Within each functional division are advisory committees; for example, the personnel and industrial relations function will have advisory committees on safety, training, industrial relations and so on. It might also have *ad hoc* working parties on particular subjects. The membership of these advisory committees is drawn from within the head office functional divisions and also from specialists within the product divisions. These advisory committees and working parties service the functions' policy-making role. An advantage of these head office advisory committees is that they permit participation by product division and works group management. In the words of the same executive quoted above, 'the debate can start anywhere. It can start in the works and go to the divisions, the product divisions, it can start at head office and go down into the divisions and from there into the works and works groups.' But it is clear that as far as general corporation policies are concerned it is within the head office functions, and within the advisory committees, that policy determination takes place.

As suggestions emerge from the various specialist functions, a major filter exists before any alternative is finally formalized as corporation policy. The chief executive has his own advisory committee, of which the twelve divisional managing directors are members.[6] It would appear that it is in this committee that ideas are finally discussed and accepted, and decisions taken relating to the operational management of the corporation.

Before turning to discuss the role of the product divisions, reference must be made to the external constraints upon decision-making. No business organization can be viewed as a closed system; a number of variables such as the firm's product market influence the outcomes of the decision-making process. In the case of BSC the system of external constraints also included the role of government policy. For instance, a recent select committee report has set out the relationship between government prices and incomes policies and the commercial freedom of BSC. The committee pointed out that BSC had had to submit to outside direction on prices on five occasions in less than six years. 'This perpetual interference . . . must reduce the morale of the corporation in its competitive environment.'[7]

PRODUCT DIVISIONS AND DIVISIONAL BOARDS

As we have seen (Table 6–1), the product divisions are large organizations in their own right responsible for running particular areas of the corporation's business. This responsibility, however, is held within the corporation's jurisdiction and the divisions are constrained by the corporation's statutory obligations to ensure the primacy of overall interests, prevent inter-divisional conflict and 'take into account overall regional considerations'. Moreover, the way in which the corporation was organized, as we have seen, ensured that it played an active role in the direction of the divisions. For example, at the time of our field work, capital expenditure for items over the sum of £150000 had to gain the approval of the corporation. Nevertheless, most capital expenditure planning, other than that ensuing from global restructuring of the shape of the industry, emanated from the divisions.

There were several ways, however, in which divisional

managements could lessen the impact imposed by the corporation's constraints. Firstly, as members of advisory committees, they could present ideas, control the flow of information, and change suggestions so as to produce more desirable outcomes.[8] It would appear that the presentation of ideas into the advisory committee system could be extremely influential, and this can be well illustrated by decisions dealing with plant closures and rationalization. On reorganization, the divisions were charged with the responsibility of rationalizing their production processes and capacity. Generally this meant that rationalization plans were discussed and formulated in the divisions, before moving into the central system of advisory committees and the main board for approval. Secondly, local divisional and works managers have the ability to modify policies as they are implemented. Throughout the period of the research, it was evident to the research team that local variations emerged around policy constraints which, on paper, appeared to offer only limited degrees of flexibility. Indeed, it is interesting to note that a number of worker directors saw it as part of their role to police the implementation of certain corporation policies. Finally, it was possible for national committees and working parties to emerge as a result of divisional initiatives, or some crisis in a particular works, and this enabled the division to exert influence over the terms of reference of such committees. In other words, whilst the control of head office over the divisions is great, the divisions also have control over head office.

The Third Report on Organization, explaining the organization of the corporation into product divisions, states that 'the divisional managing director will be personally responsible to the chief executive of the corporation for the running of his division'. Necessarily, the managing director must rely upon advice from both specialist and line management, and to satisfy this need a system of advisory committees and *ad hoc* working parties developed along similar lines to that existing in the central structure of the corporation. Over and above these committees, however, the Third Report on Organization states that the managing director 'will be assisted and advised by a divisional board'.

The worker directors who form the central concern of this book were members of these divisional boards. In a later chapter we shall examine the role they played on the board. However, the impact of their activities can only be assessed in the context of the role which the board played within the division. The divisional board was composed of all divisional executive directors, worker directors, and outside part-time directors; the outside directors were drawn from a variety of fields; local industrialists, university vice-chancellors or professors, ex trade unionists, and local notables. Each of the boards varied in size, but the norm was ten executive directors.[9]

We have made the point that in formal terms the divisional board was only advisory; responsibility for the conduct of the divisions lay with the managing director and both the managing directors and the chief executive of the corporation defined this reponsibility in personal terms. The board might be able to offer worthwhile advice, but in the final analysis that advice could be ignored. The point was forcefully put by a very senior executive. 'The chief executive doesn't hold the divisional board responsible for anything; if [he wants] to kick anybody's behind [he kicks] the managing director's behind.' In the view of this respondent the role of the board was merely that of long stop; a final sounding point for the managing director. The chairman of the corporation, however, took a somewhat different view. Whilst emphasizing the advisory role of the board, he went on to say, 'That's the point where, if there's any sort of policy making done below this office, it's done'. The divisional managing directors also appeared to attach some importance to the board, partly in so far as its backing gave the managing director additional weight in any disagreements with head office, although the influence of this support to some extent depended on the status of the outside directors. More generally it was felt that whilst the managing director received advice from a number of sources, the board was able to be more general and far-ranging in its scope. This is the spirit of the following comment by one managing director when asked to define the role of the divisional board: 'It is not for me to define the role of the divisional board. I am only conscious of how I use it. . . . I would say that it is one of the means by which I obtain advice and the ideas for running the division and make recommendations to head office. I emphasize that it is one because there are others, but the board is the most formal and rounded in its character.'

The divisional directors, who formally derived no 'special authority' from membership of the board, above and beyond that vested in them as line and functional managers, also tended to see the board as relatively unimportant (Table 6–2). Only 8% considered the board to have a policy-making function, although some positive advantage could be secured from the existence of the board, if it ensured that plans and decisions were open to criticism from outsiders with considerable experience of finance and industry. Mostly, however, the board's functions were defined in formal terms as simply advising the managing director.

Table 6–2

DIRECTORS' VIEWS ON THE ROLE OF THE DIVISIONAL BOARD

	%
To advise divisional managing director	25
Overall considerations of directors' operations/a monitoring exercise	11
Policy-making	8
To present plans and operations to outside (non-executive directors) consideration	19
To formally note actions and plans	17
Nothing/derisory comments	6
Other	10
No answer	4
N=48	100

In reply to a more specific question about the importance of the board in relation to policy-making, 69% saw the board's involvement as either extremely limited or non-existent. Indeed, for the 21% who argued that the board had some importance, it appeared that the importance was again indirect in the sense that the board's approval could be helpful in any further discussions which were likely to take place in the same topic area. In addition, the directors attached only a restricted significance to the board in terms of divisional operations. 75 % of these who answered considered the board as either not being very important, or not at all important.

What were seen as important, however, were the divisional management committees, which generally met monthly, and worked to almost the same agenda as the divisional board meetings, although pursuing each item in greater detail. These were meetings of full-time directors only, and can be seen as the most formal of the regular contacts between directors. The DMC meetings were cynically regarded by some part-time directors, including worker directors, as an attempt to develop common excuses prior to the board meeting. Certainly the DMC provided an opportunity to agree a common strategy before being confronted by part-time directors.

Given the system of constraints to which we have made reference, the DMC appeared to be the most influential body within the division. A main board director defined its role in the following terms: 'To a large extent, it is a policy-making body for the division, within a policy for the corporation.' Similar comments were found in the views expressed by the divisional directors, and comparisons were often made between the importance of the board and that of the DMCs.

'I think no doubt at all, in this nationalized structure, divisional boards as such do not play the part of their equivalent in private enterprise. I think this is quite clear, and I think in terms of decision-making more of that, within the power of the division itself, evolves in the divisional management committee.'

If, as suggested by both the corporation and divisional directors interviewed, the divisional board is of only limited importance in terms of policy-making and the operations of the division, an immediate constraint upon the opportunities for worker participation becomes apparent. Furthermore, in relation to the formal organization of BSC the question must be posed as to why it was felt necessary that the divisions should have a board of directors. We have argued that one of the attractions of the initial group boards was that they gave a certain status and legitimacy to the directors in dealing both with other organizations and with subordinates. To this extent, the boards can be seen as largely symbolic, a point made by a corporation director. 'The managing directors who are the heads of those [product] divisions are responsible for the running of the businesses, and because you use the word "business" meaning a division, which makes and sells some specific product or products . . . it was felt that he should have a board.' If the board is symbolic, it could mean that the opportunities for participation are equally symbolic.

However, while those with inside knowledge may see the divisional board as unimportant, it does not follow that other groups within the organization will have the same perception. In the sample of workers we interviewed, we found a certain confusion and haziness about the formal structure of BSC. This is very much what one would expect, both as a result of the rapid changes which had occurred since nationalization, and also as a result of the remoteness of the higher levels of the management structure from the working lives of those employed in steel. For instance, only 26% of the general sample of employees, when asked about the board structure of the corporation, were able to refer by name to the divisional board. The level of awareness was greater amongst shop stewards, 36% of whom were able to refer to the product division set-up.[10] Necessarily this general lack of knowledge about the organization of BSC was also reflected in the level of detailed knowledge about the worker-director scheme. Only 9·5% of the sample of ordinary employees realized that the worker directors were members of the product division boards.

Whilst the various types of boards and their roles were not clearly identified, it was apparent that a board was seen as significant, even if its functions could not be fully stated. The main area of board activity was defined in terms of policy-making by more than 40% of each sample (see Table 6–3). 'Policy-making' was perceived as an important exercise; an additional indication of this was provided by the views of the shop-steward sample; they were asked the type of decisions

Table 6–3

WHAT DOES A BOARD DO?

	Ordinary employees sample %	Shop stewards %
Determines policy	45·0	48·0
Deals with financial matters	5·0	11·0
Deals with commercial/sales matters	3·0	2·0
Future planning/new investments	2·0	6·0
Personal matters	1·0	—
Production/efficiency matters	5·0	3·0
Derisory comments	4·0	7·0
Other	2·0	4·0
Don't know	31·0	9·0
No answer	2·0	10·0
	100	100
	N=2579	N=317

which are made by the board and which directly affect workers. Given the major economic and technological changes which were occurring in the steel industry, the responses are again not surprising. 27·1 % of the total responses referred to the board's importance in relation to closures and redundancies and a further 29% mentioned the closely related topics of development and capital expenditure. The board, then, was considered significant, and despite the level of confusion which existed, it was seen as having some immediate influence upon workers, particularly in terms of impact upon job security. As for the worker directors, it became clear by implication that the vast majority saw the worker directors as members of boards, which acted in the way they had described in general terms. In other words, worker directors were part of an important structure.

The other two groups interviewed were managers and those full-time trade-union officials who had membership in the steel industry. Both these groups appeared to have a more detailed knowledge of the role of the divisional board, although their views differed, mainly it seems as a result of their differing structural positions. For instance, the managers tended to relate the functions of the board to their own role as manager. Whilst 61 % of managers considered the board to be important to them as managers, nearly half of these translated this importance into the functions of co-ordination and the establishment of policy guidelines. It was within the administrative framework determined by directors that the manager performed his task.

As a group, the full-time trade-union officials were much more likely to regard the board as of limited significance, in relation to the interests of their members. The reasons given for this viewpoint are of some interest, as it was the corporation which they saw as the focal point of decision-making. In relation to our previous analysis of policy-making in BSC, it could be that the full-time officials adopted the most realistic appraisal of all those groups not directly involved in the divisional structure.

Any explanation for this realism must be largely speculative, but reference can be made to the trade-union officials' involvement in those areas of decision-making dealing with investment, closure and wage negotiations. It is in these aspects that decision-making appears to be most centralized, and it is this centralization which has caused a number of problems for union officials. Indeed, both the lay and full-time representatives in the industry referred to the bureaucractic tendencies of the new corporation as a major obstacle to performing their representative functions. Information appeared not to be made readily available, but, more importantly, it was now claimed that it was impossible for a local manager to make any decisions relating to industrial relations. Generally speaking, this seemed to be the case, and it could be argued that, by reducing decision-making possibilities at local level, BSC, despite their formal commitment to the idea of participation, had effectively reduced the opportunities for participation.

THE ORGANIZATION – AN OVERVIEW

It is clear that divisional boards were generally considered by those connected with the industry (with the exception of directors themselves and possibly full-time officials) to be of importance in the policy- and decision-making processes. Our analysis has suggested that this was not really the case. We have tended towards a view that the divisional board was unimportant in these processes and in so far as it had any value this was symbolic. We have argued that policy alternatives are discussed and agreed upon within the system of advisory committees which exists at corporation and divisional level. Furthermore, we have suggested that a final appraisal of policy suggestions takes place at the chief executive's advisory committee. In reality, this body seemed to give the final sanction to proposals although formally such sanction could be given only by the corporation board. Through the advisory committees, the divisions were enabled formally to participate in determining those policies which acted as a constraint upon their autonomy in managing the division. Nevertheless, control was not totally from the top; the divisions had some freedom and scope for initiative, and this manifested itself in terms of interpreting and implementing corporation policy, in controlling the upward flow of information, and in making decisions relating to the day-to-day operations of the division. Within these limits, a further system of advisory committees, of which the divisional board was part, had been established to advise the divisional managing directors. Amongst those intimately involved in the divisional structure, the divisional management committee or equivalent, of which only the full-time directors were members, was considered of particular importance. That importance derived both from its involvement in the management of the division, and its ability to finalize reports and recommendations before discussion in the divisional board meetings. One managing director made it clear that he would encourage conflict between directors in meetings, other than those in which part-time directors were present; in that case, no such conflict was acceptable. The divisional boards, and to a great extent the corporation main board, were perceived as highly formalized meetings in which few, if any, decisions were taken.

A COMPARATIVE VIEW OF COMPANY BOARDS

The previous discussion of the role of boards in the BSC structure leads us to two main conclusions: firstly that the boards had relatively limited involvement in policy-making and were highly formalized and ritualistic in their operation; and secondly that management committees existing at levels lower than the board were mostly responsible for the production of policy and in effect took policy decisions. This general view can perhaps best be summed up in the words of one director who, when asked about the role of the board, replied, 'I don't know what its role is, it is not significant, it's an event only'. A further and perhaps paradoxical point might, however, be made here: whilst the majority of directors found it difficult to articulate what the role of the board was, in so far as it had any significant potential, this was seen as emerging from the interaction of executive with part-time directors. High value was placed on having outside directors of sound calibre at both main and divisional board level. Ideally they would be 'experienced businessmen, expert financiers'; at the moment there were 'too many academics, not enough businessmen'. Their function was seen as sharpening up the management view, giving an uncommitted outside view, widening the degree of knowledge available in the board room. They were considered as potentially key figures in the board, although the board itself might be considered unimportant.

We now go on to examine how far the characteristics of the situation we have described in BSC are unique to that situation, or how far they are more widely applicable. A recent survey by the British Institute of Management[11] tends to support a suspicion that, despite being a nationalized industry, BSC must not be viewed as a unique case. The BIM survey elicited a response from 200 British companies, ranging in size from 500 to 10000 employees. Of these, 70% had management committees which vetted and processed policies and data before presentation to the board meeting. Pahl and Winkler in their recent study reported a similar finding. They emphasized particularly the ability of key groups of directors and managers to control the provision of material for board meetings and to engage in what they term 'manipulation strategies'. They concluded that 'this situation is so commonplace that it has become the norm; the standard expectation of most of our directors (if not yet of management textbook writers and journalists) is that the board collectively does not seriously decide or even seriously discuss anything'.[12] The existence of this set of practices has two implications: firstly, and to a great extent paradoxically, the part-time director, who was generally welcomed, found it almost impossible to reopen discussion which had already been concluded. The BIM report comments that the widespread existence of management committees 'inevitably meant that very often decisions were largely cut and dried before the full board meeting, as far as the executive directors were concerned, and they were, therefore, difficult to reopen and recast at full board level'.[13]

Arising out of this difficulty relating to the presentation to the board of policies agreed upon by some directors and senior managers, there exists a second implication for the relationship between the board and management committees. Quite simply, there is a general confusion as to the purpose of board meetings. This was found in BSC, and similar viewpoints emerge from the BIM study. 'It was hard to establish what a board actually did. . . . Many board meetings were clearly relatively formal affairs preceded by formal or informal committees and group meetings of various sorts.'[14]

Again, as in BSC, the system of outside part-time directors won nearly universal approval. The man of considerable business experience cast in the role of part-time director could operate as a 'candid friend', that is a person who understood the running of the organization, and yet who would not be so intimately identified with particular policies, to be unable to ask the searching objective question. In addition to acting as a candid friend, the part-time director could also represent, in theory at least, the interests of a wider public by preventing the full-time directors acting as judge in their own court. So, the role of part-time director could be seen 'first, as a guarantee to the shareholders (and to some degree to the community at large) that the company was being run in a reputable and competent fashion with the shareholders' interest to the forefront; and second, as an objective force in the board able to offer independent criticism of the company's performance and future plans, and to advise from a neutral standpoint on senior executives' salaries, promotion and adequacy in general'.[15]

Unfortunately, the practice differed from these theoretical aspirations because of the existence and role of management committees, and the nature of the process of appointment to the role of part-time director which was largely controlled by the company chairman. This is not to say that only friends and admirers were appointed (though this often applied) but rather that appointees generally shared common backgrounds and more importantly held similar definitions of the problems facing the organization (and the objectives to be sought). To lessen this practice, the BIM report recommended the establishment of a centrally approved panel of potential part-time directors, with the company having to select from that panel. This represents a desire for professionalization of the role of part-time directors; a similar desire was often expressed by BSC directors. Part of this process of professionalization is to define the part-time director's role in terms of bringing a particular expertise to the board. We will return to this point in a later chapter when we discuss the ways in which worker directors were defined by the executive directors of the Steel Corporation.

CONCLUSION AND IMPLICATIONS

The similarities between management practices in BSC and those more generally, as represented by the BIM reports, would appear to be greater and more noticeable than the differences. Necessarily there are differences, and these tend to arise out of BSC's status as a nationalized enterprise, and particularly the formal relationships with government and the appropriate trade unions. Nevertheless, from the discussion of BSC in particular, and other companies on a more general level, a number of implications seem to emerge for worker participation at the level of the board. If the objective of participation is to increase the level of worker influence upon decision-making, then it necessarily follows that the workers' representatives should be involved in the discussion of policy alternatives. The locus of power in any organization has to be detected, and it cannot just be assumed in some formalistic manner (as evidenced by the discussion on the structure of the proposed European company) that the board is the locus of power. This must equally be true if the objective of participation is not concerned with questions of power and particularly the distribution of power, but merely sees the worker director as providing yet another expert input into the decision-making process. Again, it would seem necessary that the input should occur at a stage before policies have been formalized, and whilst alternatives are still open to influence. The significance of this chapter would be to suggest that the board is not necessarily the organizational point at which alternatives can be readily influenced.[16]

Notes

1 This excludes subsidiaries to parent companies
2 The members of this were drawn from both steel and non-steel circles and they later formed the British Steel Corporation Board
3 British Steel Corporation, *Second Report on Organisation*, HMSO, March 1969
4 It is possible to imagine a situation, however, of grave organizational crisis and strain in which the board would play a more active role than the one we have described. However, we feel our description would be valid for normal situations and would comprise the usual role of the board.
5 PAHL, R. E., and WINKLER, J. T., 'The Economic Élite: Theory and Practice', in Stanworth and Giddens (eds), *Élites and Power in Britain*, Cambridge University Press, 1974
6 After the completion of the field work, a further change took place in the organization with the establishment of a 'corporate office', which

was responsible directly to the chairman, and included board members and certain staff units. The new unit was concerned with board policy and future planning.

7 First report, Select Committee on Nationalized Industries, Session 1972–3, British Steel Corporation

8 For a more general discussion of 'power from below', see MARCH, J., and SIMON, H., *Organisations*, Wiley, 1958; MECHANIC, D., 'Sources of Power of Low Participants in Complex Organisations', *Administration Science Quarterly*, 7, No. 3; PAHL and WINKLER, op. cit.

9 During the time we were observing these boards, some of them did not have their full quota of outside part-time directors because it was found difficult to recruit people 'of the right calibre'!

10 For information on these samples, see Appendix. A maximum of two answers were coded for each respondent. In the table only the first answer has been used. Second answers were offered by 23·9% of the shop stewards, and the pattern of these was similar to the pattern in the table.

11 *Boards of Directors in Small/Medium Sized Private Companies*, Management survey report No. 10, BIM, 1970

12 PAHL and WINKLER, op. cit., p. 108

13 BIM, op. cit., p. 14

14 Ibid., p. 3

15 Ibid., p. 12

16 An earlier version of some parts of this chapter was contained in a report submitted to the BSC and the TUC in the summer of 1972. As and from April 1973, the divisional boards in BSC were abolished. The divisional management committee became the formal apex of the division's management structure and the worker directors are now members of this.

7 The worker directors I

The previous two chapters have looked at the way in which the idea of a worker-director scheme developed, and the nature of the organization in which it was to operate. In the chapters which follow, we go on to look at how the worker directors actually operated within the organization. But this requires that we first consider the people who emerged as worker directors; the kind of people they were, and the ways in which they defined their role.

Any form of social action is a function of both the way in which the actor is oriented towards his act, and the social structure in which the action takes place. Whilst in the past much sociological analysis, particularly in the industrial field, has concentrated on the structures in which action was located, whether it be the organizational structure or the technological structure, and seen action as largely determined by these structures, there has recently been a movement away from this type of analysis. Emphasis has been placed on the actor's orientation towards his role as a major determinant of behaviour in that role. Some writers have seemed to have seen the purpose of sociological writing as being merely the exposition of actors' orientations[1]; others have seemed to see orientation as static and unchanging.[2] Whilst emphasizing the importance of orientation, we would see a dialectical relationship between orientation, structure and action. 'There is a complex two-way process in which men's goals, ideas and beliefs influence and are influenced by the social structure.'[3] Something of this process, in one particular case, we hope will emerge in this and subsequent chapters.

As we have indicated in the last chapter, different unions had differing degrees of commitment to the worker-director experiment. The system for appointment assumed that nominations would come to the TUC from the relevant trade unions. No guidelines were laid down either by the TUC or by the BSC as to the ways in which nominations might be sought; consequently this was carried out in different ways by different unions. In some cases, branches were invited to forward names, in other cases, the unions asked lay members of their executive to compile lists of suitably qualified individuals, in yet other cases full-time officials proposed names.

It is clear that the method of finding candidates would have implications for the status of the scheme at works and branch level. It is equally clear that within some unions the method of nomination effectively reduced the opportunities for membership participation in the scheme and enhanced the popularity of the cynical view that worker directorships were 'jobs for the boys'. This feeling was certainly partly justified in the sense that in particular unions, the nominations had latent as well as manifest ends. For example, in certain cases candidates were put forward who it was thought might be able to assist in union recruitment and organization. In the words of one union official,

'at that time there were drives going on to recruit . . . in the steel industry. It was felt by some people . . . that this might assist with recruitment. . . . In that particular area there was a pretty large works . . . and there was a lot of business to be done there . . . and there was pretty fierce competition for recruitment.'

This is not to argue that nominees were not thought to be of suitable calibre to be worker directors: and indeed the official just quoted went on to make that point.

Individual unions submitted nominations to the TUC. The total number of nominations received by the TUC was in the region of eighty-eight. These nominations were sifted by the TUC and they in turn submitted a short list of eighteen names to the British Steel Corporation, followed by a supplementary list of sixteen names. It was evident that the Steel Corporation, having excluded the electoral process, would have to establish criteria by which to evaluate particular nominees. The problem was probably more difficult since there was no previous experience in this country on which to draw. It seems that the criteria used to assess individuals were as follows. First, it was felt that the individual should have the necessary intellectual capacity to make a positive contribution to the board. The individual should also be acceptable as part of the directorial team. To these ends, the opinions of local management, trade-union officers, and any educationalists who might have come into contact with the individuals were sought. The chairmen of the group boards were also closely consulted and they were asked to make recommendations from the list of names submitted from the trade unions. In addition, they also made recommendations from middle-management grades. Whilst the recommendations from group board chairmen were not necessarily accepted, it does seem that they had the power to veto appointments. Trade-union experience of the person nominated was taken into consideration and also membership of local authorities and public bodies. Given that steel is a multi-union and multi-occupational industry, a balance of these factors also had to be achieved within the universe of those selected. Finally, some account also had to be taken of regional factors and the old company structures.

In March 1968 twelve worker directors were appointed. Whilst the actual mechanics of appointment varied slightly, the general situation is well illustrated by this quotation from one of the worker directors:

'Personally I don't know how I got on . . . I'll tell you a story. One morning at about half past eleven our general manager sent for me and said, "Oh, the managing director wants to see you." "What the hell for?" I said. "I haven't done any bloody thing." He said, "I'm serious." I said, "Would you like to check it, I think you've got the wrong name." I was scared out of my wits. He checked it. At two o'clock I was called back to him. "The name's quite correct. Will you please see the managing director next Wednesday at such and such a time." I went over there and there was [the managing director] and in fairness to him, he treated me as though . . . very nice you know, had a chat, he knew what I was employed on, [asked me] how things were going and so on. Then he said, "now, the reason why I have asked you to come over is that your name has been selected from several names and we would like you to represent us on the board as a worker director . . ." and then he mentioned the terms of office and so on. "If you agree, you need not make up your mind straight away – if you agree, we'll arrange for you to see the deputy chairman [of the corporation] to see him and have an interview." Now that's precisely how I got on.'

Most of the worker directors expressed surprise at their appointment and the manner in which they were told of that appointment although they must have been aware of their nominations. None of those selected, however, refused the appointment.

The process of selection and appointment utilized was clearly bound to affect the kind of people who were eventually appointed. The stages of the selection process were a series of filters and apart from letting through those who fulfilled the criteria we have already mentioned, it was also likely that it would allow through only men who were middle of the road or towards the right of the trade-union movement. This is not to suggest that the people appointed were homogeneous, but certainly they did not reflect the diversity within the trade-union movement in the steel industry.[4] One of the worker directors put it like this:

'But you know the twelve of us came together originally and we were twelve strangers; each of us has reacted slightly differently but responsibly; and I was thinking the responsible side is very much probably the by-product of the form of selection. I feel that a lot of very good representatives, with whom I am in daily contact (without being egotistical at all, I want to stress this), really they would have had a great strain to have fitted in. I think their reactions would have been probably wrong; but conversely I know quite a number whose background and experience would have fitted them just as well as my own. I would think that looking at the background of all the people who have come in, they have all had fairly broad committee experience and they have had outside experience representing groups and organizations and they have all been able to express a point of view.'

We now turn to look at the characteristics and background of the men appointed as worker directors. Twelve men were originally appointed, although one resigned after only a few months in order to enter parliament.[5] Their average age was fifty-three; the overall age distribution was as shown in Table 7–1.

Table 7–1

AGE DISTRIBUTION OF WORKER DIRECTORS

Age	40–	45–9	50–4	55–9	60+
Number of worker directors	2	2	2	3	3

Eight of the twelve were from production unions, two from craft unions, and two from general unions, broadly reflecting the distribution of union members in industry as a whole (Table 7–2).

Table 7–2

TRADE-UNION REPRESENTATION IN BSC AND TRADE-UNION AFFILIATION OF WORKER DIRECTORS

	% of members in steel 1968		% of worker directors	
ISTC	55	} 65	50	} 68
NUB	10		18	
NCCC	12	} 14	8	} 16
AUBTW	2		8	
NUGMW	7	} 16	8	} 16
T&GWU	9		8	
Others	5		0	
	100		100	

It can be seen from Table 7–3 that amongst the worker directors there was considerable over-representation of staff grades and under-representation of manual grades. One reason for this has already been mentioned – the white-collar and supervisory fields were seen as fertile recruiting grounds by many unions in the early days of nationalization, and there was considerable and bitter rivalry between them; the worker director scheme was to some extent utilized in that conflict.

Table 7-3

TYPES OF WORKER IN 1968 COMPARED WITH
OCCUPATION OF WORKER DIRECTORS

	% workers	% worker directors
Process workers	44	33
General and maintenance workers	32	25
Administrative, supervisory, technical and clerical	24	42
	100	100

But other and perhaps more powerful reasons can also be adduced. One key national union official describing criteria for selection in his union said:

'Now what they [union officials] were asked to do initially was to, "please let's have a list of names from you . . . give us the names of people who you think you know would have the qualities that one would say would be required for a chap that was to be considered for appointment to a worker director." One would expect him to have at least an elementary knowledge of economics if you like, one would expect him to be able to decide the bottom of a balance sheet from the top, to be able to read figures and understand what they meant.'

Criteria of this kind certainly made it more likely that a staff candidate would be considered suitable material for a worker director than someone from the manual grades. Moreover, there were within the Steel Corporation pressures to have worker directors who were representatives of all managerial and staff categories. The occupational distribution of the worker directors emerged from this conjunction of interests.

The worker directors came from working-class backgrounds. One-third had fathers who had worked in the steel industry, and another quarter, fathers who had worked in the mines.

Table 7–4

FATHER'S OCCUPATION

Supervisory	1
Self-employed manual	1
Skilled manual	2
Other relatively skilled manual	5
Other manual	2
Not known	1
Total	12

Largely, they came from backgrounds which Lockwood has characterized as 'traditional proletarian';[6] backgrounds in which, he argues, there is a heightened sense of communability, solidarity, and class consciousness. All except one had left school at fifteen or earlier. Seven had had some further experience of the education process through evening classes, the WEA, trade-union courses or university extra-mural departments; in all but one case, however, these had been relatively brief encounters. Interestingly, several said that they had aspired to further education and that the possibilities had been there. However, the need to supplement family income with their earning power, or the extra drain on family resources which support of a non-wage-producing child entailed, had prevented the fulfilment of those aspirations. Most had entered the job market during the depression and the experience of the depression was formative for many of them; several had had great difficulty getting jobs, all had had experience, either themselves or through relatives and friends, of unemployment.

The 'traditional proletarian' syndrome is completed if one looks at their political and trade-union behaviour. All of the worker directors (with one possible exception) were Labour voters. Nine were card-carrying members of the Labour party; four of these were or had been Labour councillors and two others had at various times entertained the possibility of entering local politics. Three of the worker directors had been mayors. Of the nine card members of the Labour party, all had been, or were, party activists of one kind or another;

minimally as canvassers at local elections, but usually more actively in ward or constituency organizations.

Finally, we turn to trade-union activity. Not unexpectedly (as this was one of the criteria of selections), all of the worker directors had been, or were, active in the union in one way or another. Half of them had been members of their national union executives and another quarter had played some other role at national level within the union, e.g. member of national negotiating committee. All of those who had been active nationally had also played an active union role at local level and had usually been key members within the plant trade-union organization. Of the three who had not held national union office, one was a member of a craft union, very involved with his own plant, but with little interest in the union's problems in industries other than steel. For him membership of district or even branch committee was not perceived as relevant. The other two were white-collar workers, relatively recent converts to trade unionism and working within relatively under-developed trade-union structures.

Having looked at the background of the worker directors, we now turn to an examination of their general orientation towards participation. Before they were appointed as worker directors, the majority said they had given little thought to, or were unconcerned with, ideas of worker participation. Nevertheless, they had a distinctive, particular and reasonably unified set of views. None of their views, or sets of views, were perhaps coherent enough or integrated enough to form a philosophy, and in this respect, as we have pointed out in an earlier chapter, they were like most of the people we talked to in the industry. We start this examination of their views on participation with a quotation from one of them who probably had a clearer and more unified view of participation than many of the others.

'I've preached it [participation] for more years than I can remember. I've got a fundamental belief that the aims of the man on the shop floor and line management, and management all the way up the line (I'm not talking of course about the owners of the industry) are exactly the same . . . I do believe that people in the main are after the same kind of objectives. The only problem I find is the frustration on the shop floor when in fact decisions are taken they don't agree with altogether; and in the main the reason they don't agree is that they are not aware of the problems facing management . . . I've had a great deal of experience with ordinary shop-floor workers, and providing that they are told, you haven't got to say, "Yours is not to reason why" – you know the old saying "yours but to do or die" – provided that they are allowed "to reason why", I think the response from them would be terrifically surprising on the efficiency side of the industry. A man will do his job with a great deal more heart, with a lot less of the monetary incentive and a lot more of the pride and dignity kind of incentive; these are the things that I think must come through sooner or later. If you're consulted, you've got your dignity. This is the kind of philosophy I've always believed in.'

Much of this also reflects the position which the other worker directors took. There are three linked elements within this position, and while examining them in a little more detail, we can build up a picture of the way worker directors saw participation and the nature of relationships within the industrial enterprise.

The first element is authority. None of the worker directors would challenge the legitimacy of the authority structure in industry; what they did challenge was the ways in which that authority was exercised. It was often perceived as being exercised in a mindless, impersonal, inhuman way; a way which created frustration, resentment, even fear on the shop floor. 'I was in favour of [worker participation] because arbitrary decisions can affect a man's life. The great thing on the shop floor is the fear of the unknown.'

The second element centres around the words 'consultation' and 'co-operation'. Worker participation is 'involving' people, consulting with them and informing them. The following quote from one of the worker directors shows the way in which authority and consultation are linked. 'I agree with Joe [another worker director] about the importance of consultative committees. The greatest problems are that managers can make independent decisions.' Participation was necessary to modify these authority structures but not to radically change them.

The third element can be related to the words 'efficiency' and 'profitability'. A major reason for arguing in favour of participation is results that are thought likely to be brought about in terms of the efficiency of the industry. This is indicated in the long quotation with which we began this section. It is also illustrated in the following quotation: 'We've been talking about participation since 1928. But now [with nationalization] there was a change of emphasis – before it had all been a question of profitability. But now there was a new emphasis; profit was not possible without people and good relations with them.'

These quotations are taken from a series of group discussions held with the worker directors just over a year after their appointment. Two years later in a series of interviews with individual worker directors in which they were asked to define participation, we found no difference in terms of their definition. Participation in these interviews was to do with 'communication', 'co-operation', 'harmony', 'exchanging ideas' and 'introducing common ground between management and the shop floor'. The authority structure in the industry was still considered legitimate, but in the case of three worker directors it was felt that the making of policies for the industry should be a joint exercise, that is that workers should be part of the locus of decision-making. The basic philosophy, however, remains. 'If you involve someone, you get better co-operation. It's human relations.'

Further light can be shed on the perspectives of the worker directors by a brief consideration of their views of the aims of the nationalized steel industry. Basically, all of them subscribed to the view that the industry should be run as an efficient, profitable concern. Half of them saw no basic difference between the aims of a nationalized steel industry and one that was in the hands of private enterprise. 'The aim must be the same, to get the best return possible on capital.' The industry's job was 'to make steel as cheaply and economically as possible and to try and make a profit in the process. The aim of any industry is profit.' The other worker directors laid more stress on the need to take into account 'the national interest' and 'social responsibility'. 'The statutory obligations of state ownership mean a more responsible attitude.' 'While you're still being motivated by profit [in a nationalized industry] there is a degree of latitude which they are being afforded whereby they sort of take stock of the implications of their decisions.'

The model which the worker directors held of industry approximates to the unitary framework which we described in an earlier chapter. They saw the interests of management and workers as being basically the same and felt it important to develop a sense of shared purpose. Efficiency was a prime objective; but for the achievement of this, work satisfaction was important. Frustration and dissatisfaction within the work force were largely due to lack of communication and low involvement. Worker participation was therefore seen as an important key to unlocking the doors of harmony and co-operation and building up an effective industry.

In looking at the background of the worker directors, we suggested that the majority had come from what David Lockwood called a 'traditional proletarian' culture. One aspect of this culture is a dichotomous perception of society, that is a model that views the world as divided into 'us' and 'them', and sees the primary form of interaction between the two sides as being categorized by conflict. Clearly, this did not hold true for the worker directors. They still saw an authority structure which divided management from the workers, not because power was unequally divided, but because this power was often arbitrarily exercised. At the same time, they felt this to be an unnecessary situation; a situation which existed only because there had been a lack of the right kinds of communication; because management had not sought to consult with workers and inform them of the reason for particular kinds of decisions. Basically, the interests of both workers and management were the same and centred around the efficiency and viability of the enterprise.

We first talked to the worker directors a year after they had been appointed. During that time they had been on training courses organized by the BSC and the TUC and they had become to some extent accustomed to their board-room role. It might well be argued that the views they put forward about the industry and participation were merely reflections of their recent socialization into their directorial roles. Certainly this is true in part and we shall look at this later in the chapter.

One other point, however, needs to be mentioned here. All of the worker directors had one thing in common which we have not yet touched upon; they had all spent the major part of their working lives in the steel industry. None had been in the industry less than fifteen years and few had had much industrial experience outside the industry. (Those that had worked in other industries had done so in the early part of their working lives.) Steel workers, along with miners, shipbuilding workers and dockers, are classed as traditional workers. Unlike mining, the docks and shipbuilding, however, steel has a history of industrial peace. At least until recent years, disputes have been relatively few and the major union (ISTC) has only had one official strike since the war. Steel workers have *not* as a whole shared in a conflict orientation; this is indicated, for example, in studies which have been carried out on their attitudes to technical change.[7] The existence of rigid promotion ladders ties the worker not only to an industry but also to a particular plant, 'by establishing a pattern of aspirations and promotion for working life [it] gives him a feeling that he has a real stake in the firm'.[8] What this means is that, in contrast to mining communities, the overlap of work and other roles serves to foster a more consensual approach to industry in many steel communities. Whilst steel workers are not 'deferential', neither can they be described as a militant section of the working class. In other words, the worker directors, at least initially, could not be seen as atypical in comparison with their fellow workers.

Having looked at the worker director's general orientation towards the industry and worker participation, we are now in a position to examine his definition of his own role as worker director. On appointment, the worker directors were given minimal information about what their role was to be. The initial letter of appointment made it clear that the post was part-time, attracted a salary of £1000 per annum and was for three years' duration. The worker director would continue his normal employment. Formal union positions were to be relinquished and the worker director was not allowed to take part in (parliamentary) political activities.[9] It was pointed out that board members undertook not to disclose confidential information nor did they give interviews on steel matters without permission of the group board chairman.

This was the sum total of their formal role prescription. Perhaps the major delineation of their role, or at least the major attempt to socialize them into their role, came in the training course which they received at both the Steel Industry Management College at Ashorne Hill, and at the TUC College over a five-week period.

The Ashorne Hill part of the course, if it was to help to fulfil the overall BSC aims for the worker-director scheme, had to initiate the worker directors into an awareness of the corporation's problems and the manner in which the corporation was thinking; it had also to help them understand the management philosophy of the corporation, the management techniques utilized by the corporation and the reasons for these techniques. In these respects, the course which was put on appears to have been successful. The content of the course mirrored, to a large extent, the courses which the college ran for middle management. It was with some some pride that the worker directors reported: 'It was said by one tutor that we were putting into five weeks, what is normally done in nine weeks by middle management. If this is true, and we were told that we did at least as well as middle management, then one must accept that what happened at Ashorne Hill was a good thing for us.' In addition, the course also attempted to develop the directorial role of the worker director; firstly, in terms of their personal development and, secondly, in terms of giving the worker directors an opportunity to discuss and develop their own conceptions of the nature of their role.

The TUC part of the course was primarily concerned with the relationship between government and industry, the experience of participation in other nationalized industries and also collective-bargaining issues. It appears to have been more strongly directed towards a general consideration of industrial relations and the problems of participation than the Ashorne Hill course. While the latter emphasized strongly the directorial aspect of the worker-director role, the TUC laid greater stress on the participative nature of that role. Not a great deal of enthusiasm, however, was shown by the worker directors for the TUC course. 'Five sessions of statistics and one session of participation' was how one worker director described it.

Criticism was also expressed for the Ashorne Hill course, but this was generally overlaid with praise.

'Most of us here are ex-trade-union people and we always had a tendency to examine problems from the trade-union angle, and on accepting this appointment, when told I would be asked to attend the course at Ashorne Hill . . . I thought why should a man of my age attend school again? I thought I knew as much about the steel industry from the trade-union angle as I wanted to. . . . Nevertheless, my only criticism is that it was a crash course that put too much into too short a time. But nevertheless it gave us an insight into costing, capital investment, etc., which I think we wanted a refresher on; at the same time, it conditioned our minds to the job we would come up against in the board room and the problems of management.'

Another worker director put it this way:

'We were sort of thrown in and told to swim and if you can't swim, sink. There's a psychological approach to this; [if we hadn't been thrown in] we would probably never have been jolted out of our attitude that we had on the shop floor.'

In our discussions with the worker directors, several of them used the word 'conditioned' to describe the effect of their training experiences. But as one of them pragmatically explained, 'Any meeting, of course, conditions people, even this we are having here [a discussion group]. I mean life is one continuous conditioning. . . . In fact [the end result was] we were much more appreciative of the problems of management.'

It is certainly the case that the training courses prepared them for their board meetings. They did little, however, to prepare them for their role as worker directors, and this can primarily be related to the fact that in the early days of the scheme no one had any clear ideas as to what the role was about. The worker directors' own perception of their role, whilst also initially not very clear, derived from their general images of the firm and their definitions of participation. In this sense, the training courses served to reinforce and fill in perspectives which already obtained.

Given their general view of the nature of relations in industry and of participation, it was to be expected that the central feature of the worker director's perception of his role and of the directions in which his role should develop, was related to his idea of communication.

'The directors go for profit maximization but we see a communication problem. The functional directors don't care about communication.' 'I would say the objective of these functional directors is to make a profit, to make the industry profitable. Now our objectives are rather split. Make it profitable, also profitability with dignity for working men; somewhere along the line he's always been the casualty. When it's been profitability, it seems to me the working man has always been expendable. Now in this day and age, this has got to stop and I think this is our function, to make sure that his voice is heard in the board room. Exactly the implications of decisions they make, how it's going to affect the man on the shop floor. And it's our job as I see it, and we've been told this more than once, our job is to reflect the shop-floor point of view to the managing director, and I think this is a fair summary of what I think my job is.' 'To my mind our main objective is to bring shop-floor opinion to the board, that is our main objective as worker directors. . . .' 'It so happens, of course, that the end product of the objectives of us as worker directors, of the worker directors themselves and the management themselves, come to the same thing in the end, that it's an efficient industry, it is a profitable industry. . . . So we always argue with management at the top level, in fact, I think all of us do this, that the involvement of people down below will have a better effect on profitability than in fact your methods, which have normally been the stick and the carrot.'

In these quotations the major elements of the worker directors' orientation towards their roles are clear. They are middle men who will try to link together management, especially senior management, the unions and the work force. In this way, they will attempt to create more harmony and understanding in the industry; this in its turn will lead to greater efficiency. Indeed, the only way in which greater efficiency will be achieved is through the greater involvement of workers in the industry and the expansion of participation.

Management must be more sensitive to the views of the work force and, to a greater extent than in the past, must make shop-floor opinion part of their decision-making process. In this way, the natural unity of interests will be developed.

These are the major elements in the way in which all of the worker directors defined their role; they are also the most universalistic, in the sense that they obtain in most situations. However, all of the worker directors belonged to numerous groups and operated in a variety of situations. It is clearly to be expected that the actor's definition of his role will vary according to the context in which that role is being played. Moreover, it is also likely that the definition of the role will change over time, particularly if the role is being played out in a highly fluid situation. There is some evidence to suggest that this happened in the case of the worker directors. This is not to suggest that there was any major change in what we would call the central element of the role definition; however, the interpretation of other aspects of the role, especially what we might call relational aspects, varied over time.

As we pointed out earlier, the involvement of both management and the unions in the appointment of the worker directors varied considerably. In the early days of the scheme some of the worker directors felt strongly that they had a representative role. 'Officially we are not accountable to anyone, we are not actually representatives, but I don't think we've actually accepted that. I felt obliged to feel myself a representative of the shop floor. I'm a worker director. I'm a middle link of communication between top and bottom and I can't justify my appointment if I'm not a representative of the people below us.' Some two years later this same worker director felt that 'we're accountable to BSC: this is the [organizational] tree; we're not representative of the unions at all'.

Earlier in the chapter we said that social action and role definition interact in a dialectical process. As the worker-director scheme evolved, so too his self definition. Whilst the core definitions of their role remained relatively constant over time, the worker directors tended to stress increasingly the directorial aspects of their role rather than the worker aspects. In the early days of the scheme they were very much outsiders to the management system. As time went by, they necessarily became very much more involved. In the following chapters we explore some aspects of this involvement and its effect on the ways in which the worker directors defined and acted out their role.

Notes

1 SILVERMAN, D., *The Theory of Organisations*, Heinemann, 1970
2 GOLDTHORPE, J. H., et al., *The Affluent Worker: Industrial Attitudes and Behaviour*, Cambridge University Press, 1968
3 HYMAN, R., *Strikes*, Fontana, 1972, p. 73
4 This is not to suggest, however, that they were atypical of workers in the industry; indeed we go on to make this point later in the chapter. Whilst we have no research evidence about the orientations of the new worker directors who were appointed after the introduction of a modified selection procedure in 1972, there is some reason to believe that there is a wider range of political attitude amongst them than among the original group of worker directors. The modified selection procedure has also produced a different occupational distribution. Amongst the current sixteen worker directors, seven (44%) are process workers, five (31%) are general or maintenance workers and four (25%) are staff grades (compare Table 7–3).
5 The general background data is based on the original twelve worker directors. Later in the chapter the discussion of attitudes and orientations is based on the eleven worker directors who were in the post when we began this research. One of these during the course of the research was appointed to the main board, and ceased to be a worker director.
6 LOCKWOOD, D., 'Sources of Variation in Working Class Images of Society', *Sociological Review*, 14, 1966
7 SCOTT, W. H., et al., *Technical Change and Industrial Relations*, Liverpool University Press, 1956
8 Ibid, pp. 252–3
9 This rule also applies to top management generally in nationalized industries.

8 The worker directors II

Talking of the early days of the scheme, one of the worker directors told us: 'Initially it seemed that no one connected with this experiment could give us any clear line as to what our actual role should be; and because of this we were left to develop it to the best of our ability.' Given that the role of the worker director was a new role, and given the way in which it emerged, this is hardly surprising. Moreover, it was a role whose content and purpose was not only ambiguous but a role which was not accepted as legitimate by many in the industry. A lot of people were ignorant that the worker-director scheme had been launched on the industry; others, while knowing about the scheme, were unclear as to what they should expect from it and as to how to treat the worker directors. In the circumstances it would have been surprising if the worker directors had not encountered difficulties initially. Indeed within a few months the initial enthusiasm of the worker directors had been dampened and their early illusions shattered. The problems which arose in the early days of the scheme can most conveniently be discussed in relation to three main areas: the board, the trade unions and the work situation of the worker directors.

Attendance at board meetings was in the early days of the scheme the only clear feature of the worker directors' role. The worker directors naturally had a certain amount of trepidation about initial board meetings and board members were also uncertain about the nature of these new part-time directors who had come on to the board. Certain directors had fought very hard against the whole idea of employees sitting on the board. One of them expressed it in a particularly strong form: 'I think one saw this initially as just the final straw; we had been nationalized and now we were to have worker directors, we were going into the salt mines – it was communism coming at us.' Looking back upon their initial reactions to the scheme, only two or three of the forty directors asked thought they had reacted favourably to it; 47 % said they had been positively against it. At the time of our interviews many of those most opposed to the worker directors and to nationalization had left the industry; others who said they had reacted neutrally or favourably were not board members at the time. Paradoxically, despite a general antipathy to the scheme, it seemed that the worker directors were well received and many directors went out of their way to be helpful.

Nevertheless, the worker directors felt they were not fully accepted. There was a feeling of being second-class directors; in addition to this they felt they had a very limited involvement in the actual formulation of policy. Reports at first board meetings were not considered to be as full as worker directors would have liked and board meetings, they thought, merely performed rubber-stamping functions. Some months after their initial introduction to the board they wrote a document to the chairman of the corporation which stated: 'We soon realized that if our contribution was to be confined to attending board meetings monthly or bi-monthly it would be impossible to justify our appointment as worker directors.' There is probably some justification for the worker directors' view that they were not fully participating on the board. This, however, was to some extent true of part-time directors in general, and relates to points which we have made in an earlier chapter about the nature of the board. At the same time in the early days of the scheme particular items, for example on industrial relations matters, which would normally have been brought up at the board meeting, were not discussed because of the presence of worker directors. (We discuss the board-room situation of the worker directors more fully in the next chapter.)

The worker directors also had certain problems with the trade-union movement. At national level the TUC after processing nominations and arranging part of the training course seems to have lost interest in the worker-director experiment. There was no contact between the worker directors and the TUC in any formal way until a year and a half after they had been in office. The worker directors felt very bitter about this. They saw the TUC as 'having no interest in us' and some of the national union officials 'as thinking the scheme a bloody waste of time'. The general reaction of the TUC is possibly best summed up by one very senior official who in answering questions from the worker directors as to what connections there could be between the worker directors and the TUC replied: 'Make your own way now you are grown men.'

As we have said earlier, the worker directors were required to relinquish their lay trade-union positions on accepting their new post, and were also advised not to attend branch meetings. This was a quite traumatic experience for some of them: 'It suddenly struck me after accepting the directorship that I could never get to another trade-union meeting at my works.' Whereas formerly they had been in the position as lay union representatives to initiate meetings of their members and to attend consultative meetings these facilities were now formally lost to them. Reactions to the worker directors at local level varied very much from works to works and from area to area. In general, however, the sudden dropping of positions in the union by men who had been active within their local unions, in order to take on a post which was little understood by the unions, created a great deal of suspicion. In the words of one union official: 'The shop-floor workers realized that the worker directors did not represent them, that they were not in the same position as a shop steward or a branch official. A worker director was only responsible to the steel board and for that reason the workers were not interested in such a man.' There was a feeling that the interests of the worker directors and of any particular union were incompatible and also that the worker directors and the trade-union movement in general were incompatible. The worker directors, in the words of one full-time union official, were 'out on a limb'. 'The whole trouble lies in the Steel Corporation having asked these people to disassociate themselves from all trade-union work. The men immediately get suspicious.'

This feeling of disassociation was also strongly felt by the worker directors themselves. They were faced basically with two problems: first, how to relate to members of their own branches with whom they previously had had both an official and personal relationship; second, how to relate to other unions, for the worker directors saw themselves as being above loyalty to any particular union and as relating to the whole trade-union movement. In a very real sense, although the worker directors had been chosen largely because they had close connections with the trade unions and indeed had been nominated by these unions, they had to start from scratch after appointment as worker directors. In certain areas there were still connections with their branches and officials of these branches would come and ask them for advice; but this was on the grounds that they were ex-trade-union officials, rather than because they were worker directors. On the other hand, with other unions and other branches, they not only suffered from the disadvantage of not being a member, but also of being treated with suspicion because they were worker directors.

Moreover, there were some doubts in the minds of the worker directors as to how much contact and how much involvement they should have with the trade unions. The formal dropping of trade-union positions emphasized that their contacts with the unions were to be limited; they were not to be seen as union men, they were not to be too involved with the unions. At the same time they were expected to present a shop-floor view at the board. These seemed to them to be conflicting or at least partly conflicting behavioural imperatives; the worker directors therefore were very much in a state of anomie, of uncertainty, and it is possibly this that made them feel so bitter that neither the TUC nor the Steel Corporation offered them guidance. As one of them said, 'The success of the experiment depended as much on the BSC and the trade unions, including the steel committee, as it did on the worker directors. In the early stages we got little assistance from either party. The real problem was to define a role for ourselves.'

Finally worker directors were also faced with problems in the work place. In the past many had been trade-union officials and therefore probably had had more freedom of movement within the work place than ordinary employees. The role of lay union official, however, was well known and understood by both the work force and management, and the norms about behaviour here were generally agreed by both parties. Worker directors by comparison had to cover new and different territory both geographically and functionally. It was, therefore, inevitable that there would be some problems in the work place both in relation to their own work mates and in relation to management.

Most of the worker directors felt that when they assumed their new role there was some jealousy and some suspicion on the part of their work mates. People were unsure what precisely their status was. One worker director recounts the story of how, as he was walking through part of the works after being appointed, people hurriedly put away their newspapers as though he was a 'gaffer'. There was also a certain envy by other people and a feeling that perhaps they should have had the job; or at least they could not explain why that particular person had got the job. This is, of course, a situation which occurs even with trade-union elections, but there, at least, the reasons for any particular person getting the post are relatively clear. The process of appointment of worker directors was shrouded in a certain amount of mystery and consequently left the way open for accusations of corruption and back-door manoeuvring. It also, of course, quickly became known that the worker directors were being paid a substantial fee and there was a strong and inevitable feeling that they had in some way sold out.

This suspicion and jealousy was perhaps heightened because in the early days the worker directors spent a lot of time away from their work places on training courses and other duties; naturally their relationships with the work force became looser. Moreover, there were small but significant changes in their life styles which emphasized their new role and created a certain social distance between themselves and their work mates; for example, the receipt of documents and mail at work which had to be read, transport in chauffeur-driven cars, time off work to attend meetings, and because of worker-director commitments less frequent appearances in their regular haunts.

Relationships with management presented perhaps more complex, though not more difficult, problems for the worker directors. Broadly, these problems were of two kinds; problems of authority and status, and problems of work organization. Middle management in particular were unsure initially how to treat worker directors. One works manager asked a particular worker director to go along and see him and asked his advice, 'How do I now deal with you?' The relationship of management to worker director as employee was clear, but what was not clear was when in fact the man was employee, and when he was director, or indeed if the roles could be differentiated. As one foreman put it, 'If I told X off I knew I had to be careful that I was 100% right. I had to be careful because I knew he had a voice upstairs.' There was also a feeling with some worker directors that middle management resented the fact that they had been made worker directors. The board of director status is the top of the management career structure, and as such it was quite natural for middle management, who felt themselves qualified, and who were working their way up the ladder, to resent people of lower status in the organization suddenly achieving director status. Some worker directors felt that middle management attempted to take this out on them. 'I found out that there was this conflict; if they could possibly find something against you, if they could put the thumb on you, then they would do so.' Another said: 'Middle management definitely resent this kind of thing; they don't register a complaint about it, they only have a bit of a snipe now and again.'

There is no doubt that worker directors posed some very real problems for management. It was clear to management that worker directors were members of the board and did have access to information which was probably not at the time available to them. It was, therefore, difficult for them to treat worker directors on the job strictly as employees. As one senior manager said: 'I think the local manager would find it difficult on many occasions to treat a worker director in the same way as he treated other employees and to apply

the same discipline to him as to other members. I think he is
bound to be treated in a preferential way.'

Some management clearly saw the worker directors as a
threat to the normal authority pattern within the work place,
because it was difficult to treat a worker director as an ordinary
employee. One member of lower management said:

'I've learnt to live with things. I have to live now with the fact that
he can move around, go off the job, go and see people, without my
being able to stop him. I know that I have no recourse in this
matter. If I refuse permission then he can always go higher up the
hierarchy and as he goes higher up the hierarchy senior management become less and less aware of my problem. I have no recourse;
he is really a law unto himself.'

Another manager saw the worker director as a threat to the
normal communication channels, particularly in relation to
industrial relations matters. He thought that when people lower
down the hierarchy had access to information which their
superiors did not have, then the normal communication
channels were threatened and a general distrust was spread
throughout the department or even the works. This is a point
which management also make against senior lay trade-union
officials. In the case of the worker directors, who had access to
papers and discussions at the top of the hierarchy on a regular
basis, it was felt more fiercely. One manager who did not have
a worker director in his department thought of it in this way:
'Membership of the board confers authority. The man who
has a worker director in his department, well he has got quite
a lot of problems.'

One particular problem area, that of having time off from
the job, will suffice to illustrate this and also to illustrate the
organizational aspect of the problem. In the early days this
was an area which although in some senses trivial, caused
quite a lot of trouble. There are really three aspects to the
problem of time off. Firstly, the question of the gap to be
filled in the production process caused by the absence of a
worker director; secondly, the decision as to how much time
off the worker director should have; thirdly, the problem of
who should make the decision to give the worker director
time off. The first and third aspects of the problem caused a

lot of concern, especially to members of lower management. In certain instances the worker director's job was changed; in others manning scales were altered so that the worker director could be absent without production being disrupted. Occasionally the manning problem had already been faced and solved when the worker director had been a lay union official. Time off, however, is a frequent bone of contention even between lay union officials and management, and in the case of the worker directors, because there were no rules and no precedents, the problems were both different and more acute. In particular the issue of what was a legitimate amount of time to have off, and who should authorize this, was raised in a new form. Could the worker director's immediate manager query the fact that he wanted to have particular times off or did the matter have to be dealt with higher up the hierarchy? There was quite a lot of confusion about this in the early days. Lower management felt there ought to be a clearly defined policy but it was unclear who should lay this policy down and indeed what the policy should be.

It was these kinds of problems, problems in the work place, problems at the board, problems of relations with the unions and the strain this put upon both worker directors and individuals within the corporation, which began a movement to create a clear and more defined role for the worker directors. The worker directors themselves felt very strongly that their status was not equivalent to that of other members of the board, that they were not being involved in the creation of policy, and that they were remote from the trade-union movement which neither understood their role nor perceived what its possibilities were. Moreover, those at the top of the corporation who had been most responsible for the introduction of the scheme were also worried at its lack of impact. At the same time the change in organizational structure from regional groups to product divisions was being planned and this provided an opportunity for looking more closely at the role of worker directors.

During the spring and summer of 1969 a series of meetings took place between the corporation and the worker directors in which these problems were discussed. Out of these meetings emerged a formal job description. This was discussed with the TUC steel committee and finally agreed in December. This job description seemed to go quite far towards meeting the original complaints of the worker directors. It clearly specified that they could attend and participate in advisory committees, working parties and study groups. They could also attend formal and informal meetings of functional directors and local management. In both cases, however, it was to be at the invitation of the (new) divisional managing director after consultation with the worker director. Worker directors had also been unhappy about their relationship with the unions. The job description allowed them to attend their own and other trade-union meetings. It also established a right to attend consultative meetings as observers. This new job description took account therefore of some of the initial problems of the scheme. Although it did not formally come into operation until the organization change to product divisions in April 1970 it provided from a much earlier date a set of ground rules for future action.

We now go on to consider the way the activities of the worker directors developed after the inception of the new job description. In parenthesis it is perhaps important to point out that the amount of time that worker directors spent on activities which could be related to their worker-director role, varied between individuals. For some it was 35% as workers, 65% as directors; for others these proportions were reversed. The difference in activity was related to both orientation towards their role, and the constraints in their own social situation. To a great extent the worker directors created their own activities and provided pressure for creating spheres of activity. At the same time the social network of individuals was of crucial importance in terms of ability to act. By and large the wider, more varied and inter-connected the social network of the worker directors, the more active they were as worker directors. The worker director who was incapsulated in a narrow network, based for example within his own shop and union, found it difficult to operate in a role that lacked definition and had no generally accepted status within the social structure of the industry. In the present discussion, however, we do not take account of individual variation but examine activities in aggregated form.

The worker director's activities can be seen in relation to two main aims, influencing policy and problem-solving (and in doing so legitimating their role). In one sense both of these emerge from, and are related to, a more general value of easing strains in the organization and promoting co-operation between the parties involved in the industrial enterprise. Whilst the board meeting was, and remained, the central feature of worker-director activity, they moved out from this to a wider involvement in committee work at national and local level. The degree to which they could effectively contribute to these committees was largely dependent on access to managerial information – that is, access to people and files. It was also dependent on having access to, and being to some degree supported by, the unions. An isolated worker director, the worker directors understood, was of little use. It would, of course, have been difficult for the worker directors to have relations with both workers and unions without being exposed to their problems; and having been exposed, it was difficult not to be involved. Indeed the majority of the worker directors saw it as a central part of their role to act as something of an 'ombudsman'.

In a previous chapter we have located the role of the divisional board within the organization and broadly sketched in the contours of power and policy-making. As we have pointed out, when they were first appointed, the worker directors were only envisaged as playing a role within the divisional board. Whilst they were never totally clear about the extent of the influence of the board, it was soon obvious to them that there were several forums of debate and discussion within the organization where policy-making and decision-making took place. They were particularly sensitive to activity at national level, and felt they ought to press for influence there; they also knew that, given the sponsorship of the personnel function at head office, they had a better chance of obtaining membership on the national committees, than on committees at divisional level.

Amongst some managers and directors there was a certain sympathy towards this position. In the words of one head office manager who was central to much of the development of the worker-director scheme,

'they [the worker directors] in certain of the groups felt that they were just being used like rubber stamps and they didn't have the information on which to come to an assessment of the situation themselves, and they found it difficult to break through the mass acceptance by the majority of people on the board of the recommendations which were coming from management and a host of directors. . . . The thing we came up with was advisory committees. And we have pushed all along in the personnel function at head office to get them involved in advisory committees. . . .'

Formally, the rights of the worker directors to be involved in advisory committees and working parties was written into the new job description, though with the proviso that attendance was 'at the invitation of the divisional managing director'. However, as the above quotation suggests, even within a 'friendly' head office function, resistance was to be found amongst management to having workers on committees within the management structure. The expertise required of management, and the right to manage, these were powerful ideologies to overcome. In particular their presence on committees dealing with industrial relations issues was resisted. It was argued that this would place the worker director in an invidious position, as they would be privy to the bargaining strategy of the corporation and its constituent parts. Some of the worker directors also took this view, but others felt that it was crucial to be on these committees. Despite a great deal of pressure, during the period of our research no worker director sat on an industrial relations committee at either divisional or national level.

The worker directors were interested in policy-making and decision-making rather than the details of management. However, the distinction between policy-making and management is not always clear, especially in standing advisory committees with relatively specific briefs. During the period covered by the research the number of committees on which the worker directors served increased dramatically. Before divisional reorganization only two worker directors had been represented on one working party at national level, and one worker director served on a committee at a lower organizational level. By the end of the period covered by the research only two worker directors had not sat on a working party or advisory committee at national level and two (a different two) had not sat on an advisory committee or working party at divisional level. We now go on to consider the range of committees sat on, and the influence of worker directors on these committees.

At national level the worker directors sat on both *ad hoc* committees and standing committees, convened to consider specific problems or problem areas. All of these committees were in the field which broadly would come under the heading of 'personnel'. Some of them were highly specific, for example a committee to consider an appropriate policy for time off work for civic or other public duties; others were rather broader in their scope, for example a committee to consider social and regional policy. That they were concentrated within the 'personnel' area was partly a function of the sympathy of the managing director of this division at head office and his ability to exert some pressure on committee chairmen; he himself set precedents on committees that he chaired. It was also, however, a function of what was considered 'appropriate'. The worker director was not seen as a representative, or as a watchdog of worker interests, but rather as someone with a certain expertise derived from his experience on, and knowledge of, the 'shop floor' (this is expanded on in the next chapter). The situation being so defined, there could be no point in his being present on bodies formulating policies on matters related to finance, production, commercial policy or forward planning. Given a rather different definition, however, of the role of worker director these central policy-making areas would be precisely the areas where worker representation would be most important.

At divisional level the situation was rather similar. In one division no worker director served on any committees; in another they served on only one committee on which they formed the majority and which appeared to have been set up specifically to occupy the worker directors. In the other two divisions the committees served on were all within the 'personnel area' and were concerned with such topics as training, welfare and accident prevention. In other words, at both national and local level, the areas where the worker directors were involved in committee work were the sorts of areas where traditionally management has come to feel that joint committees serve some purpose. In this particular case it was the organizational level rather than the policy area which was unique.

The range, therefore, of committees on which these worker directors sat was rather narrow. However, within these areas it is important to ask what kind of impact they had. Without exception the worker directors themselves felt that they had affected either the tone of discussion, or particular issues within the scope of the committee work. One saw the worker directors' presence as sharpening the discussion; others, in reply to our questions on their impact on these committees, suggested ways in which they had affected particular outcomes; one, for example, had fought for the retention of a particular kind of long-service award, others had made contributions to national safety policy, others felt that they had added new dimensions to the discussion. For example, they had made BSC executives at national level aware of the difficulties and problems for young craft or production trainees in having to combine hard manual work with off-the-job training. In only one case, however, was the claim made that their contribution had been crucial to the outcome of the working party. Half of the worker directors felt that they were still on the fringes and felt they ought to be more involved in the central policy-making committees such as the divisional advisory committees; the rest were either opposed to much further extension into other committees or ambivalent about it.

The majority of the chairmen of committees on which worker directors sat were not enthusiastic about the contribution worker directors had made. Most felt that they had made little or no impact on discussions or on the outcome of the meetings. The only exception to this at divisional level was on a committee dealing with accidents where it was felt that the worker director was a useful sounding board for union reaction to policy and played an active role in promulgating committee decisions. The chairman of this committee, like most of the other chairmen, also emphasized that management was a technical affair and that the worker directors could play little part in the specialist discussions that took place. Another manager commented:

'I was horrified when I first heard that they were coming onto my committee . . . I regarded them with suspicion. They were union people. How would they fit in. And what for? It [committee work] was all cold facts. They get even more cold facts when they sit on national committees. I can see no value in them being there as they were no value on my committee. One of the worker directors generally gets involved in the discussion but there is so much they cannot speak about.'

At both national and divisional level the general management feeling was that worker representatives, whether they be called worker directors or anything else, could contribute very little to what were often technical and detailed discussions. At national level only one chairman felt the presence of worker directors on a national committee had been useful. 'However much management may try, it's extremely difficult for management to be close to the shop-floor view and the feeling of the shop floor. I would have thought that this [committee] was a very clear case of where they made a very useful contribution to thinking.'

Of course, management's view of the usefulness of having worker directors on committees and their contributions is a sectional evaluation. A worker director who was vociferous in challenging the prevailing view-points on a committee and taking up positions unacceptable to management would not usually be seen by a chairman as being a useful member of the committee.

However, in this case many of the points made by management were borne out by our observations of committees. Comments made by worker directors were generally fewer than comments made by other committee members and only a limited number of comments manifested disagreement with items under discussion. The majority of contributions related to the personal work experience of the worker directors, although in certain cases extra-work experience, for example on local authorities, was drawn upon. The worker directors

148

made little use of information which they might have obtained within the board room in these committees. In all the cases we observed, the aims of the committee, the direction of discussion, and the outcome of meetings and documents produced were kept firmly within management control. This was the case even in one working party which collected evidence from both management and unions. Here, although the worker directors often played a key role in questioning and discussion and were encouraged in this, the framework of discussion and the final policy outcomes were those of the management members of the committee.

During the period following the new job description therefore the worker directors moved out from attendance solely at board meetings to involvement in committees whose job it was to advise on and formulate policy. Initially, certainly, there was a great deal of resistance by management to this and their presence on committees was not considered relevant to management needs. The worker directors themselves consistently stressed in their conversations with us the need to prove themselves; to prove that there was a role for them and that they were able to fill it confidently. Their expanding role in the formal committee structure of the organization imposed upon them the necessity to keep abreast of changes and movement within the industry generally, within their own divisions and within their own works. Not only did they need to keep abreast, but they needed to feel and be involved. These needs patterned much of their activity.

Arising out of involvement within the formal committee structure, both boards and advisory committees, came a set of meetings with managers at various levels, which were intended to prepare worker directors for meetings or to give them background information. The majority of worker directors had regular meetings with at least one executive member of the board. Usually this would be either the personnel director or the director of the local works group. The normal function of such meetings would be to go through board papers or discuss issues arising out of the board's business (in one division the function of going through board papers was undertaken by a senior manager and not a director). The pressure for such meetings had usually come from the worker directors in an attempt to get to grips not only with the technicalities of board papers but also with the thinking that lay behind particular proposals. But management also found such meetings were useful in that they were able to clear issues (particularly technical) which otherwise would have been raised at the board and thus they facilitated the smooth management of board meetings. As one director put it in a comment that was not intended to be pejorative: 'These chats mean that the sharpness of debate is lacking in board meetings because the questions are already decided.'

Other regular meetings with executive directors were used to review in a general way what was happening in the division and to allow the worker directors to raise any particular issues they wished; or in some cases to sound out the worker directors on particular issues (usually within the field of labour relations) which were currently facing the division. One worker director described these meetings as 'a trusted heart-to-heart discussion with the directors, the power boys, who are really in charge of the division'. Over and above scheduled meetings all the worker directors had other occasional *ad hoc* meetings with the directors; these meetings were usually at the worker directors' request and ranged from the desire to find out how a particular function operated, to wanting to get information about rationalization plans or redundancy issues.

Apart from these meetings the worker directors, of course, also met the directors informally at least once a month at pre-board dinners or luncheons after board meetings. And occasional opportunities for discussion would arise when, for example, a worker director and an executive director who were located within the same works group would use the same transport to go to a meeting in another part of the country. A guide to the amount of interaction is given by Table 8–1 which shows the frequency of contact between worker directors and directors, as reported by directors.

To some extent this table under-represents the amount of interaction in that in two divisions the worker directors spent the evening prior to the board meeting with the rest of the board at a pre-board dinner; previously in one of the divisions

Table 8–1

WORKER DIRECTOR/EXECUTIVE DIRECTOR CONTACT

	% of executive directors
Only at board meetings/lunches/dinners/ other committees/or by chance	22
Occasional discussions other than at the board	44
Regular or frequent meetings (at least bi-monthly)	27
Not asked	7
N=45	100

the worker directors had had fixed meetings with some members of the board but their presence at the monthly dinner and the opportunities to talk afterwards were seen as substitutes for this. Nevertheless, the table indicates a high level of interaction between the worker directors and executive directors; certainly higher than that between executive directors and other part-time directors and probably higher than that between some of the executive directors themselves.

As well as developing and routinizing a set of activities in relation to the executive directors, the worker directors also developed a set of routinized activities in relation to management. Half of the worker directors had regular meetings with some members of their own works management, usually either the general manager or the personnel manager. For the worker director the function of these meetings was to keep informed of what was happening in his own works, in terms of production, planning, and industrial relations. In certain cases they saw themselves or were seen by management as the spokesmen for that particular works on the board. As one worker director put it: 'He [the works manager] hopes I will stress on the board what he has stressed to me.' This was particularly the case with works whose future was in doubt. Of the rest of the worker directors, all except two had a reasonably well-developed set of contacts with some of the senior management in their own works, and would see them at not infrequent intervals. From the perspective of the worker directors, the major function of such meetings was to obtain information: 'My job as a worker director depends on the information I get. I go to [the manager] and he updates me on everything.' Or in the words of another, these contacts 'are vital for information purposes'. All of the worker directors felt it was 'essential' to have good relationships with management.

We interviewed a number of key members of management in the worker directors' own works (see Appendix for details) and the pattern of reported contacts between the worker directors and management was as follows (Table 8–2).

Table 8–2

WORKER DIRECTOR/MANAGEMENT INTERACTION

	% of managers
No contact	10
Only by chance/at social functions	20
Only at meetings	16
Occasional general discussions	10
Discussions over particular problems	17
Regular discussions	23
Other forms of contact	4
N=90	100

Whilst the amount of contact the worker directors had with their own local managements was not as extensive as that with directors, and some of the worker directors felt that they needed more contact, at the same time the figures indicate a reasonable degree of access to and interaction with management.

So the worker directors had access to sources of information at their own works and at divisional level. However, they defined their responsibilities as division-wide, and not works-specific, so that in their view it was important to become familiar with other works in their division and problems associated with these works. During the period of our research, other than board meetings, visits to works were one of the main sets of activities for worker directors. These visits started during the days before divisionalization and stemmed from the worker directors' concern that they be aware of what was going on in the division. Programmes of visits to works within the division were arranged usually by either the board secretary or the personnel director, and the details of the visits were arranged by local managements.

In the early days of the scheme visits typically consisted of detailed tours of the works, with an emphasis upon the technology and production process. The worker directors would arrive at a works, usually have an initial discussion with the works manager and senior management, and then be taken on a conducted tour of the works by management. Occasionally during the tour a union representative would be introduced to them, but the schedules were usually very tight with little time to stop and chat. Lunch and occasionally dinner would be laid on and were normally attended by senior works management. Generally speaking, the visits were organized by management as though the visitors were executive directors; they were managed in order to impress, and certainly due consideration was given to the status of worker directors. As the grand tour proceeded from department to department the departmental management were lined up in order to meet the visitors; precedence was often given to the visit over other managerial duties.

However, the worker directors became increasingly dissatisfied with their lack of contact with trade unionists during their visits; one of them told management very forcibly that their first prority should be to meet men and trade unionists, their second priority was to talk to management, and only as their third priority should they have a look at the production process. This dissatisfaction was conveyed to those organizing the visits, and on some works visits the worker directors met and talked to groups of trade unionists, or sat in during joint consultative meetings and joint safety meetings. However, it was clear that the meetings were organized by management; indeed, on many occasions management sat in on the meetings

– and the point was not lost on trade-union officials. Where management did not sit in on these meetings the worker directors usually took up points that were raised with the management afterwards. Typically the meetings between worker directors and trade unionists during works visits started with the worker directors outlining their role. We quote from one such meeting which took place two years after the inception of the scheme.

Worker director (introductory remarks): 'We are the missing link between the shop floor and board of directors; we give the shop-floor and your view to the board; this is the reason for these visits. Something may come up at the board and we can make a contribution of your views. We're the missing link. There are specialists on the board and we contribute the practical side.'

Shop steward (interrupting): 'This was fine when it was first thought of, but the board only pay lip service to this sort of thing. It's fine as far as the worker directors are concerned in general terms, but often they're not very genuine on this sort of thing and communication fails by either union or management.'

Worker director (ignoring interruption): 'We were offered the appointment and then for a number of weeks we went on courses to help us with questions . . . so then we had less contact than we wanted to. But we're divisional representatives despite what some might think . . . and so we get round to see and talk to you about anything you have in mind so that we can make a contribution at the board on your behalf. It is genuine. There's no voting on the board of directors. It's the managing director's decision that counts but there's no distinction between directors; we can say what we like and at times we can influence decisions, for example about development and closure. We can ask about retraining and the timing of it so as to continue people's employment. This has been lacking in the past so we perform a useful role and equal to other directors.'

This particular meeting then opened out, and points were made to the worker directors about the inadequacy of union facilities, about the distinction between staff and manual grades in terms of clocking-on and pensions, about the lack of communications with management and management's tardiness about dealing with grievances; questions were also raised about manning arrangements and small-scale local redundancies and safety. The worker directors commented on all of the points made, occasionally fed into the discussion information about the way problems were being dealt with at other works, or indicated (for example, on pensions) that the question was being investigated at national level. After this meeting the worker directors had lunch with the management and brought up many of the questions that had been raised at the union meeting. Management on most of the questions suggested an alternative perspective on ways in which the problems were being dealt with. The occasional point they conceded. They also pointed out that the most vociferous of the union officials was unreliable and a trouble-maker. The worker directors did not raise the points the unions had made at that meeting in any other quarter.

Over a period of time the worker directors developed a consistent style for works visits in which they met union representatives. Firstly, they saw it as important to explain their role and to suggest ways in which they were important to trade unionists. Secondly, they used the meetings to get over to the trade unions information about certain aspects of the industry. The most important of these generally concerned the future state of a particular works. Clearly, constraints existed in this area as at times the worker directors were dealing with information of a confidential nature. This led to a situation in which the worker directors themselves were giving general reassurances; one summed up his approach quite simply like this: 'I generalize as usual, I must generalize.' It was not always the case, however, that they knew what was planned for particular works. Sometimes they went to divisional management for briefings before visits. On at least one occasion they were given information by the works convener during a visit that a particular works was to be sold back to private enterprise; a situation which hardly increased their stature as divisional directors.

In these meetings the worker directors also stressed the need for rationalization in the industry and the necessity for co-operation. A quote from our field notes on the visit already mentioned illustrates the point.

The worker director said that he disapproved of redundancy but that they [the workers] had to move with the times and investment guaranteed their future. The union official said he had written up about this and pressed for investment. Another union official said they all appreciated that the long-run benefit was greater than the short-run problems, but he emphasized that redundancy must be fair. And the worker director added: 'And must be done by negotiation and joint consultation. You're in the picture and know the consequences. Get hold of management and work out these questions.'

The worker directors saw it as another part of their function to relay information upwards in the organization whenever difficulties were brought to their notice. As a result of worker directors raising with executive directors problems which they saw as trivial, and also as a result of management reaction to this 'going over their heads', a procedure was developed whereby problems which came to the worker directors' notice were initially conveyed to local management and only if there was no satisfaction on that level would they be taken higher up. Some of the problems created by this situation, both for management and worker directors, are illustrated by the following extract from our field notes.

The works manager then asked if they had learnt anything useful from their meeting with the unions and a worker director said, 'yes, they had and there were a whole number of things they were going to raise at board level'. The works manager then said that he hoped they would come back before that and have a discussion with him as he might be able to answer many of the points put to them by the unions. Another worker director pointed out that if this was the case it was a bit ridiculous them having to tell him what the works union committee thought and should they not (i.e. manager and unions) get together? There was general embarrassment all round and the secretary of the union committee (who was sitting in on the meeting) pointed out that the manager had only been at the works a short time and really they had not had a chance to get together properly yet. He then offered to withdraw but was told not to do so. The worker director then insisted on reading from his notes some of the points that they intended to take up, and the manager pointed out that they (management) were trying to work on some of these points. Another worker director said that none of the things that they would take up with the board would put any reflection on local management; but in fact they would be, along with local management, presenting a two-pronged attack on the board. The manager did not seem particularly happy with this idea and made several comments, to the effect that he also had the ear of the managing director. . . . As we went outside afterwards [a worker director] remarked that it was a bit impertinent of the manager to expect them to get his approval for taking up matters with the board. 'He seems to forget,' he said, 'that we're directors and he's a manager.'

In the event none of these points was formally raised at the board meeting, though they may have been discussed informally with the relevant directors. Some months later the worker directors returned to this works to find out what had taken place and report back to the unions. The meeting fell very flat. The worker directors said that they had been pressing things at board level and the unions said (without much conviction) 'thank you' and there the connection between the last meeting, and that meeting, ended and the union talked about other and different problems.

This was one of the few occasions when the worker directors did try to establish some kind of continuing link with the unions in a works in which none of them was based. And on the whole the attempt failed. This was not due to bad will or lack of effort on either side. It was due, however, to the external role which the worker directors played in relation to both unions and management. They were not part of the normal structure of relations between or with either, and consequently the intervention had an *ad hoc* character which made continuity difficult and irrelevance likely.

This lack of structural relationship made relations difficult with the unions even in a worker director's own works and area. After the initial hiatus the worker directors soon realized that it was essential to build up relations between themselves and the unions. The majority of worker directors attended their own branch meetings. However, they defined themselves as being over and above individual branch or union loyalties, and saw it as necessary to be in touch with, and available to, all branches of all unions. For most of them this was a difficult if not impossible task. Three of them managed to attend, on occasion, other branches of their own union and of other unions. An easier forum, however, was meetings of joint union branches. Half of the worker directors were regular attenders of joint union meetings in their own works and others attended at least one meeting. Even when the worker directors were regular attenders of joint union meetings they were there on sufferance and because of personal influence rather than of right. As one of them stated: 'I attend my own branch regularly and others by invitation only. Such invitations are infrequent probably because of parochialism and jealousy on the part of local officials.'

Parochialism and jealousy were not the only reasons. At the purely formal level union rules often imposed a barrier. More importantly, however, many union officials regarded the worker directors with suspicion or as a waste of time. Whilst, as we have pointed out earlier, the majority of lay trade-union officials were in favour of a worker-director scheme in theory, only just over half expressed themselves in favour of the BSC scheme. The main identifiable reasons given by those who were against the scheme were that it was a gimmick without any real substance, and that the worker directors had no real influence. The majority of the shop stewards we talked to also felt that it was management who had the greatest influence over the worker directors (54%) and in so far as the unions had any influence this was exercised by national officials (24%).

All of the worker directors had been associated in the past with specific unions, and it was difficult for a production worker to get accepted by craft unions and vice versa. Their union network usually reflected their past affiliations. Most of them had reasonable informal contacts with the key union officials in their own and related unions. The majority (68%) of the key lay union official sample we talked to claimed to know the worker director in their works well, or fairly well (see Appendix for sample details). Of those, just over half claimed to meet him fairly often (at least once a month) and another third to meet him on the odd occasion. Very few of the worker directors had equally good contacts with other shop stewards. Their lack of a formal role in relation to the union structure, even in their own works, meant that their activities in relation to the union were *ad hoc* and depended very much on personal initiatives. Where a worker director took a view that any initiative should come from the unions a situation could result where there was virtually no contact between the worker director and local union representative, other than those of his own branch.

By and large, these key works trade unionists were passive in relation to the worker directors. We asked them whether they had ever asked a worker director to take up a problem for them. The majority (64%) said they had not, either because they felt they could sort out their own problems, or because no problem had occurred which they felt would be useful to take to a worker director. Of those who had approached a worker director with a problem, the majority went to him because they were having no satisfaction from other sources, or because they wanted to get above local management, or because they wanted the worker to ensure that local management carried out national BSC policy. The kinds of problems that were taken to worker directors were usually in the area of personnel, industrial relations and social policy; for example problems over time off and union facilities, redundancies and strikes. It was rare for a trade-union representative to feel that the worker directors had made any substantial contribution to the solution of their problems. The majority of them felt that worker directors were not relevant to their problems. They also felt that they themselves had little influence over worker directors. The majority saw management as having the major influence over worker directors. But they also took the view that the worker directors had little or no influence over management. If a worker-director scheme was going to be useful for them they felt that the worker directors had to have a much more structured role in relation to the unions.

The relationship between the worker director and the formal union organizations was even more tenuous. Only one union at national level acknowledged the worker directors it had nominated by inviting them to visit head office. Some of the worker directors had occasional informal contact with members of their national executives. With few exceptions relationships with full-time union officials at district and divisional level were almost non-existent. An analysis of contacts as described by union officials shows the following pattern (Table 8–3).

Table 8–3

WORKER DIRECTOR/FULL-TIME OFFICIAL INTERACTION

	% of FTO's
No contact	33
Only odd social occasion, or meeting by chance	22
Occasional general discussion	11
Occasional contact over problems	11
Regular contact	6
No answer	17
N=46	100

The general view held by full-time officials can be summed up in these two quotations.

'I wouldn't think of getting in touch with him. I wouldn't think there would be any useful purpose served and I wouldn't think of it anyway. . . .' 'They haven't got any significant link at all with the unions as far as I can see, and this goes for my colleagues in the unions as well; there are no benefits that have materialized since the worker directors have been in existence.'

At national level the worker directors did have a formal relationship with the steel committee of the TUC. This relationship consisted of a once-yearly meeting between the worker directors and the steel committee, at which the worker directors talked generally about their activities. The majority of national officials, like their local counterparts, felt that the worker directors were insufficiently tied to the unions and insufficiently influential to make further contact useful. On only one occasion, over the question of redundancies, did the steel committee try to enlist the help of the worker directors. We discuss the outcome in a later chapter.

The worker directors considered that the development of relationships with both management and trade-union structures was essential for them in carrying through their role within the committee system of the Steel Corporation. It was important for them to be informed of what was going on, and to show that they had a part to play in it. And it was difficult to confine that part to the committee room or the board room. Indeed the majority of the worker directors (though not all) felt it imperative to seek out problems and respond to them. They saw themselves not only as influencing policy, but also acting as an 'ombudsman', as a go-between. These definitions of their role, of course, both overlap and derive from a more general goal of easing strain within the organization caused by (in their view) lack of communication of the views of one side to the other.

Some of the worker directors came to see this role of inter-preter as a role which they should be able to play in cases both of individual and group crisis. Whilst most of the worker directors avoided being involved in individual grievances and all were very wary of being seen to take over any of the functions of shop stewards, they would on occasion suggest to an in-dividual people he should approach, or they would informally drop a word in the ear of management. As individuals they came to have a much greater knowledge of the organization and its personnel than that available to any union official either lay or full-time; moreover they also had access to in-dividuals at a variety of levels. Whilst, as we have emphasized, their lack of a defined role in the structure led to very great problems for them, it had the advantage of leaving them free to flit from level to level.

Most of the worker directors become involved at one time or another in disputes or strikes. The extent of their involvement varied from merely talking to the parties in dispute, to chairing meetings of unions and management in the middle of the strike and addressing strike meetings. In some cases the worker director was brought into the situation by management:

'I asked him [the worker director] to intervene in the strike which he did reasonably successfully. . . . Before the strike was out I wanted the message clearly got over to them that we meant business and whatever happened we couldn't go over the wages figure, this kind of thing. And when we had the strike we had no contact with the shop stewards and we used him as a liaison for that to try and get some of our points of view over and bring about a conference, which he didn't do badly.'

In other situations (and more rarely) the unions, often the unions not on strike, asked the worker director to intervene. In every case the worker director was an extra figure in the drama, another line of communication, perhaps someone who could find a key to an impasse. The reaction of various parties to the worker directors' intervention varied. However, it is generally true to say that those, both on the management and union side, closest to the dispute least welcomed the intervention of worker directors. Management and union officials, more remote from various strikes, felt, however, that the intervention of worker directors had had some beneficial effect on the situation.

Involvement in strikes and grievances was not written into the worker director's job description. Indeed, such involvement was formally frowned upon by senior management at Steel Corporation head office. At the same time it provided a dramatic and relatively public activity for some worker directors. It was a means of establishing that they had some functions; it was activity which meant simultaneous interaction with both unions and management and pointed to the duality of their role. Moreover, it related very strongly to their own definition of their role, to their job orientation.

Most of the other major activities of the worker directors were written into the job description. Indeed, the job description and the ground rules it established for action provided the legitimation and justification for their actions. This is not to argue that once the job description was agreed it was automatically translated into action. Like the worker director scheme itself, the job description was imposed by senior and central management upon the local and divisional managements. And the worker directors were encouraged to fight for its full implementation. The job description could not, however, be imposed on the unions. Whilst it gave the worker directors rights in relation to management and formally established their status, it could do no such thing in relation to the unions. It had been seen and discussed with the steel committee of the TUC but it was very much a management document.

Paradoxically then, whilst the job description on the one hand gave the worker directors a weapon against management, it also incorporated them more firmly into the management structure and steered their activities in a managerial direction. As a result of the job description their involvement in the policy-making structure of the industry grew – their access to management and to information was made easier, and their relationships with management stabilized. A very much larger amount of their time was spent with management; they were increasingly dependent on managerially defined information. The worker directors' fight to establish their role was a fight largely with management to work within the management structure. To legitimate their activities they had to work within specific confines.

This is not to argue that their relationships with the unions did not also increase. After the initial hiatus with the unions, relationships were gradually renewed and expanded – but they were re-established, so to speak, from the outside. The new job description allowed the worker director to attend union meetings; whereas the worker director had a formal position within the structure of the Steel Corporation he had no formal position within the unions. Nor, as we have stated earlier, did he have any forum in which, as of right, he could listen to and exchange information with the unions.

This was one reason why the worker directors were fervent advocates of the establishment of a comprehensive and effective system of joint consultation in the industry. Joint consultation along with the worker-director scheme and the extension of collective bargaining were the three main planks in the industrial relations policy of the Steel Corporation. Consultation was to be established at all levels within the industry. However, the process was slow, and in many places consultative

163

committees had fallen into disrepute with both unions and management. On works visits, at meetings with the unions and at meetings with managements the worker directors argued for the establishment of consultative committees, and in certain cases were directly instrumental in getting committees launched. By the end of our research period all but two of the worker directors were regular attenders at consultative committees within their own works; of the two not attending one was chairing a joint committee of inquiry into the failure of joint consultation in his own works group, the other felt that the committee was not working well and therefore it would be a waste of his time. This worker director did, however, on occasions attend consultative meetings at other works as did several others.

The worker directors saw consultative committees, especially if established at levels above the works, as forums which they could attend as of right, in which they would be able to sound out workers' views and union feeling. (Consultative committees, they felt, ought to be trade-union based.) One worker director expressed it this way:

'This is his [the worker director's] rightful place, at joint consultative committees, in spite of the fact that they are not very good at the present time. In fact this is the best, in fact the only practical venue he can have, because it is pretty impossible for me to attend all the numerous branch meetings. I don't know how many branches there are in the division, there must be thousands. But the consultative meeting is the one place he can go. . . . The worker directors will in time be accepted by the joint consultative structure as part and parcel of it. What we have got to be accepted by is the joint trade union people so that we will be able to discuss freely with the joint consultative committee.'

Of course, an effective system of consultation also related very closely to the general orientation of worker directors towards participation and worker–management relations which we discussed in the last chapter. We suggested there that the demands of communication, co-operation, and efficiency were central to their own role definition, but that certain emphases within the role definition changed over time. It is clear from the data which we have presented earlier in this chapter that the worker directors had a much greater degree of interaction with management than with the unions. They were continually exposed to managerial definitions of situations. They also felt the need to prove themselves as able and intelligent as management. Increasingly, therefore, they employed a managerial vocubulary. Linguistic behaviour must be seen within its social context and as having social functions.

The linguistic behaviour of the worker directors had the effect of emphasizing their director status over their worker status. Given a value system in which co-operation and unity of interest were stressed, and an increasing involvement with management and acquaintance with management policies, it was likely that the emphasis would be placed upon the interests of management rather than those of the work force and that over time the directorial role would be underlined rather than that of worker. Indeed, the logic of the social situation and the structure of the scheme would have made any other outcome unlikely. In the following chapters we explore these themes more fully in relation to the board room and the critical case of large-scale redundancies.

9 The worker directors III

In a previous chapter we outlined the importance of the divisional board in terms of decision-making. We also outlined the differences in perception of board powers of those groups who were more or less directly involved with the board compared with those who had little or no contact. The former largely saw the board as irrelevant, whilst the latter emphasized that it must be important even though its functions were unclear and never adequately defined. The worker directors' view of the board reflected both perspectives. Displaying on the one hand what we might consider a shop-floor or lay trade-union view-point, they felt that the divisional boards must be important because company boards are always important. Furthermore, for the worker directors to argue that the board of which they were members had no influence, would have been a negation of the value of their own role, as it was in this formal context that the workers' voice was to be heard and was to influence decisions.

This optimistic appraisal of the board's role was, however, tempered with experience. Initially, as we have pointed out, there was a feeling found amongst nearly all the worker directors that decisions had been determined prior to board meetings simply to prevent the discussions being reopened. Later that view-point seemed to change, perhaps as a result of the worker directors feeling more a part of the directorial team, and perhaps because of the new job description which gave the impression that more opportunities for participation in decision-making were to be created. Nevertheless, experience brought with it a greater awareness of the structure of the corporation, and particularly an awakening to the importance of the main board and its related advisory committees; and in the division an increased acceptance of the centrality of the divisional management committees. In some cases this led to what would appear to be a realistic appraisal of the divisional board and this is well illustrated by the following fairly typical comment:

'I think if the board meetings were never held, nothing in particular would in fact go different to what it is at the present. . . . It is hammered out at the divisional management committee meeting and then I believe a lot of our board stuff – it is a word I hate to use and I said I would never do it – is a sort of rubber-stamping.'

A lack of involvement in decision-making created a number of potentially difficult situations for the worker directors in which they met groups of workers without knowing the full background of particular decisions, and the implications of those decisions for the workers. Two examples of such situations were decisions to sell parts of the British Steel Corporation to private enterprise; in meetings which followed the announce-ment of these decisions the worker directors had to make it clear that they did not have access to all the information and that the policy had never been discussed at the board. Their lack of involvement seemed, however, to be typical of part-time directors in general and could be seen arising out of a centrally-based decision-making process (which in this particular case, because of the political and commercial problems associated with 'hiving off', was emphasized).

Whilst both this type of circumstance, in which it was clear to the worker directors that the divisional board had been bypassed, and also their increasing knowledge of the structure of the corporation, led the majority to recognize the constraints upon the board, they were still optimistic about the board's role. Perhaps the board was not all-powerful, it certainly was not autonomous, but since it was a board it remained amongst the most influential of the advisory bodies. In describing his perception of the formal situation in the following terms, the worker director concerned felt it almost impossible that a recommendation from the divisional board would be turned down: 'The British Steel Corporation holds the ring. There is a need for this, otherwise there would be chaos. The planning committee makes the decision, but the divisional board makes the recommendation about closures.' The same worker director was convinced that decisions could still be influenced when they came to the divisional board. This worker director was not atypical and, as with the majority of worker directors, the paradox in attitudes was near complete. The constraints upon the board were perceived, noted and criticized, yet at the same time, somehow, the board had to be important. It could perhaps not be otherwise, since an admission that the worker directors had only limited opportunities to influence would amount to a partial condemnation of the role itself.

THE DIRECTORS AND THE WORKER DIRECTORS

Social interaction can be viewed as a series of transactions between individuals involving both rewards and sanctions: it is a reciprocal process in which a feedback occurs between participants so that they mutually accommodate their behaviour. In the extreme case, however, one party may be unwilling to adjust his behaviour to that of other members of the social group and the other members may not have relevant sanctions to bring to bear. But conflict of a totally disruptive type is not a regular part of social relations; society could not exist if it were. Most social interaction is not played out as a zero-sum game. This will only occur when the actors concerned are in total disagreement over particular general values.

In most social situations the actors within the social system will share some values in common, although the degree and nature of their commitment to them may vary. There may nevertheless be interests which, at least initially, are partly overlapping and partly incompatible. In such situations a process of negotiation takes place so that the expectations of each party about the other are accommodated and stability is maintained. In these situations, whilst in some cases the actors concerned may have equal power and influence, more normally one actor or set of actors is in a more powerful position and is able to obtain more than he concedes.

Order and stability in society or, indeed, in any part of the social system is not something which is given; it is something which is 'worked at' continuously, especially in times of rapid social change; it is, in other words, something which is continuously negotiated between individuals. When worker directors were appointed to the divisional boards of BSC, new and rather different participants were introduced into a social situation which already had its own normative framework. In this chapter we want to look at this process of 'negotiation' as it occurred between the worker directors and other members of the BSC divisional boards.

From our brief review of some comparative data it was noted that BSC directors shared with directors in general a view that part-time directors, with the right qualifications in business and finance, could add a positive dimension to board discussions. Whilst it was generally agreed that BSC lacked the right type of part-time director, the concept of the 'candid friend' was still viewed positively. The worker directors, however, were not typical part-time directors, and as we have indicated in an earlier chapter, their appointments were viewed with some hostility. Indeed, the degree of hostility elicited by our interviews would be lessened both by time and experience, in addition to the retirement or resignation of some directors well known for their opposition.

Part of this hostility can be detected in a strong belief in private enterprise as the most efficient means of organization for steel. About 57 % of the BSC directors had been members of boards of private steel companies prior to nationalization; the rest were largely senior managers in those companies; only seven out of forty-eight directors agreed with the nationalization of steel. Of these, six argued in favour simply because private enterprise did not have the will, or the ability, to carry through a programme of rationalization at a sufficient pace to preserve the industry in an economically viable state. The worker-director scheme was closely identified with nationalization; it was seen as being forced upon the industry by left-wing thinkers or by new powerful men in the industry who had no experience of steel. Nationalization and loss of power were resented, and the worker-director scheme was seen as part of an intolerable new order. In the words of one group board director: 'There was a general feeling that this scheme was Melchett's idea. The board could not fight it; they weren't happy with it but would have to put up with it and make the best of it as far as they could. But almost every member of the board thought it was a bloody waste of time.'

An initial task in 'making the best of it' was somehow to fit the worker directors into the ongoing framework. As we have seen in the previous chapter, participation was considered instrumental by directors because it could provide management with a tool to help achieve the company's overall objectives. No director defined participation in terms of sharing power; for them it corresponded to the downward flow of information mostly achieved through some process of joint consultation. The worker directors could be seen as part of the communication process, but in itself this did not merit board membership.

Board members were selected according to their expertise in particular aspects of management; it would seem that worker directors lacked any such experience. Part of the original intention of the scheme had been to bring a shop-floor view to the board. The overwhelming majority of the 56%[1] of directors who favoured the scheme in principle, suggested that its advantages were to be found in the worker directors' ability both to understand and interpret shop-floor needs to the directors and to explain BSC policy to the work force. The worker directors came to be seen as 'experts' in their own right, people who could bring to the board the authentic view of the average man on the shop floor. The following quotation from a main board member indicates this process of defining the worker directors as experts:

'The part-time director who is not a worker director is usually chosen because he is a man of affairs and usually experienced in some facet of life which will lead to good sound advice; an expert financier for instance or an ex-politician or an established eminence in some field. Worker directors by comparison can automatically bring the views of the "reliable" workman in the industry, the views of men he sees and discuss with him policies and actions the corporation are following. It follows, initially, that the advice he can bring can only be within his trade or activity and it is more to do with the men's reactions to various policies, especially per-sonnel policies. So X (a part-time director) will give the board advice in certain fields and Y (a worker director) will give his opinions of the reactions to the closure of the works.'

This definition of the worker director's role as an expert on shop-floor practice and thinking was reinforced in the inter-action of the board room. By and large, the directors we interviewed were unable to consider the worker director con-tributions of any positive value; but in the board room the impressions given to the worker directors were different. They were brought into the discussions by the chairman in much the same way as other directors. Whilst one director might be asked to contribute on economic matters the worker director would be drawn into any references to shop-floor practice and attitudes. He was the expert link, the interpretive chain with the shop floor. Equally, suggestions and ideas forwarded by the worker directors were noted as being positive and worthy of further consideration. In fact it was difficult to find out whether any of their ideas were taken up, but in the vast majority of cases no further references were made to that topic area in the context of the board room; this is consistent with the directors' view that they attached little value to the suggestions of worker directors. On a small number of occasions special papers were prepared, and these were often the direct result of a suggestion from a worker director.

For their part the worker directors sought and were granted the status of expert; in effect, this helped to determine a niche for the worker directors in which they felt their contributions were significant. Furthermore, the worker directors occasionally required explanations of certain aspects of their board papers; again the directors displayed a willingness to help, by inter-preting the board papers for the worker directors. Necessarily this created a relationship of dependence, although it appeared that no worker director defined it in those terms.

Finally, the worker directors were keen to acquire some of the symbols of directorships, mainly as a means of emphasizing the legitimacy of the role; again these needs could only be satisfied by those already within the system. Increasingly the worker directors were seen on formal occasions with other directors –

for instance, in one division a works visit would always be arranged after a board meeting and care was taken to ensure that the worker directors were accorded the same status as other directors. As a *quid pro quo* for acceptance as 'proper' directors, however, the full-time members of the board required the worker directors to accept the dominant values and norms of the board. In other words a process of status negotiation took place.

The model of the board held by the directors related back in time to other boards of which they had been members[2] and to the directors' shared social backgrounds.[3] A good deal of their previous experience had been related to steel; 81% had worked mainly in the steel industry with the vast majority of these spending all or most of their employment with the same company. Taken together, these characteristics tended to lead to a common view on the aims of industry as well as of the problems facing the steel industry and the solution to these problems. Profitability was seen as the primary, and in some cases, the sole aim of any business organization. Nationalized industries were considered to be no different in terms of objectives, although policy- and decision-making might be unusual in that they operated within a system of constraints laid down by the government and civil servants. Often in the interview situation, the impression was given that the interviewer was a little naïve to ask about the objectives of business, and about whether nationalization, in any way, changes these objectives. 'This is a non-question almost; the object of any business is to make a profit – so we now have nationalized profit.' 'We are there to make money – not to supply free steel.'

For the majority, profit was the one impartial criterion by which one could judge the professional competence of a director. This meant that certain unpleasant decisions, such as closing particular works, would have to be taken in the search for profit. There was a need to rationalize existing production processes, and to build large new complexes. Differences might exist over the pace of the programme, but not in relation to its objectives.

The worker directors can be seen as holding the same general values as the directors. For all the worker directors, profit assumed the function of the main criterion of success, and this meant a willingness to argue within the economic categories determined by profit. Nevertheless, this would not greatly differentiate the worker directors from other workers in the steel industry as the data in an earlier chapter has clearly indicated. In order to argue effectively even within these categories, however, a dependence upon management information and interpretation developed, particularly as no counter-information was provided to the worker directors by the trade unions. One worker director saw the possible implications of this: 'I suppose it could be interpreted that there really is a danger of us becoming pro-management in our views, really because we are only fed this management attitude to any particular problem.' The emphasis upon profit is illustrated in the following quotation which also indicates that no basic difference is contemplated between the objectives of private and nationalized enterprises. 'First of all we are here to make money, and by making money we make steel. A lot of people (wrongly) think that we are here to make steel first and money later.'

Given the need for industry to be rationalized, resulting in many thousand redundancies, it might have been anticipated that the worker directors' ordering of priorities might change, and that profit criteria might give way to the need to make some sort of social cost-benefit analysis of each redundancy. This was not the case; during our period of observation at board meetings there was no instance in which the assumptions behind any closure were challenged, although on a number of occasions some effort was made by the worker directors to ensure that alternative employment would be available in the area. But the economic data presented by the directors appeared to be invested with impartiality and objectivity. Maybe one could sympathize with those who were to be redundant, but whilst the figures 'talked for themselves' and the industry had to be made viable, redundancy was essential.

'As an individual I think it is a bloody shame these fellows are out of a job, but talking about the worker directors on the board, I'm going to defend it as a commercial proposition put to us, and there is no argument against it and we have to support it. It is as simple as that.' 'All right then, if it is going to be good for the industry, to make the industry really viable, to make nationalization really work, then we ought to go ahead with rationalization.'

This position was maintained, even when the steel trade unions asked the worker directors to oppose any redundancies during what was a time of high unemployment. Almost without exception the worker directors denied the legitimacy of such a request, arguing that they had to be their own masters, and judge each proposition objectively in terms of its contribution to making the industry viable. Necessarily, this meant that the categories of profit were accepted and the potential opportunities for opposition severely reduced. The need to be objective and by implication behave in a directorial manner was stressed even in those situations where redundancies occurred in the worker directors' own or related works. One group of worker directors was able to look back with some pride on the behaviour of one of their colleagues in such circumstances: 'X was particularly congratulated [by the full-time directors] on his efforts at the works. . . . It has gone in the board minutes and I think it is going to be sent up to the main board.'

Consistent with the views of the worker directors to which we have already referred, we found during our period of observation worker directors forwarding suggestions that could be described as mainly managerial in tone, and which were aimed at increasing profitability. For instance, there were suggestions to cut overtime, and to reduce staff, and in one case, where staff redundancies had been agreed upon, a worker director was critical that on previous occasions the envisaged number of job losses had not materialized.

Although the worker directors were making their arguments within the dominant value system of the board, for the directors, it was still essential that the new outsiders should conform to the norms already in existence for board meetings. Again the directors shared a common view of the conduct of board meetings, which were seen as formal, ritualistic and above all trouble-free meetings. In all the cases we observed, the board meeting started promptly at the arranged time even if, as was often the case, all the members of the board had assembled well before. The agenda would be strictly adhered to, and given that the agenda almost always remained the same, the meetings followed a predictable pattern. The full-time directors would not question each other, and would rarely contribute unless asked to comment by the chairman. All remarks would be addressed through the chair.

Without doubt, the dominant characteristic of board meetings was the emphasis upon the controlled and rational presentation of arguments, and the avoidance of conflict. Perhaps the worker directors did not have to acquire new methods of presenting views, but they recognized from a very early stage, and never ceased to stress to lay trade-union officials, that a board meeting was entirely different in character from a trade-union branch meeting. A show of emotion may be a useful device in a branch meeting but would be totally dysfunctional at a board meeting. Because of what appeared to be a strong desire on the part of the worker directors to be accepted fully into the board they were quick to learn the new ritual and to respond in the right way to situations as they occurred.

A number of worker directors talked about a 'probationary' period during which the executive directors assessed their new colleagues and they came to know their new environment. Without reservation they felt that they had come through that probationary period well, and that they were now accepted as board members. As one said: 'The worker directors have acted responsibly. From what I can gather they have behaved themselves at board meetings.' In a similar manner one worker director recalled how a fellow director claimed to be impressed by them because of the 'reasonable attitudes' they had displayed.

In addition to being good students, the worker directors were also in a position of some dependence, as they had initially to rely upon members of the board for guidance on how to behave at board meetings. Nearly all thought that in the early days they had been welcomed by the chairman and had been brought out of themselves by the chairman's invitations to participate in discussions. 'It is hard to put it into words,' one said. 'It was a feeling that they would be talking of high finance and a feeling that they would not mix, that they would snub us on one side. I had known X [the chairman] for twenty years or more, and I spoke to him when I first arrived, and I felt different when he said we were all equal.' Or as another worker director recalled: 'It was a director . . . he said don't be too erratic and just jump in. See how things go and see how you feel. It was damn good advice.'

The processes that we have described can be likened to some sort of negotiation. Stated most sharply, the directors were prepared to appear to accept the worker directors as important and equal members of a team, as long as the worker directors in turn would subscribe to the values and norms of the board. This is not to say that any such understanding would be spelt out formally: on the contrary, it would arise in a tacit and symbolic manner from the interaction. Nevertheless, the fact that the worker directors were conscious of this process is indicated by their repeated references to a trial period, in which they had to prove themselves worthy of their new role.

The outcome of this process was a movement towards equilibrium rather than conflict. There was little or no 'trouble' at the board meeting; this was in sharp contrast to some of the fears initially expressed by the directors. Normative sanctions were, however, applied. The pattern of interaction can perhaps be illustrated from the following exchange which occurred during a discussion of possible areas for cutback of expenditure.

Worker director: 'There is one point I would like to make. Can we look at contractors, we have created more millionaires this way than any other. Surely we can tighten up in this area.'

Chairman: 'Yes, that's a good point.'

Second worker director: 'One always seems to talk about cutting back on manual workers, I often hear the unions complaining about the increase in staff. For a point of information is this true?'

Chairman: 'It's a fair point, Bill. It's a sign of progress I think that we take more people on staff conditions. I did say earlier we should be looking at this.'

The worker directors' ideas were acknowledged, seemingly endorsed, and yet no further action was reported back to the board. Indeed, there was no further discussion on these matters during our period of observation of this particular board.

As we have suggested, potentially critical comments made by the worker directors would have weight attached to them and any significant points would be dealt with in full and all the necessary information supplied. A director should consider such an explanation from one of his colleagues totally adequate and in the vast majority of cases the worker directors would act in the same way. An incident, however, which occurred during our observation suggests that if the worker directors were not prepared to act in accordance with the directors' definition of board behaviour, the directors would enforce that definition. One worker director had become concerned about the extent of waste on a particular process and the resulting loss of revenue. On the first occasion when he raised this at the board meeting the normal ritual was followed with the relevant director providing an exhaustive and informative answer. Normally that was sufficient but the worker director raised the matter again at the next meeting. The chairman was surprised at the worker director's refusal to accept the original explanation and emphasized that this form of criticism of a fellow director would not be tolerated. 'You bring this up each meeting, Fred. Bernard has already explained what he's hoping to do and trying to do, you can't expect any more.'

We are not saying that conflict never occurred between the worker directors and the other directors, only that it was rare and occurred even less frequently as time passed. In one director's words: 'In the first board meeting everything was what he [worker director] called "an indictment of manage-ment", so I had to struggle with that one . . . however, it's settled down now . . . within six months one could see that it was not doing any harm.' The board-room emphasis upon formality and lack of conflict can be seen as partly responsible for the worker directors' reporting, rather than representing, shop-floor and trade-union views. There were, of course, other important factors arising out of the structure of the scheme and the lack of involvement with the trade unions. Nevertheless, the role of reporter, rather than representative, was more consistent with a definition of the worker-director role as an

expert on shop-floor thinking. In what were potentially conflictual situations, the worker directors increasingly reported
attitudes towards, for example, strikes, wage claims, and
redundancies, rather than associating themselves with particular views.

What we have tried to suggest in this section is that when
employees are appointed to boards, the natural strategy of the
board will be to try and ensure that the man is defined, and
comes to define himself, as a director. Once this label is attached
to a worker the process of interaction in the board room and
the cultural and structural situation in which he is engaged
will also reinforce that definition. Consequently he will act,
be seen to act, and see himself acting increasingly as a director.
Alternative definitions such as that of, for example, representative will be minimized.

THE BOARD AND THE WORKER DIRECTORS' CONTRIBUTION

In the previous section the processes of acceptance and com-
pliance have been analysed. In this section we turn to a more
formal analysis of board-room interaction, and examine the
topic areas in which the worker directors contributed to
discussion, and the style of these contributions. The data used
throughout this analysis will be drawn almost exclusively from
the periods of observation in the four iron and steel divisional
boards; in all, a minimum of seven meetings was attended in
each case, although in one case the number was as high as ten.
For the purpose of simplicity and explanation we will try to
avoid detailed references to the differences between boards and
concentrate more on their similarities. Most of these similarities
have already been referred to. We have noted the formality, the
ritual, and the avoidance of conflict. In addition it is worth
pointing out the primacy of financial questions in all discussions. This is consistent with the emphasis placed upon
profit by the directors, and the formal position of the product
divisions as profit-making centres. Even in the one board
where the meeting was not structured around the financial

director's report, the works groups reports which predominated were almost entirely financial in character.

Some differences must, however, be mentioned. The personality and style of the chairman appeared important as a

Table 9–1

DISCUSSION LEVELS IN BOARD MEETINGS
BY ITEM ON THE AGENDA BOARD %

	A	B	C	D
Financial report	10·0	25·6	16·5	28·2
Other financial items	19·2	5·5	7·2	—
	29·2	31·1	23·7	28·2
Commercial report	—	10·6	7·3	10·7
Other commercial items	—	—	—	0·6
	—	10·6	7·3	11·3
Works groups reports	49·7	18·3	13·8	7·4
Works groups items	—	1·6	3·4	—
	49·7	19·9	17·2	7·4
Personnel reports	5·3	7·1	7·0	7·0
Other personnel and worker director reports	—	6·0	12·7	3·3
	5·3	13·1	19·7	10·3
Capital expenditure submissions	6·8	14·8	9·7	14·3
Development/rationalization	6·2	2·3	15·6	10·1
	13·0	17·1	25·3	24·4
Technical/operations report	0·5	4·0	2·9	5·1
Other technical etc.	—	0·3	—	—
	0·5	4·3	2·9	5·1
Items on corporation/ managing director's report	2·3	3·8	3·9	13·3
Total	100·0	100·0	100·0	100·0

determinant of the opportunities for discussion. In some cases the chairman would aim to link and direct contributions, whilst in others he would actively lead. The background of the part-time directors also seemed to assume some importance, particularly if they were respected in a special field and their views considered worthy of a full hearing. Finally, the financial and management problems facing each division differed to a certain extent, and necessarily this was reflected in board-room discussions. Nevertheless, in all cases, board meetings tended to be backward-looking in that they reviewed performance.

The data presented in Table 9–1 illustrate both the nature of board-room discussion and some of the potential problems facing the worker directors. In all boards it will be seen that between one-quarter and one-third of the discussion concerned financial matters. This emphasis upon financial reviews was strengthened by the fact that the discussion of works groups tended to centre upon past performances, particularly financial results. In the case of board A, whilst the meeting was structured around the works groups report, this approach provided yet another outlet for financial discussion. This strong element of financial review must necessarily pose some problems for the worker directors if they entertained any ideas of changing managerial policies.

This difficulty is further highlighted when one turns to items dealing with capital expenditure, development, and rationalization. Initially, these would appear to be important topic areas which could possibly be influenced. In fact this was not the case as often items of capital expenditure were rushed through the board meetings, and there were many examples of proposals coming to the board which had already been sanctioned and partially implemented. As for closures, these too tended to be predetermined and in some cases announcements had been prepared for local MPs and trade unionists prior to first mention at the board. This meant that the opportunities for influence were again extremely limited and even when the discussions became forward-looking they tended to become remote and abstract. For instance, both divisions C and D, which were undergoing major rationalization programmes, spent time discussing the future shape of the divisions and the siting of any new steel works: and yet whilst the discussions were useful for the worker directors in that they provided an insight into future thinking, they were also very general as no specific proposals or concrete ideas were examined.

One fact that emerges from Table 9–1 and is significant for the discussion of worker directors in steel, and perhaps for the concept of worker directors more generally, is the small amount of time spent on personnel issues. This took up a small amount of time, in terms of formal reporting, in each board. Nevertheless, as Table 9–2 suggests, despite the limited reference to personnel items in the board meetings, worker directors, as might be expected, contributed most extensively in this topic area. In terms of the structure of board meetings only 12% of discussion related to the report of the personnel director, and other personnel items; of the total contributions and interventions made by worker directors, almost three times that amount was concentrated in this particular area.

Table 9–2

WORKER-DIRECTOR CONTRIBUTIONS ON BOARD
TOPIC AREAS (%)

Items dealing with personnel, welfare and industrial relations	34·5
Non-personnel aspects of development	11·5
Production	10·0
Finance	10·0
Commercial	11·0
Items dealing with downward flow of information	6·0
Items dealing with the corporation as organization	3·0
Items dealing with the status/role of worker director	3·0
Other	11·0
	100·0

Both the worker directors and the other board members agreed that the contributions of worker directors in terms of topic area changed over time. Initially their confidence and knowledge was limited, and they tended to concentrate, often by design, on matters which related to their immediate work experience. This pattern changed, and from Table 9–2 it is clear that they were prepared to a greater or lesser extent to talk about almost all items which came to the board, whilst still concentrating on personnel and industrial relations. 63% of the directors mentioned these latter topics as providing the greatest source of activity for worker directors, although an additional 19% commented that they talked about anything and everything. To some extent this distinguishes the worker directors from other part-time directors (and also other executive directors) who tended to contribute only on topics on which they were considered experts.

Table 9–3 indicates a further distinction between worker directors and other directors in that the worker directors were much more likely to be seeking information rather than providing it.

Table 9–3

STYLE OF WORKER-DIRECTOR CONTRIBUTION
TO BOARD DISCUSSION

% of total contribution			
Seek information	39·0	Neutral view expressed	15·0
Give information	18·0	Proposed possible action	6·0
Critical view expressed	14·0	Other	3·0
Supportive view expressed	5·0		
			100·0

The worker directors' need to seek information seemed to arise from their lack of involvement in meetings other than board meetings, and in this they may be contrasted with full-time directors, though not with other part-time directors. But unlike the other part-time directors the worker directors' involvement in the industry was more immediate and situations could regularly occur in which information would be sought.

This is particularly true of matters related to rationalization and development and in this area 55 % of the worker directors' interventions were in search of information and clarification.

The earlier analysis of the full-time directors' reactions to the new board members suggested that whilst the worker directors were initially defined as creating potential difficulty, this did not materialize. Overall, only 14% of worker-director comments were critical and interestingly enough such comments were generally related to the downward flow of information.[4] This can be seen as a neutral area for the full-time directors, to the extent that new ideas which made it possible for BSC policies to be better explained to the workers would be particularly welcome. In the significant area of development and rationalization the worker directors were less critical than in most other areas.

It has been suggested that one of the strategies adopted by the directors to minimize any potential conflict with the worker directors was to define them as experts similar to every other member of the board. The worker directors' field related to personnel and the articulation of workers' views; on these topics they supplied information much more often than in other areas. For instance, whilst only 18% of their overall comments were giving information, that figure increased to 22 % and 24 % on personnel and industrial relations, and to 91 % on the upward flow of information, an area of monopoly expertise for the worker directors.

Some dominant patterns emerge in relation to the worker directors' board-room style and contributions. Firstly, although personnel and industrial relations matters were relatively unimportant in the context of board meetings, for the worker directors they provided the greatest source of activity. Secondly, the style of the worker directors differed from other directors in that they were not totally knowledgeable about all projects that came before the board, and therefore they had to seek information considerably more than other directors, including the other part-timers. And finally, given that the worker directors' background and experience was rooted in an oppositional structure, the trade union, it might have been reasonable to expect that they would be lively critics of managerial policies and plans. This did not materialize, and as we have seen, those criticisms which did occur mostly related to matters in which the executive directors' status and expertise were not at stake.

ASSESSMENT OF WORKER DIRECTORS' CONTRIBUTION
TO BOARD

The worker directors' evaluation of their own contributions suggested a similar sort of ambivalence to that found in their attitudes to the importance of the board. (In that case, it will be remembered that, whilst they held a certain suspicion that the divisional board had minimal importance, at the same time they maintained because the board existed it must and did exert influence.) On the one hand they maintained it was difficult to see how they could exert influence; the board was merely a rubber stamp, or a forum in which the workers' voice was not heard.

'We still go to the board meetings where all the talk, all the decisions are taken by someone else and where the employees' voice is never heard.' 'I find it extremely difficult to believe that we have been influential. We may be on some very, very minor aspects; matters whichever way it goes there is no concern; but on a matter of great concern then I feel myself we cannot be very influential.'

On the other hand, it is upon the conduct of board meetings that the worker directors felt they had their biggest impact.

Before their participation in board meetings, the worker directors considered the meetings to be abstract and arid, dominated by financial matters with little or no reference being paid to the practicalities of steel-making. They had changed this. They had injected a sense of realism, by asking the so-called theoretical experts questions deriving from their experience rather than from *a priori* principles. Furthermore, workers and their views were now more relevant to the discussion.

Whilst the other directors would not necessarily accept that the meetings prior to the advent of worker directors were arid, the majority did recognize that the presence of workers had made some differences to the style of the meetings. They were now more subject to questioning, if not criticism, about new plans, and a number admitted that the effect of this was to make the meetings less formal, in addition to ensuring that thought at least was given to possible reactions from workers. A form of insurance had been created by the presence of the worker directors, to ensure that decisions would be just and humane.

'They, the worker directors, react to the effect of policy changes on the shop floor. They tend to be a little bit of the Doomwatch in this situation. They stop the board from forgetting about people.' 'They contribute in the main by their presence in that this new presence ensures that there is a check in any unbridled and ir-responsible action; not that this is likely but if one was disposed not to take a responsible view, their presence acts as an insurance.'

Though agreeing that workers' views and reactions were possibly now more taken into account, a significant minority of directors felt that negotiation and consultation offered better insights into shop-floor thinking than did the worker directors. Furthermore, the majority of directors attached little weight (see Table 9–4) to the contributions of the worker directors, and only one or two could give instances of situations in which outcomes might have been altered. These instances always related to the processes of communications; and the worker directors' contributions which proved acceptable were aimed at improving the methods by which management policies were explained to the workers. Presumably, because the policies were considered correct, and only the methods of explanation inadequate, the suggestions would prove highly palatable to directors.

Even though the worker directors had been defined as experts in shop-floor attitudes and practice, only 23 % of the directors rated their contributions as of some or considerable value. This hardly seems consistent with the projected image of the expert. It was therefore possible for directors who spoke positively about the worker directors as experts, also to make the following comments upon their board contributions: 'Most of their contributions are lightweight and to a certain extent irrelevant. I don't think they have any influence on board decisions.' In other cases, while arguing that on an ideal level the worker-director role could still bring to bear some positive influence the point was made that the present incumbents of the role tended to bring to the board trivial matters, largely examined from a parochial view-point.

Table 9–4

DIRECTORS' ASSESSMENT OF VALUE OF WORKER
DIRECTORS' CONTRIBUTIONS TO BOARD

Value	%
Contributions of considerable value	4
Contributions of some value	19
Contributions not of very much value	17
Occasionally useful	23
No value	15
Varies	8
Worker-director presence important	6
Don't know/no answer	8
N=48	100

Worker directors had failed to recognize that the board dealt with the broad issues and not with questions of detail, for which there were other channels, such as joint consultative committees. In addition, it was felt that any manager worth his salt should know about these trivial matters and about the views of his subordinates. The impact of this would be to make the worker director largely redundant.

'They have perhaps said one or two things at the board room which really ought to have been said in another context such as management. Perhaps the opportunity wasn't there, I don't know, but there are things which I would have expected them to thrash out with management before they came to the board.' 'Their contributions are useless or puerile, and often problems should have been dealt with through other channels.'

Almost despite the evidence to the contrary, the worker directors themselves considered that they had exerted influence upon the outcomes of decisions, as well as upon the style of board meetings. Again, it was difficult to instance examples, but it was felt that in their formal and informal contacts with the directors they had been able to influence thinking, and inject a greater social conscience. The informal contacts were considered particularly important, as, for example, at the pre-board dinner; here it was possible to raise problems over a drink without being constrained by the formal structure of board meetings.

Given the directors' assessment of the value of the worker-director contribution at board meetings and the difficulty experienced by worker directors in offering examples of their ability to influence outcome, it would appear that the board exerted greater influence upon the worker directors than the worker directors did upon the board. Whilst the presence of a worker might not have altered the pattern of board decisions, the board-room experience of these workers seems to have drawn them closer to the directors. This is well illustrated by the following comments by worker directors.

'As worker directors we are more open-minded and it has taught us to examine both sides and sort out what we think is a sensible way to argue or what is a sensible way to answer.' 'I said Fred [a fellow worker director] has been associated with the board so long now and with management that he can't help but look objectively at every question that is put before him. You are a victim of this, but if you are looking objectively at a thing, you are not going to make a flag-roaring speech about it.'

SIGNIFICANT OTHERS AND WORKER-DIRECTOR INFLUENCE

Even though it can be argued that the worker directors had little influence, the scheme could still prove useful for management if groups of workers in the industry believed that it represented a meaningful symbol of industrial democracy. This was not the case, however; Tables 9–5 and 9–6 indicate that within each group interviewed a majority envisaged that the worker directors had limited influence.

Table 9–5

WORKER-DIRECTOR POWER/INFLUENCE ON BOARD

	Shop steward sample %	*General employee sample* %
Great deal	2·0	1·0
Fair amount	8·0	10·0
Not much	47·0	22·0
None at all	25·0	4·0
Don't know/no answer/ had not heard of worker directors	18·0	63·0
	100·0 N=317	100·0 N=2379

Table 9–6

WORKER-DIRECTOR POWER/INFLUENCE ON BOARD

	Management %	*Full-time trade union officers* %
Worker directors have no influence	32·0	39·0
Worker directors have some but not much	60·0	52·0
Worker directors have a lot/fair amount	5·0	0·0
Don't know/no answer	3·0	9·0
	100·0 N=90	100·0 N=46

The reasons given for the worker directors' lack of influence can be divided into two types. Firstly, there were those reasons which related to the structure of the board meeting itself. It was generally felt that the board voted, and because of their minority position, it followed that the worker directors must have little or no influence. For those who recognized the board as an advisory committee, it was held that while the worker director might be listened to, his advice would be ignored. The other type of argument related to the personal skills and characteristics of the worker directors, which were considered inadequate for the job of director. This was not a criticism of the worker directors as individuals, because it touched upon the concept of a worker-director scheme, and the ability of the working class to provide representatives of the right qualities. Reference to the worker directors' personal ability was most common amongst managers, with 32 % of those interviewed relating influence to skill; but this view-point was by no means limited to managers and could be found amongst all the samples.

Given the low level of perceived worker-director influence, it comes as no surprise that the worker-director scheme was seen as having little or no effect upon workers in the industry. Only 5 % of workers could perceive any change, and almost without exception the changes were non-specific and intangible, relating to the possibility of the workers' voice being heard in the board room. Turning to the shop-steward sample, we find only nine instances in which the worker directors were considered to have had some effect; these nine shop stewards referred to worker directors becoming involved in personnel and industrial relations issues and to this being of help to workers. In these cases the worker directors' utility was to be found in his ability to open managerial doors and speed up processes. This might have been achieved without membership of the board.

From the shop-floor samples, strong evidence emerged to suggest that from their perspective the power of the worker directors must be increased, if the scheme was to have any relevance (Table 9–7). It was felt that if it merited existence, then it was important that the worker directors should have some power to influence decisions in a direction desired by the workers. This desire to increase the power of worker directors must be read alongside the demand that the workers or their unions should have a much greater degree of control over the worker directors than existed at that time.

Table 9–7

SHOULD WORKER DIRECTORS' POWER BE INCREASED?

	General employee sample %	Shop stewards %
Yes	24·9	62·0
No	10·3	20·0
Don't know/no answer	64·8	18·0
	100·0	100·0
	N = 2379	N = 317

The methods suggested to increase power were largely mechanical. The worker directors should be given a vote, their numbers should be increased. Scarcely ever was the importance of the divisional board in policy-making taken into account, when designing schemes to increase worker-director power.

All groups that we talked to thought that the worker-director scheme had little or no influence upon decision-making and policy formation in the Steel Corporation. Certainly the 'trouble' which board members had initially expected did not materialize. The process of socialization into the board-room role and the structure and function of the board itself served to ensure that the stability of board-room relations was not disturbed. To some extent the worker directors constituted exceptions to the general view that they had little or no power and were ineffective in either aiding management in decision-making or representing employee interests. They felt that they were contributing fully to the directorial team and the objective of a more efficent industry.

Yet our analysis suggests that the worker directors were constrained in a number of ways, although they only partly recognized those constraints. It also suggests that it would have been difficult for the worker directors to operate unless they had accepted the broad values of the board and come to accept the specific interests of directors. At the same time, however, the pressure to accept board-room rationality made it difficult to put forward and represent worker rationality. In the following chapter we go on to explore this theme more fully in the context of the particularly critical case of redundancy.

Notes

1 Whilst most directors we interviewed said that their initial reaction to the worker-director scheme was one of hostility (see Chapter 8), at the time we interviewed them over half expressed themselves in favour of such schemes. This is consistent with the argument of this chapter that the full-time directors were able to ensure that the worker directors conformed generally to the normative code of the board room, and did not become a source of 'trouble'.

2 65% of the directors had experience of other directorships, mostly in steel prior to nationalization.

3 77% had been to public school and/or university. 76% had fathers whose occupations would be classified under the Registrar General's Social Classes I and II.

4 52% of the worker directors' total contributions relating to the downward flow of information were critical; and, on questions of communication generally, 29% were critical.

10 Redundancy: An issue and some themes explored

In this chapter we look at the role of worker directors in situations of redundancy and closure and use the analysis to draw together some themes which have arisen in the discussion so far. An exploration of this area is important for a number of reasons. Firstly, redundancy is a critical issue and redundancy situations present a crisis for those involved. For the observer the study of crisis often reveals the basic principles and basic contradictions within forms of social organization more starkly than the study of normalcy.[1] Closures and loss of jobs are perhaps the most conflictful situations in industry in that the interests of capital and of labour are brought into sharp antithesis. Within such a situation the dynamics of a scheme of worker participation at board level might be expected to be clearly revealed. Certainly this is the case if one takes two polar definitions of participation; that is that its purpose is to promote workers' interests over and against those of management, or a managerialist definition that it is an instrument for promoting co-operation within defined goals. Whether it was possible for the worker-director scheme to do either is the central issue we explore. In doing so we argue that the contours of conflict in situations of redundancy are more complex than is often suggested.

During the course of our research programme the themes of closure and redundancy were never far from centre stage within the Steel Corporation. It was an issue which posed a dilemma for all of those involved in the industry. We have seen in Chapter 4 that historically rationalization has posed a continuous problem for the steel industry; and that nationalization and the subsequent reorganization of the industry were seen as a means of facilitating this process. Rationalization is related to redundancy in a number of ways. Firstly, the move towards large-scale units employing more sophisticated and capital-intensive methods means the closure of smaller, older works. Secondly, it generally means that even those plants where there is large-scale investment often have labour surplus to requirements. The process of rationalization is complicated by a number of factors relating to the matching of supply with demand. Closure of works, in the face of a constant demand, has to be phased with new plants coming 'on stream'. Accordingly, changes in demand can accelerate or delay closures. Further, a fall in demand may lead to a reduction of shifts which, in a large-scale works can mean a significant number of men out of work. Organizational factors are a further complication in so far as they affect the selection of works for closure.

During the period of our research, accounting systems had not been rationalized hence making the already complex process of plant comparisons more difficult. This facilitated, it would seem, the operation of the old company loyalties. Further, while the new divisions were responsible for particular products some of these same products might also be produced in another division; here there could occur divisional conflicts concerning profits and the long-term strategy of divisional product monopoly. Resultant divisional conflicts could only be solved at corporation level. These demand and organizational factors complicated the closure process within the Steel Corporation. Within the industry plans were developed in discussions between head office, divisional planning personnel and divisional directors. Actual decisions might be made – effectively – at corporation or divisional or even works level. But the key factor was the overall reorganization strategy of the corporation, in which the government was not inactive. Within this broad context, two particular cases of redundancy will be considered in some detail with a view to considering the nature of the worker directors' role and the constraints and opportunities of that role within the corporation.

The first of these was the decision to close virtually the whole of one works at which a worker director was employed. This works was part of a stable community and isolated from the major areas of steel-making; it had previously formed the major part of one of the old private companies, and along with a number of even smaller works presently formed a works group within one of the divisions of the corporation. The works was a marginal one from nationalization onwards – it had been losing money under private ownership and the lack of investment in the works after nationalization served to raise the fears of both workers and management that the plant would be axed. These were further inflamed by a press story that the works was to be closed; this was denied by the corporation but within a year the intention to close was announced and a year later confirmed.

From the beginning of our research the worker director at the works was concerned about the future of the works. The men were also concerned, but the worker director in his contact with them – which was fairly close – told the men that the works was now profitable and that they should work hard to ensure the works remained viable; viability would ensure the continued existence of the plant. The press story mentioned above alarmed the workers, and as a result the worker director requested that the works group director should meet union officials and assure them that there were no grounds for such a rumour. The stewards were not satisfied with the explanation and a month later when the other worker directors of this division visited the area they were bombarded with questions and their argument that the future of the works was secure was rejected on the grounds that 'there's no smoke without fire' and the press must have got the story from somewhere. The worker-director counter-argument that the job of a paper was to sell papers was not considered convincing.

Throughout this period a number of other closures and developments were being planned in this division, and the worker directors were informed of the general pattern of plans a few days after their visit to the works; there was no discussion of the meeting at that particular works but the worker directors did plead that workers should be informed of plans at the earliest possible moment, although as one of them stated afterwards, 'We didn't behave like shop stewards, did we?' By the next month's board meeting, the worker directors had become increasingly concerned over the scale of closures, and, while accepting the need for rationalization, one of them argued that 'we have to go flat out to show we are not in-human. It is generally accepted that rationalization is a must, it is unpleasant, but it has to be done.' In view of their recent experience they also appealed that some policy should be developed to overcome rumours of closure. And they stressed the need for more information to be given to them. If they were ill-informed, they argued, 'we will be unable to carry the lads with us'.

These demands and the worker directors' concern at the psychological effects of uncertainty upon workers' morale were repeated at the next three board meetings, and increased as the worker directors became aware of the extent of concern as they visited various works. The worker director from the works in question was becoming increasingly concerned about its future, as he heard about plans for two new green-field sites, which to be fully loaded would require the demise of a number of smaller works. Within a month this pessimism was confirmed by a discussion at the board on development which failed to mention his works – other than in the most conditional terms. The new year's annual operating plan confirmed his fears that his works was to be closed and in addition put him in an awkward position in relation to his work mates; as he stated, 'I have been saying the wrong message to the unions for the past three years; I have been telling them that if they get viable they will survive. [The executive director] was saying this six months ago, too.'

He opposed the closure but only within the confines of the board – he did not inform the unions of what was to happen because he felt bound by the confidentiality of board affairs. The argument for closure put forward by the full-time directors was related to the scale of production which was to flow from the new large integrated works; he argued against this – 'I think that the corporation have got it wrong because you will have a difficult time before the new sites come on stream and you will have nothing to fall back on.' The chairman replied that this would depend upon the pattern of orders. At the next board meeting he raised the question of his works again, arguing that the annual operating plan was incorrect in its underlying strategy; but it was still an economic argument – 'I think you should try to get the maximum out of the plants rather than chop them off. We might then be forced to import at any price later.' The chairman suggested that he should discuss the question with one of the directors concerned.

Within a month the intention to close the works was formally announced. Throughout this period the local worker director had not merely been concerned about the future of his works and raised the issue at board meetings; in addition he had been in especially close contact with the general manager of the group of works which included his. They had discussed ways of ensuring the continued existence of the works, but with little success. These discussions were important, however, both for the general manager and for the worker director in terms of the development of arguments and the exchange of information. No such discussions were held with workers or union officials as the worker director felt bound by the norms of board confidentiality.

The final decision on the future of the works was announced at the board only two or three weeks before it was publicly announced, and it was part of what the chairman himself described as a formidable list of closures; 'the whole exercise', he went on, 'is aimed at homing on to the lower-cost, high-production units concentrating on single production. In other words, it is doing what the divisions were set up to do.' The worker directors admitted themselves overwhelmed by the scale of closure decisions and stated they were unable to understand the logic behind them; they therefore requested more information, so that 'we will be in a position to defend the decision *we* have made'.

The feeling of collective responsibility and involvement in the decisions was a crucial aspect of the worker directors' perception of their role in relation to closure, even though formally, given the nature of the board, there was no such responsibility. The worker director was present at meetings where the decision was announced to the unions and he admitted that 'the unions made life difficult'. However, as the chairman of the division expressed it in congratulating the worker directors on their behaviour in this matter, 'they played it straight down the middle'. They had not divulged confidential information and they had promulgated BSC policy – that profit was insufficient – it was 'profit compared to other areas' that was the vital consideration.

The reaction of the unions and the local community to the announcement of intent to close the works was considerable. A joint action committee composed of works union officials and local political figures was formed. The local worker director attended its first meeting, but felt unable to speak or even to have his presence formally noted. After the announcement and the initial meetings with the unions he became less active in the affair; he felt constrained by the decision of the division and bound by the rules of confidentiality. Increasingly his role became one of reporting to the board on developments and feelings at the works. It must be emphasized that the worker director had a good contact network with the unions at his works and was generally well respected. With the announcement of the planned closure he became a focal point for trade-union officials seeking information. At first they were reluctant to accept his argument that he could not divulge information. However, his sincerity, his obvious dilemma and the strength of personal relationships led them finally to accept the definition of the role he professed. As one of them said to him, 'We know you know but we're not going to put you in a difficult position.'

The position of all the worker directors in this division was made rather more difficult when the steel committee of the TUC developed a policy of opposition to any further closures, at least in the short run, in view of the increasing scale of unemployment in the country. While the steel committee recognized that they could not instruct the worker directors to pursue a particular policy in the board room since they were formally not linked to the unions, they informed the worker directors of their policy in the hope that they might pursue it. Indeed, they went further than this and two representatives of the committee sought a meeting with the worker directors involved in this particular closure. The meeting was brief, largely because of a prior commitment of the worker directors to see a film on counselling workers over redundancy. However, the worker directors felt that they could not support the arguments of the steel committee. As one of them explained, 'Although we sympathize with the steel committee during these times, we have been involved in a dialogue leading up to the closures; we don't think we should press on them [the Steel Corporation] to delay it. . . . Realizing the financial position of BSC, to delay it is only going to make matters worse. You have got to generate some cash. . . . We agree it is very hard for people who have got to suffer for this, but in the long term it does mean security for the people who are left.'

The major sources of opposition to the closure of the works were the unions and the joint action committee. The arguments put forward by the unions in the works primarily concerned the possibility of making the works profitable; one of their major steps in fighting the closure was to put forward proposals which were essentially similar to those that had already been considered by divisional directors (and rejected), namely the introduction of electric arcs furnaces. What effectively the unions were arguing was that the criterion of profitability *was* important but that if there were to be investment at this works then it would become competitive. Their arguments were primarily economic and accepted the basic philosophy of the corporation. This was less true of the opposition expressed by bodies outside of the industry who argued more in terms of the social effects of the closure. Within the context of the corporation such arguments were secondary.

Opposition within the works did not only come from the trade-union side. Managers as well as workers were critical of the lack of consultation over the decisions, and amazed at its scale. Some were involved in the fight against the closure decision. Certainly they felt equally helpless and thought the impact upon their lives would be considerable; one manager, for example, told us that he could not see how BSC could justify absorbing redundant managers because they were padded enough already. 'If I was offered a job by BSC I know it would be a job made for me.' He did not think he would stay in BSC because the industry was contracting but the problem was that he was too specialized for many other jobs; this was a problem for many managers in the industry.[2]

We now turn to our second case, that of a small Scottish works where a small hand mill was to be shut down, making a hundred or so workers redundant. This was essentially a short-term, commercial decision which flowed from the action of a different division in withdrawing its orders from the division under whose control this works came. The decision was announced briefly at a board meeting; no questions were raised at this meeting concerning the closure, and the worker directors concerned, while they noted the decision, did not comment upon it. However, they had visited this particular works a few months previously; on that occasion they had made a general commitment to be of any assistance they could to the works.

The reaction of the works to the announced closure was strong. The Scots, particularly since the change to product divisions, had felt increasingly concerned about their future. The closure of this mill within the context of the more general rationalization programme going on in the corporation led shop stewards to think that this was the beginning of the end. These fears were shared by management, who discussed strategies of opposition with, and gave information to, the workers concerned. This small closure was defined as a threat to other works and indeed to Scottish steel-making; local politicians and academics became involved in the conflict.

Opposition was again phrased in primarily economic terms. Given the interlinking of production processes, it was argued that the disappearance of this mill meant there was little economic logic for keeping other processes; such investment as there had been at this works was of a 'mobile' kind which could easily be shifted south of the border. In addition, it was claimed that Scotland had not received its share of investment (and this meant lower profitability) despite earlier assurances from both the corporation and the government. Nevertheless, they argued, profits at the works were good, especially if one made allowances for what they considered the biased system of accounting operating in the corporation. Finally, it was argued that to cut steel-making in Scotland would increase the cost of supplying Scottish customers. These economic arguments were pressed hard because of the total dependence of this part of Scotland upon steel and steel-based industry. If steel were to disappear, then they would find themselves in the position which they knew only too well: 'For the Scots it will be a choice of continued unemployment, the armed forces or emigration.' This fear was undoubtedly a key motivating force of opposition, but its expression within the confines of the corporation was muted – 'We are not asking for charity; we are demanding what is rightfully ours.'

The economic logic for investment in Scotland, it was felt, was ignored because there was no Scottish voice at the locus of power. There was no Scottish representative on the divisional board or even a spokesman for Scotland; nor were there any Scottish 'influentials'. (The fact that the chief executive of the corporation was a Scot and that there was one member of the main board with special responsibility for Scotland does not seem to have been considered relevant.) It was because of this that on their previous visit to this works the worker directors had been fed with arguments concerning the greatness of Scottish steel production and the depth of anti-Scots feeling within the corporation. Workers, and more particularly managers, had urged that the worker directors should represent the Scottish interest on the board. This they said they would do because of their role as representatives and they gave assurances that they would try to help with any problem that came up.

When the mill closure was announced union officials at the works first approached a Scottish worker director in another division – he felt he could not become involved. They therefore took up the offer of the worker directors from their own division and asked them to come to Scotland. The worker directors agreed to go. It is of interest that prior to their visit they found it necessary not only to gain the agreement of the executive director responsible for the works but also to be briefed by him concerning the arguments for the closure. At their meeting with union officials the worker directors were forcefully confronted with the arguments against closing the mill we have outlined above and further information was sought from them. They were, however, limited in what they could tell the workers – they agreed to take their points to the board, 'and push them as hard as we can at the highest level'. However, the union officials were critical of the worker directors because they could tell them very little, because they were 'English and did not really care' and because they 'had not done their homework'. Further, while the worker directors did commit themselves to supporting the demands of the Scottish steel workers, they also pointed out that other areas too were suffering short time and redundancy and that the corporation had to be made profitable.

On their return south of the border the worker directors took up the points put forward by the union officials and management with the executive directors concerned – but their role was primarily one of reporting the feelings of the men rather than actively lobbying for them. They felt powerless in the face of the structure of the corporation through which the decisions had effectively come about and which they would have to confront in order to challenge the decision. More importantly, on their return – indeed at the board meeting two days later – the worker directors learnt that there were to be sizeable redundancies in their own area for precisely the same reason, that is the withdrawal of orders by another division. Accordingly, their action was diverted to fighting this decision, but again with no success.

As for the Scottish works after one or two further meetings with the executive director concerned one of the worker directors reported formally to the board – 'we promised to bring their [the union in the works] point of view to the board. There are good economic reasons for closing there. The works' director thinks they will close some mills there, but we met some very upset and disgruntled people there and they want to make a plea for investment there – but I can't see it happening.' The chairman agreed that 'we must take note of their concern, but I am afraid our future plans . . . do not include that works'. The mill was closed and one hundred less jobs were available in an area of high unemployment. After the board meeting one of the worker directors summed up their own dilemma: 'I just don't know what the future holds, I don't know what we can do, but I am going to fight for [his own works] because there is a danger there will be no steel-making there in the future.'

A number of conclusions can be reached from these and our other studies of redundancy situations. The position of the worker directors rested upon their access to the divisional board; all other things stemmed from this, most importantly their ability to discuss issues with directors. Whilst the process of decision-making on redundancy varies according to its 'causes', consistently the divisional board itself was of little importance in decisions on closure and redundancy. Rationalization formed a small part of board discussions, as we have noted in an earlier chapter. At divisional level, decisions were made outside of the board – by informal discussion between certain directors and in a number of key committees.

The worker directors' knowledge of the general trends of rationalization (as well as some specific closures) came from board meetings, and corporation documents, particularly the five-year plan and the annual operating plan. The worker directors were scarcely, if at all, involved in the development of these plans (though final drafts were discussed at some board meetings). In some divisions informal discussions were also a crucial source of information, particularly discussions with key executive directors. Of equal importance, however, were managerial (and to a lesser degree union) lunches and gatherings which provided opportunities for the worker directors to pick up hints, listen to new arguments, and sort out their own ideas of the future pattern of the industry. Such informal discussion was important for the worker directors not only as a source of information but also because it indicated acceptance. But these discussions, while being an important source of hard information, arguments and probabilities, also served to limit the activities of worker directors. They could not push too hard for information if they wished to remain acceptable; access to discussion depended upon playing the game. In one instance where a worker director made a strong challenge in this situation, managers reacted as a group, his behaviour was reported to a director and he was reminded of his role and the way things were done in such circles.

The conclusion suggests itself, therefore, that the structure of the worker-director scheme was such as to limit significantly the possible influence of worker directors upon closure decisions. But, in addition, the role conceptions of the worker directors themselves meant that frequently they were not predisposed to challenge decisions. The worker directors accepted the overall goals of the corporation; in many respects they saw themselves as missionaries carrying the message of profit for viability and the unitary interests of men and management. Their message emphasized that it was only profits that could ensure a works' survival, and since interests were common, there was no *real* conflict – the goals of management and men could both be achieved by an efficient and viable industry. This message was challenged by large-scale redundancy. There can be little doubt that the worker directors were at a loss and dismayed by the scale of closure; they nevertheless maintained that rationalization was the only possible course of action – a few would inevitably suffer, but the jobs of the majority would be made more secure. They saw their role, therefore, as being to ensure that the decisions which were made were economically sensible; that the proper process of consultation with the unions was undertaken; and that, if possible, new investment should be directed to those areas most hit by redundancy.

In terms of the first of these goals it has been seen that the worker directors lacked the necessary access to information. A number of them felt increasingly that they were not involved at the point in the organization where key decisions and plans were formulated. In discussions on redundancy with senior management their first questions therefore concerned the underlying economic rationale of the decision. In addition, they sought to make clear the number of jobs which would be lost and the extent to which natural wastage would avoid the need for redundancy. In relation to the second goal, the worker directors were insistent that the reasons for the decision should be made clear to workers and that they should be told of plans at the earliest possible moment. The worker directors saw good communication as vital; the careful management of information and communication was seen as reducing uncertainty, boosting morale and maintaining good relations. It was particularly in this area that worker directors felt they could contribute – as they were workers themselves, other workers would be more ready to believe their statements.

Many managers accepted this role for the worker directors but with the qualification that the primary responsibility for communication was management's. Hence, frequently managers agreed that worker directors should meet trade-union officials on closure questions. Many union officials welcomed the principle of discussing such matters with worker directors – they expected information from them and a commitment to their cause. The worker directors could put their case at the highest level. It would be true to say that generally workers were disappointed in the worker directors – they 'had not done their homework', they doubted whether they had any real power or influence and some questioned the extent to which the worker directors were committed. One shop steward summed up his contact with worker directors over closure as follows – 'When a man's drowning, he'll clutch at any straw.'

In terms of their second goal, therefore, the worker directors had only a marginal success; the same is even more true of their third goal. While they accepted the primacy of economic arguments, the worker directors felt it important that the corporation should attempt to alleviate social hardship – they were strong supporters of the Steel Corporation social policy unit which was set up to provide alternative sources of employment in high redundancy areas and develop redeployment and retraining plans. Beyond that, however, there was little they could do to ensure that new jobs were created in redundancy areas – they simply did not have access to those situations where such decisions might be made.

In redundancy situations, as in other situations, the worker directors were also concerned with the maintenance and promotion of their own role. This was not merely self-interest, but also a belief that their role was the beginning of a social revolution. Hence it was important that they be acceptable to management and workers. We have already pointed out that the source and structure of the scheme was primarily managerial and this meant that the primary constraints upon their activities were from the corporation. Hence, the very activities which might have served to strengthen the position of workers fighting closure – the breaching of confidentiality, the public statement of opposition, etc. – these the worker directors rejected. Similarly, they felt bound by the decisions made, despite the fact that there was no collective responsibility and that they had not been actively involved in the decisions. They increasingly stressed two aspects of their role; first, they saw themselves as communication channels rather than representatives. Their role was to inform management of workers' reactions to proposed redundancies, 'how they were taking it'. Secondly, they stressed their directorial role and the need, as an expert, to put forward one's own view and to filter information. They should not support, or even mention, all the arguments of workers, but merely those that were 'sensible'. Accordingly, workers' protests at redundancy were on one occasion reinterpreted by worker directors as caused by 'low morale' and 'being upset'.

In terms of the polar definitions of participation mentioned at the beginning of this chapter the worker-director scheme could not be seen as a success. The extent to which they promoted workers' interests was very limited and the degree to which they fostered harmony and co-operation, while greater, was still marginal.

But are things really that simple? We would argue that they are not. The argument concerning workers' interests assumes a particular objective definition and ignores how workers define their interests in a pragmatic manner. It therefore defines the idea of workers' representative in a particular way. The argument also tends to assume that the contours of conflict are non-problematic; once the 'true' nature of interests has been defined, then one has automatically solved the question of the 'real' lines of conflict. Conversely, therefore, once perceived interests are taken as the focus the membership of conflicting groups becomes a question of empirical research.

Previous studies of steel workers have shown that they are ready to accept technical change.[3] We also found this to be the case; particularly from stewards it was common to hear the phrase 'you've got to move with the times'. The level of international competition, the seniority system, the traditional system of payment compounded with the continual stress upon the vital need for rationalization by the corporation are major factors in this. But, at the same time, workers are primarily

concerned with the industry as a means of achieving a livelihood
– while individuals may volunteer for redundancy, no group of
workers volunteers their works for closure. Indeed, there is
invariably opposition to closure, and that opposition finds its
mainspring in workers' fears of unemployment. But the
opposition is not primarily articulated in terms of the need and
right to work.

The cases for keeping a works or department open which we
looked at showed amazing similarities – it was invariably argued
that they were profitable; or they could be profitable if only
they had some investment; or the overall economic strategy
of the corporation was mistaken; or that the decision was
political not economic. In other words the arguments against
closure put to the corporation were primarily of an economic
nature; they were *argumenta ad hominem* based upon the values
and priorities of the corporation itself. Arguments in terms of
the social effects of closure were secondary and directed much
more towards the government than the corporation. It was
not workers *qua* workers but in the guise of local councillors or
community action groups who put the social case. Wright Mills,
in talking of vocabularies of motive,[4] points to the manner in
which an actor puts forward different reasons for his behaviour
to different audiences. The extent to which workers 'really'
believed their arguments is open to question – and indeed is
not relevant, for it was the corporation whom they had to
convince. The corporation and possibly the government, held
their future in their hands; they were the powerful organizations. In other words, unless a head-on challenge backed by
the exercise of shop-floor power was to be undertaken, the
structure of power required that workers adopt the sorts of
arguments which were legitimate in the eyes of the powerful.
Workers, like worker directors, were constrained by the
structure of power.

In only one case did we find an exception to this. This was a
works which was more properly an engineering rather than a
steel works; it had a tradition of shop-steward militancy and
radicalism, having been a key works in the shop stewards'
movement in the first world war. Here a work-in of sorts was
instituted when redundancies were announced. These were

associated with the selling of part of the works to the private sector and the subsequent closure of some sections and it was largely upon these points that the challenge focussed. However, here, as in the UCS work-in, we find a fusing of radical arguments with the dominant values. Given that the corporation is nationalized, workers were again able to argue not merely that they themselves believed in the principle of nationalization but that they were fighting to protect the very essence of the corporation; they also, however, argued that the planned closures were not in the general economic interest. In this they were echoing the case put to the corporation by some of its major customers.

Not only did workers in closure situations utilize primarily economic arguments, but they also frequently built alliances with other groups. In joint action committees staff and manual unions often came together for the first time. But more interestingly often managers and workers co-operated to fight the closure decision. That this should be so is not surprising, for the impact of closure upon managers could be equally drastic; they also could lose their jobs and many of them had specialist skills which were applicable solely to steel where job opportunities were declining. However, their opposition had to take a less overt form – they were, after all, part of the management structure which was implementing the closure. At works level, therefore, co-operation with workers was informal – managers did not lead opposition outside of management channels. Managers, like the worker directors, were constrained by the nature of their roles.

Other managers and directors were opposed to particular closures because they meant a decline in the size of their empires with consequent risks to their careers. At the same time, they were more constrained in their opposition. If they were to step out of line too much the costs could be significant loss of promotion or at worst, the sack. Coalitions against closure were, therefore, complex but they were not, of course, constant. Workers, for example, might turn against their managers seeing their lack of ability as the cause of their problem. It was nevertheless the case that some management, particularly works management, formed an opposition group along with their workers; what differed was the visibility and style of their opposition. It is misleading therefore to think of closure situations as necessarily highlighting differences of interest between managers and men. The contours of common interest may be vertical as well as lateral. The organization of opposition largely reflected the organization of the corporation. At times, the lines of conflict became works versus works, each arguing that the other was less efficient and should therefore be closed; similarly at times the conflict was a divisional one.

These points suggest important conclusions concerning the worker directors, and serve to modify points that we have made earlier in this chapter and in previous chapters. Firstly, the lack of effectiveness of worker directors in situations such as we have described reflects not only the structure of this scheme of participation and the orientations of the worker directors themselves; it also reflects the structure of power and system of values and legitimations in the economic system more generally. In closure situations the arguments workers themselves adopted followed essentially the same logic as those which the worker directors employed and those which the BSC itself utilized. Moreover, arguments against closing a particular works or mill also tended implicitly or explicitly to be arguments in favour of closing someone else's mill. For a worker director to work for the interests of one group of workers often meant not working in the interests of another group. Support for one group's case may often mean opposition to another's. The problem of representing workers' interests becomes extremely complex. Nor, as we have pointed out, were the issues simply of a worker versus management kind. Within the context of the present system the lines of conflict are sometimes vertical rather than horizontal; even when they are horizontal the exact line or division varies according to the level at which closure decisions are taken. We cannot therefore talk simply in terms of conflict between managers and workers; managers are also employees.

A further point is related to this. For the worker directors to have fought against closures would have meant utilizing a different and more radical set of ideas than those generally held by steel workers. In that sense they would have had to be less representative of shop-floor modes of thought, or of shop-floor interests as conceived by the majority of the work force, than they were. Of course, as we have pointed out throughout this account, the worker directors were not formally representatives of the work force, nor were they defined in this way by workers or management. And whilst they did at one point in time feel themselves that their job was to represent shop-floor interests they increasingly moved away from this self-definition. But if they had been formally representatives, or if the structure of the scheme had been different, we would argue that the amount of impact they had upon closures and redundancy would have been little different.

It is perhaps ironic that in those situations when workers become most conscious of the power structure of the corporation, they may also become more attached to the employment of a vocabulary which is the very source of their problems. Given the structure of our industrial system, and its acceptance, wholeheartedly or resignedly, by workers, it might be argued that the impact of any participatory scheme will be limited because of the inevitable primacy of particular definitions of what is economic or profitable. Without raising more general, social questions within economic organizations rather than only outside of them, and without the direct backing of shop-floor power, no scheme of participation can hope for more than a marginal impact upon the life chances of workers, either on the shop floor or in management.

Notes

1 See for instance TURNER, V. W., *Schism and Continuity in an African Kingdom*, Manchester University Press, 1956
2 The closure went ahead. However, the opposition resulted in a retiming of the operation so that it started later and was carried out in two equal parts phased over a period of two and a half years.
3 See SCOTT, W. H., et al., *Technical Change and Industrial Relations*, Liverpool University Press, 1956
4 MILLS, C. W., 'Situated Actions and the Vocabulary of Motive', in I. L. Horowitz (ed.), *Power, Politics and People*, Oxford University Press, 1963

11 The European experience

The BSC worker-director scheme has been unique in this country as an attempt to have worker involvement in the upper echelons of a large-scale, modern manufacturing organization. As we have suggested in the first chapter of this book, however, there is increasing interest in this country from political parties, trade unions and employer organizations in the topic of worker participation, whilst Britain's entry into the European Economic Community has accelerated the debate and sharpened discussions of board-room participation. Discussions in the European Economic Community have turned towards questions of company structure and the role of workers. Proposals have been issued for a European company law which would operate on a voluntary basis for those companies with trading activities in more than one EEC country. Part of these proposals envisages a two-tier company board system with the possibility of one-third worker representatives on the supervisory boards. In addition, the fifth directive on Company Law circulated by the EEC Commission recommends in its draft a mandatory system of worker participation for all companies employing more than 500 workers. These proposals are still being discussed and are still flexible enough to allow alternative models of worker participation.

Experimentation with participation has been bolder in Europe than in this country, and there is a greater amount of systematic research undertaken. We therefore intend to examine some of this material and relate it to some of the themes which have emerged in the BSC case study. In particular, we will be concerned with questions of authority and conflict, the role of worker representation in the upper echelons of management, and the degree to which ordinary workers are involved through this role. It is not the intention of this chapter to provide a review of European institutions, these are readily available elsewhere,[1] but rather to pick out certain relevant aspects of the working of these institutions. To this end we will concentrate upon Norway, Germany and Yugoslavia, all of which have had considerable experience of worker representation at the governmental level of the enterprise.

We start our review of European experience by looking at Norway and the conclusions of research undertaken in that country on worker directors. In Norway the introduction of worker participation took place after the first world war when, as a result of industrial unrest, a law was passed to establish works councils in industrial organizations. Later, during the thirties, national collective bargaining machinery was established between employers' organizations and unions and after the second world war this was extended to cover not only the right to bargain but also the right to be informed and consulted on major company affairs. However, the results of works councils, production committees and suggestion systems were not considered impressive and the machinery has been modified from time to time. Partly as a result of the relative ineffectiveness of consultative machinery, legislation was passed in 1948 to provide for worker directors on the boards of some large enterprises owned or partly owned by the state; this was seen as a way to open up radically new possibilities in industrial democracy. Studies were carried out on these worker-director schemes by the Work Research Institute in Oslo. Several interesting and pertinent themes arise from this work.

In analysing the behaviour of employee representatives, in the context of the board and the organization more generally, the researchers concluded that

although they legally share in the power of the board, they find it very difficult to see how to use that power in ways that are in accord with the usual board purposes, and also make a direct impact on the working life of their constituents. The power of the board relates to, and is appropriately used for, the economic prosperity of the firm. Most of the known and obvious ways of furthering the employees' interest at board level involve an increase in labour costs, with no assurance of an off-setting economic gain for the company; or they involve interference in managerial execution of board policy which a board will be naturally reluctant to do. As a consequence, the representatives find themselves in a position where they can do only one of the following:

1. Work along with the rest of the board hoping that increased prosperity for the firm will result in greater job security and increased rewards for the employees. In this way there can be a genuine sharing in the power of the board, but this is at a personal level and does not depend on them being representatives of the employees. The responsibility that they assume when they act in this way is a responsibility to the board.

2. On issues that concern employee interest the representatives could, in line with the preceding alternative, act as a member of the board who happens to have some information about the temper of the workers, etc., which might help them decide on their strategies.[2]

Whilst we would not necessarily feel that these alternative strategies for the worker directors are either mutually exclusive or comprehend all possible strategies, the description of the circumscription of worker directors reflects our own findings. We have indicated in earlier chapters the ways in which worker directors are socialized into their roles, not only through training programmes but through their interaction with other board members and their exposure to the culture of the business organization in general and the board in particular. In the Norwegian context Emery and Thorsrud argued that the introduction of a worker representative on to the board took place in such a way that he found himself under pressure to become a 'regular' board member. At the same time his relationship with the unions was weakened and he no longer had the status of a trade-union representative. Nor was it appropriate or possible to take up personnel problems regarding particular employees. Such problems were referred to the personnel department or to the trade-union representatives.[3]

The forces in the situation, therefore, tended to push the representative into the role of an ordinary board member:

On balance, it is easier for him to avoid playing the part of the union representative than to play it. Furthermore his constituents seem less active in pressing for allegiance to their interests than are the other members of the board in asserting its requirements. Examining the evidence of those who have occupied this role, we find that they have generally changed their outlook towards that of a board member and have tended to find participation easier the further they have developed this role.[4]

Given that participation becomes easier, it is reasonable to conclude that this arises out of the absence of challenge to the traditional authority structure. Some support for this view is to be found in the following quotations from a number of Norwegian worker directors:

Obviously when you get a wider perspective you see what a company consists of, and you understand more. . . . We have many good things to protect in this company and we are striving to get a viable economic situation in which to develop further. On important matters I would get many requests from people asking me to do something. . . . I had to be careful. I could not take sides. I had to be independent.[5]

The emphasis, strikingly similar to that which we found in steel, and others have found when talking to worker directors in Germany, is less upon the need to be a representative and more upon adopting a balanced and responsible view; a position which is in practice supportive of management. Independence seems to lead paradoxically to new dependencies. Authority would appear to remain unchallenged, with any marginal modifications arising out of the symbolic nature of the worker-director scheme. Indeed, it could be argued that the exercise of managerial authority might be facilitated if the worker-director scheme increased the workers' commitment to managerial objectives. However, from a managerial perspective, the Norwegian experience again suggests limited impact: the worker directors were reported to be under insignificant pressure from their constituents for whom the traditional collective bargaining machinery seemed more relevant. The degree of worker involvement through the worker directors would therefore seem to have been limited.

Because of this inability on the part of the worker-director schemes to generate interest and commitment, the Norwegians have turned increasingly to direct forms of participation. The research to which we have referred already was broadened out to examine the possibilities for implementation of job enlargement in a number of work situations. The approach, based upon the socio-technical systems thinking associated with the Tavistock Institute in this country, emphasized the need to develop worker commitment by allowing greater autonomy in the immediate task environment. In that way it was hoped to modify the prevalent authority systems without, in any way, restructuring overall objectives.[6]

Many of the conclusions drawn from the Norwegian studies reflect our findings in the British Steel Corporation, despite the fact that the BSC worker directors were never intended to be representatives. In particular, it is clear that the appointment of worker directors has in no way interfered with management's ability to manage – paradoxically this might well have been strengthened. The worker directors themselves have become socialized into adopting a managerial perspective; indeed, the logic of the situation would appear to make it difficult to do otherwise. The authority structure of the industry remains intact, the value orientations of management remain unchanged and the position of the worker is unaltered.

Similar conclusions can be drawn from the German experience, although the historical and cultural conditions governing worker participation in that context are rather different from both Norway and Britain. The German system of worker participation has three main components: the labour director, the supervisory board and the works councils. Legislative attempts to introduce worker participation can be dated back to the revolutionary period immediately after the 1914–18 war, even though the legislation cannot be described as revolutionary in character, and is better seen as a reaction to demands for increased workers' control. Although the effective machinery of worker participation was abolished during the period of National Socialist domination, it was revised and updated during the social reconstruction of the early 1950s.

The new machinery was established by two separate pieces of legislation, the Co-determination Act of 1951 and the Works Constitution Act of 1952. This latter act has recently been revised by the Works Constitution Act of 1972 which increases the powers of the works councils. Discussion is also under way which will lead to the revision of the Co-determination Act. Under the Works Constitution Act a works council has to be elected in every establishment with more than five workers. The works council is not a joint body but represents exclusively the work people. Though the representatives do not have to be union members, in practice the majority are. The works council has a right to co-decision on social matters and on aspects of internal work regulation – on, for example, job evaluation, wage structures, training, discipline and welfare schemes. Personnel matters, hiring, firing, promotion, transfers and so on all need the approval of the works council. In matters affecting the actual conduct of the business the works councils are generally limited to the right to have information.

In addition to the works councils there is a graduated system of co-determination at board level in joint stock companies and all other limited companies with more than 500 workers. Unlike the unitary board Anglo-American system, German companies have two boards: a supervisory board (Aufsichtsrat) and an executive or management board (Vorstand). The supervisory board meets generally four or five times a year, appoints the management board, supervises the end-of-the-year accounts of the company in addition to being responsible for all basic policy decisions, such as mergers, takeovers or vital labour organization schemes. The management board conducts the day-to-day business of the company. Its members are full-time. They are not allowed to sit on the supervisory board and vice versa.

In all joint-stock and limited companies outside the coal and steel industries one-third of the supervisory board must be elected labour representatives. They have a direct control over the firm's activities and enjoy the same rights and obligations as all other board members. Usually one of them will be the chairman of the works council, but also trade-union officials from outside the company may be elected, so that there will be the means for automatic communication with both works council and unions.

Special rules apply to the coal and steel industries. Here the

H   215

Co-determination Act 1951 stipulates equal representation of shareholders and workers on the supervisory board. All boards contain an uneven number of members: eleven, fifteen or twenty-one. Thus, in a supervisory board of eleven members, five are appointed by the shareholders and five by the workers. The eleventh member – known as the neutral man – is co-opted by the two sides of the supervisory board. In the coal and steel industries the workers are also represented on the board of management by an elected labour director. He has the same responsibilities as the other executive directors and is usually entrusted with wage, personnel and welfare questions.

In 1968 an independent expert commission was set up under Professor Biedenkopf to examine and evaluate previous experience with co-determination. Whilst the results of the inquiry, which reported in 1970, are still a matter for some debate, the commission was unequivocally clear on one thing. No evidence was found that co-determination enhanced the power and influence of the trade unions to an extent where it could create a threat to the employers' freedom of action. They also refuted the argument that co-determination was detrimental to the profitability of a company. On the contrary the commission established that the workers' representatives on the supervisory boards were committed to company objectives and profitability. A similar conclusion was arrived at by Furstenberg in a review of the German experience. 'For several years the coal industry in the Federal Republic of Germany has been suffering from a structural crisis which has led to the shutting down of quite a few mines and a long-range policy for the replacement of personnel and other jobs. Facing these severe problems employees' representatives seem to have shown remarkable understanding of economic necessities.'[7] The last part of this quotation is of particular importance in that it indicates an obvious orthodoxy in tackling economic and social problems; the similarities with the BSC and Norwegian experience are noticeable. Criteria of profit and efficiency appear to be the main ones to be applied in relation to the utilization of economic resources; an alternative view based upon job security and the need to maintain particular communities is not considered tenable.

Two major reviews of German experience, then, have indicated that at board level, even in situations where worker directors are equal in number to shareholder directors, neither enterprise objectives nor managerial ideologies are undermined. There appear to be few, if any, contested decisions. Blumenthal has described how supervisory boards have tended to develop an informal division of labour within which the labour representatives confine their attention to pay structures and conditions of employment, whilst other areas of decision-making are left to management.[8] Daniel argues that there is no evidence that coal and steel workers who have fifty-fifty representation on company boards receive any greater increases in earnings as a result than workers in other industries.[9]

The evidence available on the functioning of works councils is similar. In law they have a dual function both to support employee interests against employer interests and also support the employer in realizing the functions of the enterprise. They are both agents of management and opposition to management. They have both to represent and reconcile interests. In practice the available evidence would suggest that they do neither. Furstenberg concludes that they are very open to the interest of management and 'management usually tries to utilize their functions for its own ends and integrate them wholly into the existing social system of the factory'.[10] Dahrendorf argues that they have taken over many aspects of what traditionally was a foreman's role – they help in the upward and downward flow of information, they mediate in individual quarrels, they play some part in hiring and firing. They are perhaps a more efficient instrument than the foreman in performing these functions. As such they form part of the system of authority in industry and have contributed little to the redistribution of authority.[11] Similar points could be made about the labour director. His position is by definition part of that cluster of roles which have authority in the enterprise. Whilst it has been argued that there is some merit in recruiting a labour director from the trade-union side of the enterprise, in itself this does nothing to modify the authority structure of the enterprise.

AUTHORITY, PARTICIPATION AND INVOLVEMENT

The reviews we have undertaken of Norwegian and German experiences of worker participation, especially in the upper echelons of management, suggest that the ability of management to manage has not been impaired nor have overall enterprise objectives been changed. A process seems to take place in which workers' representatives' orientations take on a managerialist colouring, and in which their activities become increasingly supportive of management strategies and goals. Although the worker-director scheme in BSC is different in a number of crucial respects from the institutions we have described in Norway and Germany, the general social dynamics appear surprisingly similar. The question arises of why the behaviour of worker representatives is shaped in this direction. Dahrendorf has argued that the central feature of industrial enterprises is that they are 'imperatively co-ordinated associations', that is they are structures based on authority and the arrangement of roles into levels of super- and subordination. The efficiency of our present industrial system has arisen from an increasing rationalization of the production process, a central feature of which has been the subdivision of labour. Parallel to the subdivision of labour has been the subdivision of authority. For the purposes of organization and co-ordination a system of authority relations between various positions in the structure is necessary. So that 'wherever there are industrial enterprises there are authority relations'.[12] Dahrendorf argues that implicit in a differentiation of power and authority is a differentiation of interest, so that a unitary view of the enterprise is objectively false. Employers who assert that they represent the interest of the total enterprise whilst unions only represent a partial interest are taking up positions that are both ideologized and false. At the same time, the interests of the most powerful group, those at the top of the authority structure, assume the character of accepted values.[13]

As an illustration of the implications of this analysis Dahrendorf takes the role of the labour director within the German co-determination system. The labour director is a member of the senior management team in the enterprise with executive functions. His position is one of super-ordination. In the rather unusual case of a welder, for example, becoming labour director (only 10 % of labour directors are drawn from the ranks of manual workers) he would move from a position of subordination to one of authority. The interests related to that role would be different to the interests related to the role of welder, for, Dahrendorf argues, interests relate to structure and positions not to individuals. In so far as the welder-cum-labour director attempted to act as a welder he would be a bad labour director. No matter what his personal sympathies he would have to learn to act as labour director or return to the role of welder. In the same way the worker director becoming a member of the board takes on the interests of that board. In so far as the worker pressed specifically worker interests, then he would be a bad board member and indeed, as was clear in the case of Norway, it would be difficult for him to act as a member of that board. That, however, the transition is not difficult is suggested in Dahrendorf's argument, that the interests of those at the top of the authority structure, assume the character of accepted values. Or, to put it another way, the dominant vocabularies are those of the powerful.

It might however be argued that the analysis in the preceding paragraph confuses roles in differing areas of decision-making within the enterprise. A commonly used distinction is that between legislative and executive decision-making. Whilst any hard and fast distinction cannot be maintained in a dynamic situation (as we have indicated in an earlier chapter), it might for the present discussion be desirable to recognize a degree of differentiation between decisions which are concerned with the general objectives of the enterprise and those which are concerned with day-to-day situations. Given that the role of the worker director is more likely to be concerned formally with legislative rather than executive decisions, is he not in a more open situation than has been suggested? In order to answer that we must refer to the wider social system within which the business enterprise is located in the countries we have referred to. The individual enterprise is part of a capitalist economy. Within this economy the logic of the market is central and profit necessarily assumes primacy as an objective. The board of any enterprise must then work within the logic of and the priorities of capitalism. As Marx has pointed out, 'Capitalism subjects every individual capitalist to the immanent laws of capitalist production as external coercive laws. Competition forces him continually to extend his capital for the sake of maintaining it';[14] or, as Shenfield concluded in an empirical study of company boards, 'none of the companies had any doubts that their primary objective was to be efficient and profitable and that being socially responsible would serve no useful purpose if it hindered those overall company goals'.[15]

Production for profit then must be the prime goal of the company and the performance of those in positions of authority will be judged in relation to that goal. The interests of the board must be related to profitability and the worker director can only operate *qua* director within that constraint. In so doing he is estranged from the interests of those he represents. This is not to say that management and workers do not have common interests. They do. But these are in the sphere of production, not of profit. So that at the most basic level, while a wage is income for a worker, it is a cost for management and the imperative of profit demands that costs are kept down. We are not arguing that in general terms workers do not often subscribe to the general values society puts on profitability and efficiency. Indeed, we have pointed out in earlier chapters that they do. But they also strike, stay absent from work, break work rules and so on, and it is by these actions that their different interests are revealed.

This analysis also illuminates another aspect of European experience of worker participation in the upper echelons of management. We noted earlier that the Norwegian worker-director scheme had led to no marked increase in worker involvement; the same appears to be true in the German situation and in the BSC. Furstenberg, summarizing the studies carried out in Germany says that

all the available studies indicate that most employees had a limited perception of co-determination. About three quarters of the workers knew that co-determination had been introduced within their undertakings but only half of the interviewed workers had any concrete ideas about the actual meaning of co-determination and most of these just knew the name of the labour director.[16]

Quoting from a study by Poppitz he goes on:

> Though concrete knowledge about co-determination practices was rather limited, the great majority of workers showed a positive attitude towards these institutional changes, through which they hoped to obtain better wages and fringe benefits, greater job security and better personal treatment.[17]

Similarly, in the case of BSC nearly 40 % of the workers we interviewed had heard of the worker-director scheme; only 5 % of workers, however, felt that the scheme had changed things as far as they were concerned; only 1 % felt that they had any influence over worker directors and worker directors were felt to be a less effective means of influencing management than either collective bargaining or joint consultation. At the same time a large majority of the workers were in favour of the *idea* of a scheme of board-room participation. One can conclude that, whilst there is a great desire within the work force for institutional change, actual changes which have taken place leave them with very little sense of involvement and little feeling that their interests are being represented. In terms of our analysis they have a realistic appreciation of the situation.

The arguments in the preceding paragraphs almost inevitably lead to a pessimistic appraisal of higher-level participation. Is Dahrendorf's structural determinism justified or is it merely that within capitalist economies higher-level participation creates contradictions which are resolved in favour of management? Yugoslav experience allows us to take these themes a little further and to suggest that the answers are by no means clear-cut.

INVOLVEMENT AND AUTHORITY: THE YUGOSLAV CASE

The background to the Yugoslav system of industrial democracy is somewhat confusing. The Yugoslavs claim an ideological basis in 'the Marxist theory of socialization of the means of production according to which producers themselves must govern these means thereby bringing about democratic and socialist relations in production'.[18] In addition, there were the pressures of the break with Russia, and the need to speed up the process of industrialization in what is still mostly a 'peasant' economy. The status of the Yugoslav enterprise, as established in 1950, is that of a community and the law states that 'on entering employment in an organization a worker shall become a member of the community of workers on an equal footing with other members and shall incur the obligations and acquire the rights attaching to and deriving from his work'.[19] The highest authority within the enterprise is the workers' council, comprising at least fifteen and up to one hundred and twenty members and elected for two years by direct and secret ballot from and by the workers in the enterprise. Candidates are mostly proposed at workshop assemblies, but lists may also be put forward by other groups of workers; lists normally contain more candidates than there are vacancies and in practice there are wide differences in the votes cast for the candidates. In 1966 there were workers' councils in 6809 enterprises.[20]

The research work undertaken to examine the Yugoslav system has not produced any clear-cut conclusions in relation to the themes we are examining. To a great extent this is not surprising, as the system has evoked a good deal of ideological commitment and antipathy. In addition, one would expect the workers' councils to function in a somewhat uneven way, with some being successful and others less so. Nevertheless, there does seem to be some degree of unanimity in the view that workers' councils have increased the workers' sense of involvement in the running of the enterprise. In many respects, this arises naturally out of the machinery; in 1966, for instance, there were 150 389 council members.[21]

However, a recent review of research suggests that the extent to which workers participate in the structures for workers' self-management is considerable.

In 1968 out of 2·5 million persons working in undertakings of seventy or more workers, 145·5 thousand were members of workers councils (about 6%). A survey of undertakings with a total of

750000 persons showed that 228641 of these (about 32%) participated in various self management bodies. . . . A survey of forty industrial establishments with 52262 workers, 1980 of whom were questioned, showed in 1967 that 60% of the workers attended the meetings of the working people of their units and 42% attended the meetings of the collective of the enterprise.[22]

As one would probably expect, the composition of workers' councils does not accurately reflect the composition of the total labour force, with unskilled and semi-skilled occupations being under-represented as the following table indicates.

Table 11–1

PARTICIPATION IN WORKERS' MANAGEMENT BY
LEVEL OF SKILL, 1960 [23]

Level of skill	% in labour force	% on workers' councils
Highly skilled	10·1	19·6
Skilled	38·3	53·3
Semi-skilled	25·0	17·6
Unskilled	26·6	9·5
Total	100·0	100·0

Kolaja's study of two Yugoslav factories concluded that there was a high degree of apathy towards the workers' councils, although this might be accounted for by the large percentage of women in the labour force in the factories he studied. But Blumberg adds what appears to be a necessary caveat to these conclusions: 'that over half the workers questioned in one factory [by Kolaja] believed the workers' council to be the single most influential force within the enterprise'.[24] Findings along similar lines were produced by one Yugoslav survey of 5000 workers. In that case, 74% attributed an improvement in the workers' position in the enterprise to the role of the workers' council: 76% believed that the workers' councils had sufficient power to maintain complete control over the management of the enterprise, and 82% thought that there were no serious obstacles preventing their representatives from playing a more active role. Even if these figures are not typical of all Yugoslav industry, they do nevertheless demonstrate a higher degree of commitment than apparently exists in the other countries we have considered.

Though the Yugoslav system seems to engender a greater degree of involvement, how far has it altered the orthodox pattern of authority relations in the enterprise? Kolaja in his case study found that the plant director, although formally responsible to the workers' councils, was able to control almost unilaterally the major investment and technical decisions.[25] Zupanov has suggested on the basis of his research that the system of workers' councils and self-regulating enterprises has not altered the oligarchic structure of power and authority in the enterprise.[26] Rus has brought together seven studies on the distribution of influence in the enterprise and has concluded that in all seven situations studied influence is perceived as concentrated in top management. The works councils he suggests are being transformed into transmission belts for line and staff instructions, losing their function as representatives of workers' interests.[27]

Further evidence of managerial dominance of the self-management system is to be found in the composition of the management board, a sub-committee of the main council which is most intimately involved in the running of the enterprise. According to Blumberg, whilst 48·4% of the labour force can be classified as highly skilled and skilled, 80·42% of the management boards in 1960 fell within these categories; again, whereas 20·5% of the total labour force has benefited from university or advanced education, 34·2% of the management board have experienced these advantages.[28] It is often suggested that this dependence upon a managerial elite can be accounted for by the relatively underdeveloped state of the Yugoslav economy; about half of the employed population is to be found in agriculture, with less than one-eighth in manufacturing.[29] Moreover given that twenty years ago Yugoslavia was a largely peasant economy with high levels of illiteracy, it can be argued that 'a large proportion of workers are incapable of understanding – much less supervising – the operation of an enterprise'.[30]

Whilst there is some substance in this argument, it ignores

the increase in managerial domination which has followed from the Yugoslav decision to allow market forces to allocate resources within the economy and to use material incentives to motivate workers to compete with other enterprises. As an American economist has argued in a recent study of the Yugoslav system,

commodity production with exchange or a market induces competition amongst enterprises and, most importantly for this experiment in participatory socialism, competition amongst workers employed in different enterprises. This competition, as with competition in capitalism, induces an 'efficiency fetishism' with the resulting detrimental impact on social relations within the enterprise. Experts and technicians ascend to power in the enterprise at the expense of blue-collar workers. . . .[31]

That this managerial elite has a different perspective on the goals of self-management from that of the work force more generally is indicated by the findings of a recent study by Zupanov.

Interviews conducted in ten Croatian factories in 1966 . . . showed that the majority of workers favoured the continuation of price controls. Only in the managerial group did the survey find a majority in favour of the elimination of price controls and even in this group one third wanted controls to continue. . . . In response to the question whether an unprofitable enterprise should be kept going with government support in an attempt to improve it or close down, the majority of workers opposed closing. White-collar employees and supervisors were approximately evenly divided in their opinion while the majority of managers and staff were in favour of closing down unprofitable enterprises.[32]

There is however data pointing in an opposite direction suggesting that the director is effectively constrained by the workers' council. Unfortunately most of this material relates to an earlier period, prior to the introduction of greater market pressures in the Yugoslav economy. For instance, the 1962 ILO report accorded growing power to the workers' council, particularly in such areas as recruitment, dismissal, regulation of remuneration and the distribution of profits. Specifically on the role of the plant director, it was reported that the position had 'lost some of the material and political attraction and prestige it once had'.[33] Blumberg detected the power of the workers' councils in forms of non-managerial behaviour, which often have proved to be dysfunctional for the system of economic planning. For instance, he referred to the pace of wage increase, which exceeded the growth in productivity. In addition to behaving like workers, the workers' councils assumed some of the entrepreneurial characteristics of Western capitalism, and indulged in monopolistic practices. 'As a result of monopolistic pricing, price collusion and other devices to create favourable market conditions, the government resorted to anti-trust legislation which prevented the formation of cartels and established maximum prices on a great number of items.'[34] These and other abuses (as Blumberg terms them) provide some evidence of significant workers' power, as they 'almost always take the form of actions which benefit the workers [or their representatives] directly, and were almost invariably, from their very nature, the concoction of the workers' management representatives'.[35]

As we have previously commented, most of this research dates back to an earlier period in which the 'market' played a smaller part to the Yugoslav economy. It would appear that there was a real growth in managerial power in the late sixties with the development of market forces. However, in the last few years the regime seems to have returned to the sort of ideology which gave birth to the workers' councils. In addition, there has been a deliberate attempt to lessen the power of the so-called technocratic and managerial elite. Their power has been under attack in the party, in the state apparatus and in industry. Real attempts appear to have been made to strengthen the control of the workers' councillors. These have culminated in the new Yugoslav constitution which was proclaimed early in 1974. This excludes executives from workers' councils; it also precludes any manager or executive from becoming a parliamentary deputy. The Yugoslav regime appears to be trying to have both its market and its self-management system.

The data on Yugoslavia do not allow for any definite answers on the relationship between orthodox authority structures and participation. The weight of evidence suggests, however, that, whilst the authority of the enterprise director and his management team declined considerably in the early days of self-management, the gradual extension of the market principle has led to a re-emergence of that authority. The paradox of the introduction of the market principle into the Yugoslav economy is that, whilst it has devolved power within the context of the total society by giving greater autonomy to the enterprise in relation to the state, it has strengthened the movement towards hierarchical government within the enterprise.

This is not to suggest, however, that the self-management system is bankrupt. The workers' councils seem not only to have formal power within the enterprise but also to exercise considerable control. None of the empirical studies we have looked at has denied that the workers' councils have power nor that the work force feels it exerts control through the councils. It is clear from the evidence that the workers' council system does draw forth a very much higher degree of worker involvement than the other high-level systems of participation we have looked at. It is also clear that in this situation enterprise objectives are given a high degree of legitimacy by the work force. The Yugoslav economy has undergone a remarkable improvement in performance since the introduction of the self-management system. Whilst we would not wish to fall into the *post hoc ergo propter hoc* trap, we would cautiously agree with Blumberg that as 'large increases in labour productivity have taken place alongside the development of the system of workers' management, the two have not been incompatible. . . .'[36]

CONCLUSION

The review that we have undertaken in this chapter has underlined a number of themes relevant to the discussion of worker participation in the upper echelons of organizations. Firstly, it has emphasized that such participation does not *in itself* alter the basic authority structure of the enterprise, though it is possible that it might lead to less authoritarian and more humanistic decision-making. The system of co-ordination necessary for technical reasons, which requires a hierarchical structure, is also normally related to a system of domination and status differentiation. Within the Yugoslav system, which differs from that of Western Europe in that it can be viewed as a system in which 'labour employs capital instead of a system in which capital employs labour', the aim has been to organize the enterprise on 'a principle of polyarchic distribution of authority, that is, authority and influence evenly distributed among groups each of which exercises a substantial amount of influence'.[37] The evidence suggests however that even within this system there is a constant tendency for the hierarchical authority system to reassert itself. Constant challenges to this tendency from the political and educational system, challenges which might be seen as a continuous cultural revolution, are felt to be necessary. Within Western Europe where participation schemes have been 'grafted on' to the existing structure of the enterprise, a structure which is both reinforced and legitimated by forces within its wider social environment, they have left the authority system largely unaltered.

The review has also suggested that high-level participation does not *in itself* affect the involvement of the work force in the enterprise. The low degree of involvement evidenced in Germany, Norway, and the BSC scheme and the high degree of involvement which the Yugoslav system has generated need to be related to the extent to which the work force feels that it is represented by the workers' council, its view of the power of the council in influencing enterprise goals and the degree of legitimacy which they attach to these goals.

Finally, a highly participative system does not mean a system without conflict. Even in a self-management system, within a state system which is socialist in character, there is conflict within the enterprise. 'Experience within Yugoslavia indicated that self management does not remove conflict within organizations. Where a dispute cannot be settled by the provisions made for the settlement of disputes by internal arbitration or by tribunals outside the enterprise, there may be a public protest, work stoppage or strike.'[38] It is interesting that as the market principle has developed there are signs that the Yugoslav trade-union movement is changing its role within the enterprise from that of a largely educational and welfare body to a body with protective and pressure-group functions.

Even a highly developed participation system then does not create industrial peace. This is an important point, for much of the impetus towards participation in Western Europe arises from a mistaken notion that if you can create institutions of co-operation you will abolish conflict. The model for much of the thinking that is currently taking place about high-level participation is the German system. One of the reasons for the popularity of this system is Germany's low record of industrial conflict as measured by strikes. Since the war, Germany has had the lowest strike record of any industrial nation of its size. If industrial democracy is about preventing strikes, then Germany appears to be doing well. We have already suggested that *in fact* the co-determination scheme has done little to alter the authority system of the industrial enterprise. Moreover, as we have indicated, there is not a very high degree of involvement of the ordinary worker in co-determination. It would appear that other variables are needed to explain the low strike record. Several can be suggested. During the period 1948–72 economic expansion took place at a high rate. For most workers there have been yearly salary increases and a growth in real income. Prosperity evenly spread is a damper on militancy. In addition, there has also been a low rate of unemployment.

Factors related to German industrial culture need also to be considered. Dahrendorf has argued that the search for industrial democracy in Germany has been intimately related to the desire to build an industrial utopia free from conflict. 'Instead of industrial relations the main issue in all clashes between employers and workers in Germany was and is the constitution of the industrial enterprise.'[39] This search has been intensified during periods in which particular political groups have criticized and challenged the existing distribution of power. Industrial democracy has represented a reaction to open conflict and a search for co-operation; but more than that, it has enabled employers to resist attempts to establish collective bargaining in the work place. This has weakened the unions, although they are firmly established at industry and national level, as strength in the work place has depended upon the state and not upon membership. The system of industrial relations and the institutions of collective bargaining have remained largely under-developed. But this does not mean that there has been no conflict in industry. 'In industry too there are more quiet, almost inaudible and yet effective manifestations of conflict.'[40] Conflict is redirected into mass individual reactions. High rates of absenteeism, high rates of illness, high rates of suicide, high rates of alcoholism; apathy and consumerism. All of these are manifestations of conflict.

A more detailed examination of European experience does not allow us to share the view of those managerial optimists who believe that within the current economic system participation can eradicate or minimize conflict. Conflict can take many forms and seems inevitably to co-exist with institutions of participation. The system of co-ordination needed in order to make effective the division of labour within the industrial enterprise, itself leads to differentiation of interest. Where, however, the co-ordinating hierarchy is also related to the system of power and status, the degree of felt conflict is likely to be higher, though not necessarily more visible.[41]

The themes that have been raised in this chapter do not, if they are valid, suggest a very optimistic future for high-level participation in the current socio-political context in Western Europe. In the final chapter we go on to discuss them further and relate them to other issues which have been touched on in the book.

Notes

1 See, for example, BALFOUR, C., 'Workers' Participation in Western Europe', in Balfour (ed.), *Participation in Industry*, Croom Helm, 1973
2 EMERY, F. E., and THORSRUD, E., *Form and Content in Industrial Democracy*, Tavistock, 1969, pp. 83–4
3 Ibid., p. 75
4 Ibid., pp. 75–6
5 Ibid., p. 18
6 See QUALE, T. U., 'The Industrial Democracy Project in Norway', *International Industrial Relations Association*, September 1970
7 FURSTENBERG, F., 'Workers' Participation in Management in the Federal Republic of Germany', *IILS Bulletin*, No. 6, 1969, p. 128

8 BLUMENTHAL, W. M., *Co-determination in the German Steel Industry*, Princeton University Press, 1956

9 DANIEL, W. W., and MCINTOSH, NEIL, *The Right to Manage*, PEP, 1972, p. 142

10 FURSTENBERG, op. cit., p. 132

11 DAHRENDORF, R., *Freedom and Democracy in Germany*, Weidenfeld and Nicolson, 1968, p. 173

12 DAHRENDORF, R., *Class and Class Conflict in Industrial Society*, Routledge & Kegan Paul, 1959, p. 249

13 Ibid.

14 MARX, K., *Capital*, Moscow, 1959, Vol. 1, Chapter 24

15 SHENFIELD, B., *Company Boards*, Allen and Unwin, 1971, p. 164

16 FURSTENBERG, op. cit., p. 130

17 Ibid.

18 Congress of Workers' Councils of Yugoslavia, ed. of the Central Council of the Confederation of Trade Unions of Yugoslavia, Belgrade, 1957

19 ILO Legislative Series, 1965, Yug. 4, Act of 4th April 1965, S. 2(2)

20 Statisticki Godisnjak, SFRJ, Belgrade, 1967

21 Ibid.

22 GORUPIC, D., and PAJ, I., 'Workers' Participation in Management in Yugoslavia', *ILLS Country Studies*, No. 10, Geneva, 1970, p. 17

23 Taken from BLUMBERG, P., *Industrial Democracy, the Sociology of Participation*, Constable, 1968, p. 218

24 Ibid., pp. 226–7

25 KOLAJA, J., *Workers' Councils: the Yugoslav Experience*, Tavistock, 1965

26 ZUPANOV, J., quoted in Alexander Matejko, 'Industrial Democracy: a Socio-technical Approach', *Our Generation*, Spring 1973

27 RUS, VELJKO, 'Influence Structure and Yugoslav Enterprise', *Industrial Relations*, Vol. 9, No. 2, February 1970

28 BLUMBERG, op. cit., pp. 217–19

29 In Britain, by contrast, less than 3% are in agriculture

30 BLUMBERG, op. cit., p. 218

31 WACHTEL, HOWARD M., *Workers' Management and Workers' Wages in Yugoslavia*, Cornell University Press, 1973, p. 186

32 ZUPANOV, J., quoted in Matejko, op. cit.

33 ILO, *Workers' Management in Yugoslavia*, Geneva, 1962, p. 115

34 BLUMBERG, op. cit., p. 212

35 Ibid., p. 215

36 Ibid., p. 223

37 GORUPIC and PAJ, op. cit., p. 35

38 Ibid., p. 41

39 DAHRENDORF, 1968, op. cit., p. 167

40 Ibid., p. 164

41 Visibility will depend upon type of conflict behaviour and possibilities for the open expression of conflict.

12 Conclusions and beginnings

One of the themes that has acted as a backdrop to the discussion in this book is that of social and technological change. Whereas in previous centuries a man might expect things to change little in the course of his lifetime, this century has seen a radical transformation of the world. The dynamic of industrialism has involved a process of accelerating technological, economic, and social change. This has been particularly acute in the period following the second world war; at the beginning of this book we described some of its essential features. One effect of rapid change is that technological and economic development tends to move ahead of changes in social institutions. Whereas once our social arrangements could be allowed to develop through natural evolution now we need to plan and actively develop them. This is particularly true of the social relations in terms of which we organize production; in recent times it has been argued with increasing frequency that if we are to ensure the full and efficient usage of productive resources then we need to experiment with new forms of relationships in industry. Participation generally and the involvement of workers in the upper echelons of industrial organizations more particularly is one such type of experimentation. The extension and expansion of the existing institutions of collective bargaining has been seen as another.

The steel industry in this country, particularly in recent times, has in many ways acted as a microcosm of the more general economic and social changes we have outlined. There has been rapid technological change, increased state intervention, centralization and bureaucratization of administration, increases in the size of manufacturing plant, and changes in the occupational structure of the work force. It is precisely in this context of rapid and major change that participative measures have been introduced. Indeed, in identifying participative measures as a corrective to the industrial relations strain which rapid change generates, and in actively promoting institutional changes of a participative kind, the senior management of the industry might be seen to have acted in a manner that was prototypical; that is, they were in advance of a trend which has gathered momentum in recent times.

The engineering of social change is, however, more complex and less predictable than the engineering of technical change. It is difficult not only to control the process of change but to anticipate the outcomes. The same sets of social forces which led senior management in the Steel Corporation to espouse participation also led various trade-union groups in the same direction. While both sides saw nationalization and the consequent rationalization of the industry as both an opportunity for and a spur towards changing the relationships of production, the degree of change which they envisaged differed. Out of the interaction between these interest groups arose the worker-director scheme; whilst this was essentially the creation of management it involved compromise both between the various groups and within these groups. The compromise, however, which was necessary in order to get the scheme off the ground, meant that there was no clear unambiguous definition of what the goals of the scheme were or indeed of what the worker directors were meant to do.

The Steel Corporation, however, clearly saw the scheme as part of their armoury in the management of change within the industry. More specifically, they felt this would be achieved through the worker directors' providing a symbol of a new departure in industrial relations, helping to make ordinary employees feel involved in policy-making and allowing a shop-floor perspective to be heard in the board room. Our analysis of the social context in which the worker-director scheme operated, however, has indicated a number of social structural factors and social processes which made the realization of these aims unlikely. Nationalization brought with it great organizational changes and it was within this context that worker directors were expected to operate. Since the nationalization

233

of the steel industry there has been an increasing tendency towards the centralization of decision-making. In that sense the divisional boards on which the worker directors sat were not at the centre of power. At divisional level, moreover, formal and informal meetings of full-time directors were more significant to the decision-making process than formal board meetings. Comparison with boards in private enterprise, however, suggests that even where boards are formally and legally the apex of the decision-making structure they often seem to play a role comparable to that of the BSC boards. Our analysis of the organizational constraints on the BSC worker directors therefore has more general implications. First, it is not immediately obvious where decision-making occurs within an organization; its locus is variable. Second, and following from this, having worker representatives on a board may not, probably will not, in itself mean that they have the opportunity to influence policy-making; indeed, they may only be marginally related to it.

Even, however, if the board had been the locus of decision-making within BSC our analysis has suggested that there are a number of social processes related to worker representation at board level which militate against a shop-floor view being heard for long in the board room, let alone shop-floor interests being actively pursued. These processes are related to selection and socialization. In looking at the Steel Corporation's scheme we saw how particular criteria were adopted in an attempt to ensure an overall equitable representation of occupation, trade union, region and so on. More importantly, however, it was clear that important members of management in their concern for academic ability, local government and broad trade-union experience were seeking in worker directors those qualities which they thought would make these new men most amenable to becoming 'normal' board members. Whilst for some trade unions other criteria were important, as we have pointed out, they also demonstrated concern that worker directors should display at least some promise of those skills which were seen to be directorial and consistent with conventional board-room behaviour. The selection processes then acted as a filter which tended to let through people who had particular characteristics which can be defined in terms of responsibility, moderation, adaptability and intelligence. A self-selection process also operated in the sense that candidates were hardly likely to put themselves forward or to accept appointments in what was clearly a managerially controlled scheme unless they accepted, at least at a very general level, management's goals for that scheme.

Even if a worker had been appointed to the board who was likely to behave deviantly within the board-room context, there were a number of other social processes at work, which we can broadly label 'socialization', which were likely to either eradicate or limit the potential for deviation. Here we are not referring only to the formal training programmes which were of their nature going to help the worker director fit into the existing structure and attempt to smooth out 'rough points' in his education and behaviour, but also to the process of social exchange which occurred between the worker director and other significant social actors in which behaviour was modified so as to fit expectations. Within the context of our case study we have referred to this specifically in relation to the board room. We saw in Chapter 9 the way in which a process of negotiation over the worker directors' role occurred. On the one hand the directors expected their new colleagues to accept conventions of board-room behaviour and the overall goals of the board which they took for granted. In exchange they were willing to accept the worker directors as *bona fide* members and to listen to them as people who reflected a valid and reliable shop-floor perspective.

The worker directors for their part were concerned to gain acceptance as legitimate members of the board and to show that they had a valuable contribution to make. Their contribution, however, could only be within parameters which they had not laid down. Even within this context their impact was likely to be limited because they were playing a game whose rules were strange and with others who had played the game longer and had more expertise; more importantly perhaps, they were contributing as individuals at only one stage of the discussion process whereas full-time directors had been involved at earlier stages and were backed by the full resources of their segments of the organization. In attempting to maximize their impact the worker directors within BSC sought an increasing involvement outside the board room in committees, working parties and in information-gathering exercises of various kinds. Whilst they did through this expand the scope of their role in the Steel Corporation they could only do so by increasing their involvement with and dependence on management. They could only stress their directorial role at the expense of their worker role.

We have painted a relatively stark sociological picture of the BSC worker-director scheme and have argued that the worker directors had no effect on the decision-making process because the board was not really the place where it occurred; we have also argued that even if it had been things would have changed little; management have a monopoly of knowledge, of language; and of authority; the worker directors were individuals with no sanctions and no power. Nor did the scheme lead to the representatiom of shop-floor interests at board level or a feeling of involvement in the organization on the part of the work force.

This is not to argue, however, that the worker-director scheme left things totally unchanged. Indeed, it is clear that if one introduces new actors into the situation then by definition that situation has changed and other actors must adapt and to some extent accommodate to the new situation. In that sense, although the worker directors in no way altered the authority structure, they did perhaps have some effect on the way in which that authority was exercised, at least at board level. Their presence on the board to some extent ensured that labour as a factor of production was seen a little differently from other factors of production; it was not seen totally as a 'thing'. In other words, the presence of workers on a board induces a measure of humanism into board-room discussion. In so far as humanism is good for business at the present time, then it might be argued that worker-director schemes are an aid to efficiency. We return to this point later.

We would also want to argue that the worker directors did influence events, but only in isolated incidents and in marginal areas. In general terms these were areas which might be seen as beneath and not directly related to what would normally be considered the sphere of directorial interest. Individual worker directors were responsible in particular cases for the improvement of contact between management and unions and also between unions. Also in specific instances they were able to make some changes in working conditions. We have pointed out that they did have some effect within strike situations in the sense that they were able in a number of cases to restore communication between the various factions. They also played a role in encouraging in particular plants the setting up of joint consultative committees and in individual cases they were able to settle particular grievances. The situations where they did exert influence were usually however situations where they had the backing of management, or at least a section of management.

As we have indicated in the introduction to this study, there have been changes in the BSC scheme since our field work finished. These changes have led to a greater formal involvement of the trade unions in the worker-director scheme. We would argue, however, that these changes are unlikely to affect the general social processes we have described although they may well lead to the worker directors exerting more influence of a marginal kind. The data that we have presented on Norway and West Germany would tend to confirm our view that the general social processes which we have described within the worker-director scheme are likely to occur in much the same way in any scheme of board-room participation within our present socio-economic context. Unfortunately, in the case of Norway and West Germany we largely have research on the outcomes rather than on the social processes themselves. These outcomes in a general sense are relatively clear. There has been little sense of worker involvement through such schemes, the authority structure and decision-making process within the enterprise have been little affected. The exception to this, however, has been the Yugoslav system. There the evidence suggests a greater degree of worker involvement and a more radical assault on the traditional hierarchical authority structure of the enterprise. The latter has, however, been variable in relation to the importance given to market forces within the Yugoslav economy. We concluded that the market had important implications for the working of participation at high levels in the organization. It is worth exploring this further in order to place the possibilities of boardroom participation within a market economy, such as our own, in context.

The development of industrial society has been dependent upon an increasing division of labour both at the societal level and within our economic institutions. The corollary of the subdivision of labour within the industrial sphere has been the growth of a system of co-ordination and control. This is the basis of the function of management. The control system is hierarchically organized, but the hierarchy that is necessary for co-ordination is also related to other things. It is related to the overall setting of enterprise goals and to decisions about the distribution of rewards within the enterprise. It is also related to the amount of rewards of both a financial and status kind which individuals receive. And in that way the hierarchy within the enterprise also to a very large extent relates to the hierarchy within the wider society for one's position at work also controls one's life chances more generally. The system of status and power within the enterprise reinforces, and is reinforced by, the system of status and power in the wider society.

We have suggested earlier that one of the most important forces behind the recent interest in participation has been the view that the co-ordination and exploitation of technical skills and the acceptance of change within industry can no longer be efficiently furthered by the traditional hierarchical form of organization. There is no *a priori* reason why technical co-ordination should not take place through a more participative and less hierarchical system. Indeed, within the management structure there is increasing dependence on formal and informal meetings to hammer out questions of co-ordination and control. The basic problems posed for participatory systems are not specifically related to technical co-ordination and authority but rather the relationship of these to the wider social context of the market system.

Economic theory assumes that firms are profit maximizers

and that profits are an index of efficiency. Much recent economic writing has questioned these propositions. However, this is not to argue that firms have lost interest in profits. There is a distinct difference between maintaining high profits and maximizing profits. It is in terms of this difference that a number of economists have posited other motivations for management such as growth, security, market domination and so on. But many of these new motivations do not conflict with profit maximization but can be seen rather as a shift of emphasis towards long-run maximization. They are attempts to manipulate, fix and control the market and still to work within it. All of these operations are related to and based on ideas of private cost and benefit; they ignore the wider social costs and benefits which are external to the firm.

The presence of worker directors upon a board potentially raises non-market issues. Most means of furthering worker interests, whether it be in terms of health and safety, wages, working conditions or welfare, involve costs to the firm. In so far as worker directors press such interests, then it might be argued that they will be in conflict with the goals of economic prosperity for the firm. However, as we have seen, economic prosperity does not necessarily mean immediate profit maximization and in some cases the acknowledgement of worker interests may be offset by economic gains for the organization in the long run. There is then no necessary conflict of interest between worker directors and other directors on a number of matters. Moreover, our analysis of the forces which determine the behaviour of worker directors would indicate that they are likely to take a 'wider' view of the interests of the firm – that is one that coincides with those of their fellow directors. Board-level participation therefore is possible without there being a threat to the economic prosperity of the company. Indeed, in many cases it might be argued that this kind of participation can lead to improved efficiency. However, in a situation where the pursuit of workers' interests is in conflict with the clear market interests of the firm (e.g. in the case of large-scale rationalization) then a worker-director scheme is likely to be ineffective from the point of view of the work force or disruptive of the operation of the board. It is the operation of the market and the necessarily different interests which that creates between management and the work force which underlines the necessity for collective action and negotiation; that is for the utilization of power by the trade unions outside of the authority system of the firm. The importance of collective action in this respect lies not so much in the withdrawal of labour and the challenge to management but in the fact that it puts the arguments to management in a way which they can understand; that is it imposes financial costs upon them and therefore comes within the ambit of market considerations. A number of people have argued that workers should not be involved in the management system because it would compromise collective action; workers' interests in the work place should be represented through the exercise of collective bargaining. We would agree with the necessity of having strong oppositional groups within the organization for the logic of the market pays little heed to the interests of individuals or groups. We would also agree that influence has been exerted through the trade unions on the conditions of employment for ordinary workers, and perhaps to a lesser extent on pay.

However, the development of collective bargaining does not in any central way impinge on the traditional forms of social relationships in industry. It does not challenge the basic division of the enterprise into the managers and the managed. Indeed, it might be seen as supporting that division. The formal authority of management stems from their role as agent of the owners (whether this be the state or shareholders) and from the contract of employment in which workers engage with the enterprise. From this is derived their right to organize the affairs of the enterprise and to direct the work force. The notion of management who have formal authority is essential to the process of collective bargaining, for trade-union power is exercised from the outside, so to speak, on those who have the right to give. In this sense the rights of management receive no major challenge from the process of collective bargaining. This is not to argue that these rights can be exercised in an unhindered or unconstrained way; this is clearly not the case. But checks on the way managerial authority is exercised do not affect the principle; rather they underwrite it.

We would argue then that the larger changes which are taking place in society are creating the need for new systems of social relationships in industry. Whilst the institutions of collective bargaining will need to be maintained, they are not the basis for the development of social systems which distribute authority more widely and which acknowledge in a real way the plurality of interests in the enterprise. Developments here are more likely to stem from experiments in participation. However, particularly in the case of board-room participation, our own work and studies of European practice would indicate that such experiments are going to have little effect on the existing system of social relations unless worker directors not only have access to key decision-making points but also means of counteracting pressures towards managerialism. If worker directors are to represent, in any sense, workers' interests at board level, then they need not only pressures from workers but also the resources to formulate a view-point independently of management. Management themselves cannot be the source of such a critical approach; the obvious source of this information back-up, as well as maintaining the representativeness of the worker directors, is the trade-union movement.

However there is an apparent dilemma here. On the one hand a strong trade-union movement is necessary within a market system to prevent attacks on its members' interests. On the other hand, schemes of board-room participation, if they are in any sense to begin to change relationships in industry, require trade-union backing and support. It has been argued that the independence of the trade unions is a crucial condition for their oppositional role and that involvement with participative structures would compromise this. But what is the status of this independence? Whilst, as we have argued, the market system means that there is a basic conflict of interests between management and workers, on the other hand they do have interests in common in order to achieve gain, or prevent losses, within that system. In pursuing these common interests the trade unions engage in a wide range of co-operative activities with management. These range from the everyday problem-solving activity on which shop stewards spend a large proportion of their time, to the agreements made, for example, in productivity bargains. Such agreements not only aid management in their planning and production functions but they also impose a discipline on the labour force. What responsible trade unionism means is that the unions take over certain managerial functions in controlling their members.

The trade unions, then, are actively involved in *de facto* co-operation with management. They are also in a dependency relationship to management. At its most basic they are dependent on managment for the provision of jobs for their members; they are also to a great extent dependent on management recognition, provision of facilities for their shop stewards, and access for their full-time officials, in order to operate effectively. The trade unions then can only be described in the most formalistic way as independent of management. Their independence is more apparent than real. At the same time they still operate as effective oppositional interest groups. As one trade-union official put it, describing the duality of his relationships, 'If you can't ride two horses at once you shouldn't be in the bloody circus.' The involvement of trade unions in high-level participation then would be a change of a quantitative not a qualitative kind. We would agree with Blumberg that it is not impossible to have trade-union backing and support for worker representatives in management without compromising the oppositional functions of the trade unions.

There is, however, within our argument a contradiction. On the one hand we suggest that there are social pressures at work which have led to increased demand for, interest in, and experimentation with board-level participation. On the other hand we argue that within a market economy a number of forces are at work which ensure that board-room participation changes little. These are not only contradictions within our argument; they are contradictions within the social system. It would be our judgement that these contradictions will work out in the long run through the diminution of the power of the market system. In the short run, however, whilst it is unlikely that worker-director schemes will lead to radical change (and from that point of view neither management nor trade-union leaders need fear them) they represent the beginnings of a search and of a learning process. Through them both work force and managements may begin to understand and be exposed to the contradictions of the market system and be led to new forms of social organization in industry and indeed in society more generally. It is clear that there can be no easy route to these new forms; it is equally clear that if we wish fully to develop our industrial and our human potential, then we cannot afford not to experiment to try to find them.

Postscript: The development of participation

In the main body of this book we have noted that there has recently been a considerable body of literature on participation, and a great deal of general interest in the subject. But there have also been periods in the past where the idea of greater worker influence in economic enterprises has been the focus of many people's thoughts. It is remarkable therefore that few attempts have been made to explain why interest in participation should develop at particular periods of time. This is all the more surprising since a good deal of sociological theorizing has relevance to this question. In this postscript we do not see ourselves as providing a complete remedy. Rather, our aim is the much more modest one of trying to set out the elements of a tentative model which will hopefully form a basis for further debate and work. Space permits no more than a broad and rough sketch of certain points which appear important. A more satisfactory model would require a great deal of historical and theoretical work which are unfortunately beyond the scope of this book.

A further limitation upon the validity of our tentative model is that it is based only upon British experience.[1] We recognize that Britain 'rather than being the "type case" of either capitalist or industrial evolution, . . . represents only one among various identifiable patterns of development in the emergence of the advanced societies.' For example, as Giddens points out, while a strong workers' movement developed in this country, the strength of revolutionary class consciousness was not as strong as in France or Germany. In Britain, 'the interpenetration of nascent industrialism with a very specific social structure allowed for a relatively stable accommodation between the various classes; neither revolutionary socialism, nor militant

245

conservatism became the forces which they were in the other two European countries'.[2] Moreover, the role of the state in Britain – at least in the initial phases of industrialization – was smaller than in many other countries in fostering economic development. Participation will vary between societies (as it does between industries) according to the nature of the wider social structure as well as the industrial structure. Similarly, patterns which have occurred in the past need be no sure guide to the future.

In this postscript, we first consider briefly the broad nature of capitalist development and the significance of participation in this process, drawing upon the work of a number of sociologists. We then go on to consider one important feature of the history of participation which receives scant attention in these discussions – its 'cyclical' nature in the past. Finally, we consider the question, raised by certain more recent writers, of whether or not workers' participation is likely to be a central and stable feature of capitalism or modern industrial society in the future.

CAPITALIST DEVELOPMENT AND WORKERS' PARTICIPATION

Our attempt to develop a model rests upon the basic notion that all schemes of participation are in effect attempts to change relationships of production in such a way that they are accommodated to changes in the means of production.[3] We are not suggesting any *mechanical*, deterministic relationships. Man is both determined by the social, technological and physical world and at the same time creates that world. We are pointing rather to a tendency among human groups to react to tension between the means of production and existing social relations by reorganizing these social relationships.

Such a thesis requires a consideration of the nature of capitalist development in order to understand the strains which develop between the means and relationships of production. The essence of modern capitalism is the institutionalization, in the form of a market economy, of a particular set of values centring around the profit criterion and the cash nexus. It is associated with a relatively consistent and rational pursuit of these values involving not merely the pursuit of market opportunities but also the attempt to control both natural and social resources to reduce costs and achieve other market advantages. There emerges from this a particular concept of efficiency which leads to movement along the path of industrialization. Two related factors promote this movement. The first of these is the consistent and rational pursuit of profit maximization and growth; the second is the nature of the market. In a non-market economy there is a more direct relationship between production and consumption. With the development of a market, this relationship is mediated and indirect; to this extent it is less predictable and therefore liable to disjunction and fluctuation. The uncertainty involved fosters the development of new techniques, new products and new markets in the search for comparative advantage. The paradox of capitalism, then, is that the focal uncertainty of the market fosters attempts to increase certainty and control on the part of companies.

Analytically, it is possible to conceive of this process leading to a cumulative and increasingly rapid rate of change. The broad directions of this change were graphically described by Marx.

One capitalist always kills many. Hand in hand with this centralization, or this expropriation of many capitalists by few, develop, on an ever-extending scale, the co-operative forms of the labour process, the conscious technical application of science, the methodical cultivation of the soil, the transformation of the instruments of labour into the instruments of labour only usable in common, the economizing of all means of production of combined, socialized labour, the entanglement of all peoples in the net of the world market, and with this, the international character of the capitalistic regime.[4]

Interestingly, as Avineri has pointed out, Marx emphasized that

the capitalist form of production necessarily stresses the need for social togetherness and mutual co-operation in the production process. This statement contradicts the individualistic model on which capitalist economic theory operates and this antagonism between capitalist theory and practice ultimately causes the capitalist mode of production to fetter its own development.[5]

In the meanwhile, however, the development of capitalism has seen an increase in standards of living (despite short-term cyclical reverses), although the shares of capital and labour have remained remarkably constant. To this extent the market has helped to maintain itself and to do so has changed and developed the expectations of consumers. This has involved attempts on the part of companies to strengthen their position in the market by advertising. Further, the nature of industrial production has changed, the result being an increase in the concentration and centralization of capital, most clearly seen today in the form of the transnational company.[6]

Such concentration can in part be seen as the natural outcome of differential company success in the market. But in addition the development of new techniques and the market strategies associated with them have been important. The optimum use of new techniques often requires a large scale of operations, and in turn fosters the attempt to control both supply and product markets. For the interruption of production in units of such size, both in terms of capital and employment, can be very costly. Similarly the innovation necessary to exploit new technical developments is often a costly and risky enterprise. Large capital assets are therefore increasingly required, both to finance such activities and to spread risks over a variety of activities. Technical developments have, therefore, fostered the inherent tendency in profit pursuit to achieve financial control of other companies. The need for capital to permit these activities has seen the development of a whole range of financial structures, along with mergers, takeovers and amalgamations.

Nevertheless the uncertainties of the market still persist. For example, in the motor industry there has been a process of concentration, but there still remains a considerable amount of oligopolistic competition. This uncertainty indeed may in certain respects be that much greater. The amount of capital committed to a project is larger and the requisite time horizon longer. The long-term market predictions upon which such investments are based can obviously be wrong: one major reason can be the development of still more sophisticated techniques or products on the part of competitors.

The attempt to control and predict involves not merely companies but also the state apparatus. The state has often provided financial aid to companies, as well as being a major customer; similarly, tariff barriers have been put up to foster investment or to protect obsolescent sectors. More generally, capitalist development tends to concentrate in particular sectors, with the result that certain weaknesses exist in the general economic structure. The state therefore becomes involved in the economy in two important respects. First, it tends to become directly involved in certain weaker sectors of the economy, and, secondly, it plays a key managing and mediating role more generally in an attempt to avoid severe cyclical fluctuations.[7]

The kinds of development we have described also have implications for the position of workers in the production process. Two factors, in particular, make the position of labour important. First, the increasing use of capital means that the costs which workers can impose upon companies become that much greater. This is accentuated both for individual companies and the economy generally, because of the interdependence of processes. These facts give the worker increasing potential structural power. The concentration of workers into large factories and establishments is associated with a growth in union membership – that is, involvement in an organization specifically directed towards the promotion and protection of workers' interests. The pursuit of these interests can mean that labour is increasingly the least predictable factor of production.

Conflict between capital and labour has become, at least in part, regulated through its institutionalization. As Dahrendorf argues:

Marx displayed a certain sociological naïvety when he expressed his belief that capitalist society would be entirely unable to cope with the class conflict generated by its structure. In fact, every society is capable of coping with whatever new phenomena arise in it, if only by the simple yet effective inertia which can be desscribed, a little pretentiously, as the process of institutionalisation.[8]

Postscript: The development of participation

This process of institutionalization serves not merely to recognize the existence of conflict and strain but also to legitimate it. By developing procedures through which compromise between the conflicting parties can be reached, the conflict itself tends to be modified, and in the short term limited.

These forms of conflict regulation within the industrial sphere take the form of collective bargaining, conciliation, mediation and arbitration. But another important means is a modification of the industrial authority structure itself, or the establishment of systems of workers' participation.[9] In this way, changes in the means of production foster a change in the relationships of production, in an attempt to come to terms with changes in the balance of power and an awareness of a conflict of interests.

Social integration within industrial society is, however, problematic. Durkheim, for example, argued that the growth of large-scale industry had established two broad classes, capital and labour, which confronted one another. Unlike Marx, however, who saw conflict, in particular class conflict, as intrinsic to the division of labour in capitalist society, Durkheim asserted that conflict grew out of the incomplete development of the division of labour; in particular he designated two main 'pathologies'. The first of these related to the lack of a set of moral beliefs which was adequate to the conditions of modern economic life which he termed the anomic division of labour. He referred here to the inability of the worker to meaningfully relate his tasks to the functions of the total production system, and also to the unregulated aspirations and expectations which were generated by the production system. The search for a new basis of moral regulation in industry through participatory schemes which emphasize communication and job satisfaction can clearly be related to this element of Durkheim's perspective.

The second main 'pathology' he termed the forced division of labour. Moral regulation of the division of labour would always be problematic, he argued, as long as there existed social arrangements which blocked the actual development of the relationships of production. Primarily he had in mind here a class structure which allocated positions within the division of labour on grounds other than those of merit or ability. Social integration would only be achieved in a situation of greater social equality. Whilst Durkheim's main prescription here related to the abolition of inherited wealth he also argued for changes within the institutional arrangements of industry. An occupational activity he argued 'can be effectively regulated only by the group close enough to know how it operates, what its needs are and how it is likely to change. The only one that meets these conditions is the one which might be formed by all the agents of the same industry united and organized into a single body.'[10] There must then be within industry participatory channels. Whilst employer and employees need to have their own unions, Durkheim felt that unless there was a common organization to bring them together it would always be 'the rule of the strongest which settles conflict'. What Durkheim argued for were institutional channels where both employer and workers 'can develop common forms of regulation which will determine the relationship between them in an authoritative fashion without either of them losing their autonomy'.[11] A formally free contract was an insufficient basis for organic solidarity.

Various forms of participation can be seen as similar to these 'corporate associations'; works councils and consultative committees will serve as examples. In the main they emphasize the integrative and consensual aspects of relationships in the enterprise. At the same time whilst integrative institutions have at particular times developed, our society is clearly very far from that organic unity which Durkheim envisaged. Unequal access to wealth, status and power are very much part of our society whilst, as Mann has shown, the degree of normative consensus is open to doubt.[12] Indeed, Fox has argued that

the ultimate condition of the division of labour in advanced industrial states has come to be, not Durkheim's high trust 'organic solidarity', but inflation, the supreme symbolic expression of low trust society. By having to fight to retain what they already have in a society where they have no institution or mechanism to do this for them, men force others to do likewise and thus the process reinforces itself. The galloping contagion of distrust is well represented in the concept of galloping inflation.[13]

However, while Durkheim and others have suggested why the institutionalization of conflict, including participation, is important in modern capitalist society, we are still faced with a number of unanswered questions. These include an understanding of the exact processes which lead groups to adopt systems of participation, why participation is the mechanism chosen in preference to others, and why this should occur at certain times rather than others. It is to these questions that we now turn.

SITUATIONS AND CIRCUMSTANCES OF PARTICIPATORY INITIATIVES

In Chapter 2 we have noted the increased interests in workers' participation in the sixties. Certain writers have argued that it is in this recent period, and only in this period, that a significant movement towards workers' control has developed.[14] Briefly their argument is as follows: in the industrializing phase of capitalism, artisan craftsmen produced the bulk of manufactured goods in small workshops. Despite onerous conditions, this provided a sense of accomplishment and pride, which fostered a demand for integration into the existing society rather than demands for its transformation in the direction of workers' control. A second phase of capitalism – the mechanical – saw the decline of craft as mass production, large-scale units, new organization of work and the development of financial and state institutions occurred. Work became drudgery and, while trade unions developed, their goals primarily reflected workers' interests in higher wages and the amelioration of working conditions. Such demands fostered involvement in politics, but, it is argued, it has only been in more recent years that demands for significant changes in the authority structure of industry and society have occurred. Posner and others argue that this is because of two significant changes in the nature of work which occur under advanced technology.[15] First, the worker becomes a member of a team, which 'presides' over machines rather than directly operating them. Second, the worker is not a mere appendage to the machine – he develops his own specific skills once more which are essential to production. The worker accordingly becomes interested in work for other than economic reasons.

In the earlier phases the question 'for whom am I producing?' was not asked. In the continuous process phase the question is inescapable. . . . Meaning must be restored to human activity by activity being rehumanized and subject to human decision, and that decision must be made directly by those involved, not by obscure and distant bureaucracies.[16]

Certainly the sixties saw a renewal of interest in participation, and in a later section we will take up the question as to whether this really does mark a new stage as far as participation is concerned. But for the present we have to recognize that participation was not unknown previously. Indeed, it is possible to crudely distinguish two other periods, in addition to the sixties, when participation was important and both occurred in what Posner and others would describe as the mechanical phase.

The first period runs from the first decade of this century until about 1921. This period saw the rise of the shop stewards' movement, demands for workers' control in engineering, syndicalist ideas in mining and the railways, the flowering of guild socialism, the involvement of trade-union representatives in the running of some enterprises, government recommendations for participation in the form of Whitleyism and in the reorganization of the mines and railways. The second period covers essentially the 1940s, a period of war and reconstruction; joint production committees were established, there were new demands for workers' control, human relations philosophies of management were taking a hold; in addition the post war nationalization Acts statutorily required a certain degree of worker participation.

Any satisfactory explanation of the development of participation has to be able to account for these periods as well as the sixties. We would suggest that this requires a focus upon the periods of boom and depression which are a notable feature of the unsteady development of capitalism. It has been in particular periods of boom which have certain key elements that participation has developed. We will call these 'crisis' periods, distinguished by a situation of apparent boom and relatively full employment but not of high profits. Basic structural problems in the economic framework associated with the need for major changes due to competition and innovation, or war, prevent profits from being high and competition or the war effort demand efficient production. The need for high output – for the war effort or to keep one's place in the market – adds to problems. In such a situation employers and, more recently, governments have been loath to permit wage increases which would cut into profit margins or have an inflationary effect. At the same time employers are likely to attempt to increase productivity and profitability through the introduction of new working methods and standardization. But boom conditions and full employment mean the work force has a significant degree of power particularly in industries which are important to the general health of the economy. At the same time the goals of organized labour – goals of a primarily economistic kind – are difficult to achieve.

These are the general outlines of the 'crisis' situations. Within these situations participation comes to be seen as a solution to the strain in the relationships of production by management, workers and government. Each category is however affected differently and does not necessarily act to achieve similar goals. The situation for the work force is one of being unable to achieve its economistic goals through the normal collective bargaining processes. This creates a shift in perspective and imagery away from these goals towards goals related to the control of production.

Whilst there has recently been a renewed interest in social imagery and the conditions for the development of class consciousness we in fact still know relatively little about the process by which imagery changes. The extent to which workers espouse the dominant values of our society is open to question; many workers demonstrate what has come to be called a dual consciousness. That is their attitudes combine elements of both acceptance and rejection of society's core values. Many workers therefore merely accommodate to many of the institutionalized values – they avoid, evade and manipulate them.[17] This is facilitated by the fact that the dominant-value system is not so coherent as to permit its non-problematic application to specific situations. As Wright Mills has pointed out, 'varying and competing vocabularies of motive operate co-terminally, and the situations to which they are appropriate are not clearly demarcated'.[18]

If workers are only conditionally attached to the existing structure then it is reasonable to expect that under certain circumstances they will challenge it. If, for example, legitimate economic expectations are not met then it is quite possible that they will begin to question the application of particular values or indeed the validity of values more central to the dominant social structure. Demands for workers' control, for example, tend to occur in situations where the central value system is being actively questioned more generally. These challenges are facilitated by the availability of alternative ideologies. There are no doubt elements of cause and effect in the fact that in periods when workers' participation is on the upsurge socialist ideology also finds a new lease of life. Blumberg states that, 'the internal logic of socialist ideology means an emphasis upon industrial democracy as part of a strategy to eliminate power inequalities in industrial as well as political settings'.[19] Such demands find an uneasy ally in the ideology of liberal democracy itself. The rights to political organization and the franchise, the more recent rights of economic welfare and social security provide a partial legitimation for demands for participation in industry (although equally they may serve to restrain the development of revolutionary consciousness).

The historical 'success' of collective bargaining along with a general increase in the standard of living has strengthened expectations amongst the work force about a certain level of economic reward. These expectations are socially legitimate and form the primary attachment of workers to the system as it exists. Where these expectations are not met by employers and where the state supports the employers' stand or itself clamps down on wage rises, then attachment to the system becomes increasingly conditional and makes them more susceptible to radical modes of thought. Some groups of workers begin to challenge the prevailing structure of authority and power in a conscious and direct manner; in this they are aided by the ideologue who provides a critique of society which legitimates and extends the course of action workers are pursuing. It is in this situation that there is pressure towards greater participation in industry on the part of more militant groups although the majority of workers continue to accept the definitions of national interest, proffered by management and the government and act in a 'responsible' manner.

The 'crisis' situations we have described encourage government involvement. Employers, for example, seek the aid of the state to defend their position against international competition or to maintain production in time of war. The unions may well turn to the state, or be open to state intervention to resolve impasses reached with employers. The very nature of the 'crisis', however, is one in which the government needs to maintain the co-operation of workers and unions in the face of pressing national problems and needs to integrate them fully into the system. In situations of the kind we have outlined full employment alone is insufficient and increases in wages or a halt to rationalization are seen as impossible. Participative issues become central areas for compromise.

One of the most interesting aspects of capitalist development is that the government has played an increasingly active role in the economic life of the country. In this country increased state involvement has meant the adoption of new functions on its part. In addition to the maintenance of law and order and the protection of property, other functions have become important. Not only does the state also play an important role in promoting the ideological justification of the existing social structure, but these functions and the maintenance of the economy lead to the development of certain state institutions which 'have a conformative role, which contain and moderate the conflicts inside capitalist society'.[20]

Frequently the structural problems of the economy require that the government override the interests of individual employers; the amalgamation of companies, rationalization on a grand scale, which is seen as necessary by the government, is beyond the scope – or often the wishes – of the individual owner. The very inability of employers to put their house in order eases the task of government; the radical demands of particular groups of workers also legitimates government action. A degree of participation can be introduced into the structural changes deemed necessary in industry. The extension of a moderate form of participation has appeal both to the balancing-of-interests approach of the government, particularly in times of 'crisis', and at the same time serves to stem the extension of radical demands through a 'demonstration effect'. Furthermore, the 'responsibility' shown by the majority of workers in periods of 'crisis' encourages the view that they have earned themselves a 'place in the sun'.[21] The 'national interest' and the 'Dunkirk spirit' can be given organizational substance in the work place, whilst providing little challenge to the traditional principles of industrial organization. The principles on which government itself has operated merely find their extension into industry – consultation and the recognition of the realities of power and consciousness.

Management's interests in participation are less easy to describe. Participation has rather hesitantly been employed by management where other means of integrating workers into the organization are thought to have failed or to be impracticable. It is clear that in the past management has been less than enthusiastic about any form of participation. Both the philosophy of private enterprise, the high value on formal efficiency and on a structure of hierarchic authority are likely to incline them in this direction. Participation is likely to be considered, therefore, only when there are threats to these and paradoxically in order to maintain them. This is likely to occur in situations where integration and encouragement of the work force are not being achieved by the current levels of instrumental rewards and it is not considered possible to improve on these, and also in situations where the work force is making radical demands. There are, of course, some general trends which are likely to make management more susceptible to participatory movements. First, the increasing scale of operations has led, to a divorce if not between ownership and ultimate control, at least between majority ownership and general management. The resultant professionalization of management and an associated trend towards an achievement, rather than a status oriented management, particularly in an increasingly bureaucraticized and technologically complex organization, facilitates participation. The increasing divorce of ownership and control, along with state aid, support and involvement, makes the traditional stance of *laissez-faire* capitalism of dubious validity. There is, therefore, a long-term trend within management which means they are more amenable to the idea of participation.

Within the structure of modern capitalism participation may well become a permanent factor. We discuss this below. In the past, however, the popularity of participation has declined. A variety of reasons for this appear to exist. Essentially any of the conditions we have described in the 'crisis', once they change, may lead to the decline of participation. For example, one of the major forms of 'crisis' is war. After peace and reconstruction the superimposition of boom and emergency disappears. When emergency passes but boom continues, by definition the room for compromise increases. Employers can pass on increased wage costs in the form of price increases without damaging profits. Governments will take a more accommodating attitude towards such actions since they do not immediately endanger the economy. Where 'crisis' moves into slump the industrial power of workers is reduced while at the same time the employer becomes more ready to accept long-drawn-out confrontations with workers; with their 'backs to the wall', they have little to lose and a good deal to gain. In these situations they have tended to be supported by governments.

The general trend of worker and trade-union demands during the course of this century has been related to the 'sphere of consumption', that is to economic demands. In a situation of boom and prosperity following 'crisis' the normal institutions of collective bargaining are revitalized and the institutions of participation fade into disfavour. The demands for workers' control fall away. Where economic goals are being achieved there is little support either for radical reconstruction or for forms of participation (e.g. joint consultation) which have little bearing on financial rewards. Where slump follows 'crisis' a similar situation obtains. With reduced power it becomes important to employ the conventional vocabulary which is more acceptable to a relatively more powerful management and expresses workers' concerns more directly, while vocabularies of workers' control seem of doubtful relevance when the employment situation is so fragile.

THE RECENT PERIOD – A NEW ERA?

We have argued that, in the past at least, interest in participation has declined as 'crisis' has passed. But we have noted earlier in this postscript that certain writers have argued that the recent period marks a new era. The basis of this argument is to be found among writers of both extremes of the political spectrum.[22] In modern society, so the argument runs, knowledge and expertise have become the key catalyst to progress. Not only has there been an increase in scale of operations, but more importantly the monopoly of specialist expertise is no longer held by those in key positions within organizational hierarchies. Goldman has summed up some aspects of this in a neat illustration.

Discipline and organization cannot in fact be the same in an infantry corps as in an aeroplane or any other technically advanced thing. Any junior officer knows how to handle a rifle and can explain it to soldiers by telling them what they need to know and giving them general directions. But even a senior officer would be incompetent in comparison to a specialist soldier in the handling of an ultra modern piece of weaponry. . . . Little by little technological progress demands that hierarchy be replaced by cooperation.[23]

Goldman and others would suggest that there is a new breed of workers emerging with a high degree of commitment to their technology and to efficiency and progress. This is related to an awareness of the industrial authority structure and the definition of this as antiquated. In other words there is perceived strain between the mode of production and the relations of production which leads to increasing demands for more worker control.

Technological change is seen as causing a two-fold movement in terms of the conventional occupational hierarchy. On the one hand the formerly independent professions have experienced a process of 'proletarianization' while on the other certain groups of workers, both monitoring personnel and 'super-craftsmen' in the new industries, have become key decision-makers in practice. This group which possesses a unique body of expertise has been termed the 'new working class'.

Such analysis found especial support from the May '68 demands in France. But the French experience would appear to be rather unique, and can be explained in part by the particular industrial development of that country and its social structure, notably the processes of social mobility.[24] In other countries, groups which might be seen as constituting the 'new working class' have not demonstrated the same pattern of demands. Moreover, it is open to question how many workers have experienced this transformation in the nature of their work. The skills and demands of many continuous-process industries appear to have been exaggerated. At the same time, many other jobs have experienced a significant degree of 'de-skilling' even within such industries.[25]

Nevertheless it is useful to distinguish trends in newer or growth industries, and in older industries which suffer from a general decline and the need for radical change. We might term these 'frontier' and 'non-frontier' sectors. In the former, we would suggest that such moves towards participation as have occurred in this country have not derived from workers' demands to employ their skills in a more socially meaningful and relevant manner. Rather, movements towards participation have occurred largely at the initiative of management. These have taken two forms. First, among management the specialist knowledge of often junior managers and the frequently uncertain nature of decision-making has fostered a lesser concern with hierarchical status. Knowledge has become a crucial factor in decision-making.[26]

However, there is little, if any, evidence to suggest that such participatory decision-making has extended beyond the confines of management. Among the work force movements towards participation, largely in the form of job enrichment and related schemes, have been neither at the demand of workers nor due to their monopoly of specialist knowledge. Of greater importance appears to have been management concern with motivating workers, overcoming problems of absenteeism, turnover and labour shortage, and ensuring the maximum usage of sophisticated technology. Participation then in the 'frontier' sector can be seen as a response by management to the imperatives of technology rather than as a result of the demands of a new working class.

In the 'non-frontier' sector the general pattern has been different. The thrust of technical change has been to decrease the pattern of worker control. Even in industries where the basic production technology remains the same there have been changes in size of organization, computers and systems technology have been introduced into the planning processes, and there has been a continuous process of production and product rationalization. For example, within the shipbuilding industry over the last decade there have been a series of mergers which have led to production being centred in a few large groups, a movement from unit to batch production and changes in the system of management and task allocation which have had the effect of moving control away from the point of production.[27]

In general terms the direction of change in the non-frontier sectors has been well documented. For a large part of our industrial labour force work has become increasingly meaningless; there has been a normative breakdown within the industrial relations system.[28] There is an increasing sense of powerlessness experienced by a growing number of workers, the feeling of being 'just a number' in a vast bureaucratic structure; a sense of the failure of that structure to distribute either rewards or power in a way which is perceived as fair or even rational. Whilst very often the response to this generalized anomie has been a demand for increased wages, money is a language through which one expresses, in Dahrendorf's phrase, 'less what one wants than that one wants something'.[29] Whilst an increased standard of living has been one of the major means of integrating the worker within industrial society, the increasing anomie of industrial life casts doubt upon its continuing effectiveness. There are signs that the status of a simple performer of tasks is becoming a frustration too difficult to bear.

It is within the non-frontier sectors that the demand for

workers' participation on the part of workers themselves has been strongest. As control has decreased at the point of production it is asserted at other levels. Since the bulk of this text was written, many such moves have received the support of a Labour government. These demands largely conform to the processes outlined in the previous section.

In sum, we are suggesting, on the basis of this examination of the direction of technological and economic change, that participatory structures will remain as permanent features of our social system. At the beginning of this chapter however we suggested that although man is to a great degree determined by economic and technological forces he still exerts control over his destiny. Marx suggested that whilst the development of capitalism depended on mutual co-operation in the production process at some point the further development of the productive forces of society would depend upon the 'capitalist integument' being broken. Many observers feel that we are near this breaking point. Relations in industry are increasingly based on formal contract; but as Durkheim has pointed out contracts are insufficient basis for co-operation. Further movement in this direction might lead to a breakdown of our social system. The alternative is increasing concessions in industry to the solution of anomie and at the same time a radical devolution of authority. We feel that this gradual but radical change is a more likely outcome than revolutionary change. However, prediction in this area is fraught with peril for those on both sides of industry are increasingly aware, to paraphrase André Gorz, that workers' participation is more than just that.

Notes

1 However, it is interesting to note that at least in other countries in Europe participative movements have tended to develop in broadly comparable periods.

2 GIDDENS, A., *The Class Structure of the Advanced Societies*, Hutchinson, 1973, p. 144

3   The means of production we use in Marx's sense of the technological form in terms of which material production takes place: relationships of production refer to the sets of socio-economic relationships involved in the operation of any given production system, between production systems, and between the system of production and the system of distribution and consumption.

4   See JORDEN, A. (ed.), *Karl Marx*, Nelson, 1971, pp. 238–9. Marx also emphasizes the social and co-operative nature of capitalism.

5   AVINERI, S., *The Social and Political Thought of Karl Marx*, Cambridge University Press, 1968

6   For a fuller discussion of this and many other subsequent points on the general development of capitalism, see, among others, BARRATT-BROWN, M., *From Labourism to Socialism*, Spokesman Publications, 1973

7   GIDDENS, op. cit., p. 151

8   DAHRENDORF, R., *Class and Class Conflict in Industrial Society*, Routledge & Kegan Paul, 1959, p. 65

9   DAHRENDORF, op. cit., p. 261

10   Quoted in GIDDENS, A. (ed.), *Emile Durkheim, Selected Writings*, Cambridge University Press, 1972, p. 187

11   Ibid.

12   MANN, M., 'The Social Cohesion of Liberal Democracy', *American Sociological Review*, Vol. 35:3, 1970

13   FOX, A., *Beyond Contract: Work, Power and Trust Relations*, Faber & Faber, 1974, p. 322. For a less academic discussion of these themes see FOX, A., *Man Mismanagement*, Hutchinson, 1974

14   For example, POSNER, C., *Reflections of the Revolution in France: 1968*, Pelican, 1970. See also GIDDENS, op. cit., and MANN, M., *Consciousness and Action Among the Western Working Class*, Macmillan, 1973, for a discussion of such arguments

15   POSNER, op. cit.

16   Ibid., pp. 34–5

17   For a general discussion of these themes see, for example, PARKIN, F., *Class, Inequality and Political Order*, Jordon, 1971

18   MILLS, C. W., 'Situated Actions and Vocabularies of Motive' in Horowitz (ed.), *Power, Politics and People*, Oxford University Press, 1963, p. 449

19   BLUMBERG, P., *Industrial Democracy, the Sociology of Participation*, Constable, 1968, p. 5

20   BARRATT-BROWN, op. cit., p. 68

21   CLEGG, H. A., *The System of Industrial Relations in Great Britain*, Blackwell, 1973

22   See DRUCKER, P., 'Knowledge Society', *New Society*, 24 April 1968, and *Landmarks of Tomorrow*, Heinemann, 1959. BELL, D., 'The Post-Industrial Society: the Evolution of an Idea', *Survey* XVII (1171); TOOUAINE, A., *The Post-Industrial Society*, Wildwood House, 1974; and GOLDMAN, L., *Power and Humanism*, Spokesman Pamphlet No. 14

Postscript: The development of participation

23 GOLDMAN, op. cit., p. 11
24 See MANN, M., *Consciousness and Action*, op. cit., p. 65
25 See, for example, WEDDERBURN, D., and CROMPTON, R., *Workers' Attitudes and Technology*, Cambridge University Press, 1972, and CHADWICK JONES, J., *Automation and Behaviour*, Wiley, 1969
26 See, for example, BURNS, T. and STALKER, G. M., *The Management of Innovation*, Tavistock, 1966, p. 11
27 BROWN, R. K. et al., 'The Contours of Solidarity', *British Journal of Industrial Relations*, 1972
28 FOX, A. and FLANDERS, A., 'The Reform of Collective Bargaining: From Donovan to Durkheim', *British Journal of Industrial Relations*, Vol. VIII, 1969
29 DAHRENDORF, R., *Freedom and Democracy: Germany*, Weidenfeld and Nicolson, 1968, p. 170

Appendix:
A note on research methods

The field material on which most of this book is based was collected between October 1969 and October 1971. It was collected through a programme of interviews, observation, and examination of documentary material. This triangulation of methods was partly dictated by the research framework which we have described in the introduction to the book; we hoped, by using more than one method, to strengthen the validity of our data. We now describe briefly what was involved in each segment of the programme.

I. INTERVIEWS

The universe of people we set out to interview can be split into two categories, 'general' and 'specific' relating to their putative relationship to the worker directors; and a third category consisting of the worker directors themselves. The 'specific' category consisted of individuals or groups likely, because of their positions, to interact directly with the worker directors. The 'general' category was conceived of as the mass of employees in the industry whom the worker directors in some sense represented. The groups within these categories can be set out as shown on p. 266.

Within the specific category the numbers of people involved in each group were relatively small and consequently we aimed to try and interview all members of these groups. The general sample, however, posed problems of size and two possible strategies were available to deal with this: (a) to take general samples from the total industry, or (b) to select particular

General		Specific	
Production Craft Other	} Manual workers	Divisional directors Corporation HO personnel	Worker directors

Clerical &
  Tech-
  nical
Supervisory
	} Staff	Management
		Lay union officials	

Lay union officials		Full-time union officials	

works and to sample within these. The second strategy was adopted, and nine works selected on the following criteria:

  (i) At least two works from each division of the Steel Corporation.

 (ii) A balance between works where worker directors were employed and those where they were not.

(iii) A balance between large and smaller works in terms of numbers of employees, but all works to employ at least 2000 people.

(iv) That the works chosen should mirror a large range of technology and product.

 (v) That the works should be fairly well spread geographically so as to allow for different social and cultural traditions.

(a) *General category*

Two groups were interviewed based upon these nine works. The first group we shall call the general employee sample and the second the shop-steward sample.

The general employee

The occupational categories in our general sample were as follows: manual workers divided into sub-groups of 'craft', 'process' and 'other' workers. Staff workers divided into sub-groups of supervisory, clerical and technical. We excluded females, males under eighteen, apprentices and trainees from our sample. The sample was chosen in order to ensure a fair spread of occupations and yet at the same time to attempt in fairly general terms to allow for the effects of different patterns of work experience upon attitudes. The sample consisted of 5% manual workers in all works, and 10% of people in the foreman, clerical and technical categories, except at one works where, because of its size, we took 2½% of manual workers and 5% of the other groups. The interviews were conducted by interviewers recruited and trained by the authors. The initial sample consisted of 1577 people and a 75% response rate was achieved. A structured interview schedule was used. Tables presented in the text based on this sample have been weighted up to allow comparisons across works and occupational categories.

The shop-steward sample
This sample was stratified by type of union into production unions, general unions, craft unions and white-collar unions (for our purposes this included white-collar and staff branches of predominantly manual unions). We used the term to include broadly all lay union officials within the works. Officials who fell within the sampling frame, however, clearly varied between unions; the shop stewards as such were selected from unions with non-works based branches, lodge delegates were taken in the case of the National Union of Blastfurnacemen and branch secretaries and works representatives were taken in the case of the British Iron, Steel, Allied and Kindred Trades Association (BISAKTA). In other words, our general criterion was those lay officials who negotiated. In the larger works we interviewed 20% of each of these categories of union official, whilst in the smaller works we interviewed 60%. The interviews were carried out by the authors using a structured interview schedule. The initial sample consisted of 168 individuals and a 93% response rate was achieved. Tables presented in the text based on this sample have been weighted up to allow comparisons across works and union categories.

(b) *Specific category*

The following groups represented the specific categories we interviewed. As has been noted the criteria of selection in the specific category is different from the general category. In the latter case individuals were selected randomly; in the former case they were selected on the basis of the position they held.

The works union role set

This group consisted of the following persons from each of the works in which one of the worker directors was employed:

(i) the key union officials in the works, such as craft convenors, chairmen of BISAKTA joint committees, etc., and

(ii) the officials of the worker director's own branch where this was works-based or, where this was not the case, the senior officials of his union in the works.

In this sample we were particularly concerned to investigate the views and contacts of those union officials who were most likely to have contact with the worker directors and those whom the worker director was most likely to contact. In all 101 people were interviewed.

Full-time union officials

In this category we attempted to interview one full-time official of each of the unions in the works where a worker director was employed. In a number of cases one full-time official was responsible for members in more than one works in which worker directors were employed. The officials interviewed also covered the bulk of the works in which the general interviewing programme was carried out. In all we interviewed forty-six full-time officials.

Management

Within these same ten works we also carried out interviews with management. Two types of managers were interviewed (although in fact these types overlapped). First, we interviewed all those managers in the line of authority between the worker director in his work role and the general manager (foremen were included as managers in this sample). Secondly, we interviewed the most senior manager in the works and all those reporting to him who were either responsible for large numbers of employees (mainly line managers plus engineers) and the senior manager concerned with some aspect of personnel. The logic of this sample was similar to that of the lay union officials role set sample – namely to interview those managers who might be expected to be most involved with the worker director; again therefore the logic was to interview the incumbent of particular positions rather than interviewing proportions of those who fell within a particular category. In all ninety managers were interviewed.

Divisional directors
We attempted to interview all persons who sat on the boards of the four steel divisions including part-time directors (other than worker directors) and the secretaries of the divisional boards. Interviews were completed with forty-eight of the fifty-three members of the boards in the steel divisions. The directors we failed to interview were all part-time directors.

Other individuals interviewed
In addition to the above samples we also interviewed certain members of the Steel Corporation, members of the steel committee of the TUC and some of the chairmen of BSC committees at national and divisional level on which worker directors sat.

Worker directors
Most of the above groups in the specific categories were interviewed only once. (However, certain individuals, particularly some board members and some key lay full-time union officials had informal discussions with the research team as well as the formal interview.) All worker directors, on the other hand, were interviewed formally and informally on a number of occasions throughout the research.

(c) *Interviewing methods*
An attempt was made throughout all interviews conducted to

have a common core of questions or topics which were asked of all respondents, both those within the general category and those within the specific category. The major variations as between groups were:

(i) The extent to which the interviewing schedules were structured.

(ii) The schedules for each specific category were naturally more concerned with contact and social relationships between respondents and worker directors.

(iii) The schedules for various categories of respondents were also directed towards their particular roles. For example, the general sample were asked a number of questions concerning their own jobs and the degree of job control exercised whilst union officials were asked about their role as union representatives.

The general questionnaire had the following sections: biographical, attitudes towards work and work organization, perception of the firm, trade union involvement, joint consultation, worker participation, worker directors, social imagery. Other interview schedules were variants of this.

The interviews with lay union officials and employees were relatively structured, containing a mixture of both open-ended and forced choice questions. The employee sample interviews were conducted by trained interviewers and all the other interviews were carried out by the research team.

Interviews with other groups were essentially treated as guided discussions. The researchers used an interview guide which contained an outline of major topics and sub-topics to be covered. This guide had been fully discussed between the researchers so that the topics were covered in similar ways with similar emphasis.

II. OBSERVATION

By observation we mean non-participant observation, that is the researcher observing situations and making clear his role as researcher without participating in these situations in any other role. This was the only observational technique we felt to be appropriate within the context of this particular project. We used observation in the following situations:

(a) Meetings of divisional boards on a regular basis.
(b) Any preparatory meetings for boards at which worker directors were present.
(c) Head office meetings in which worker directors participated.
(d) Joint consultative meetings at section and works levels (in particular works) and at divisional levels.
(e) Union meetings in which worker directors participated. Other union meetings in particular cases.
(f) Official visits by worker directors to works.

Observation at board meetings began in August 1970. All boards in each division were attended for at least seven consecutive meetings and in one case, at the request of the board, the observer stayed for ten meetings.

At national level we attended all meetings at which the worker directors as a group met with senior members of the corporation and all the national meetings of the worker directors. In addition we attended official working parties on which worker directors sat and were present at most meetings of these working parties. At divisional level we attended pre-board discussions and Divisional Advisory Committees and working parties on which worker directors were involved. We also covered most of the formal visits worker directors paid to works and in the course of covering these visits also attended meetings between worker directors and management and local trade unionists. Works consultative meetings which the worker directors attended were covered in a much more random way. We also attended a variety of meetings with the unions in which worker directors participated, and went along to branch districts and other types of union meetings whenever possible to get the flavour of union activity at the local level. On two occasions worker directors had meetings with the steel committee of the TUC at national level, but we were not allowed to attend these meetings; we did however see minutes and receive verbal accounts.

III. DOCUMENTARY MATERIAL

The collection of this kind of material was carried out through the period of research. Basically it can be classified in three ways:

(a) *Historical data* – files on the worker-director scheme which were held at the headquarters of the Steel Corporation. This has proved an important source of material in its own right on the origins and early history of the scheme; it also helped us to understand the origins of a number of events which were taking place during our period of field work.

(b) *Press cuttings* were kept on all aspects of the industry. These were used in two main ways. Firstly, to keep the research team abreast of current issues in the industry; this was essential for parts of the observation programme, especially that carried out in board meetings. Secondly, the cuttings acted as a data source in their own right which provided material on, for example, public pronouncements by key figures in the industry.

(c) *Other documentary material* – during the field-work period of the research, there was a certain amount of generation of documents within both the Steel Corporation and the trade-union movement relating to the worker directors, joint consultation, and industrial relations matters more generally. As these documents had a bearing upon the work we were doing we tried to collect them. We also attempted to collect other kinds of material especially minutes of meetings which had a bearing upon the work in which we were engaged.

Index

Compiled by Gordon Robinson